The Polish Economy

The Polish Economy

CRISIS, REFORM, AND TRANSFORMATION

Ben Slay

PRINCETON UNIVERSITY PRESS

PRINCETON, NEW JERSEY

Published by Princeton University Press, 41 William Street,
Princeton, New Jersey 08540
In the United Kingdom: Princeton University Press, Chichester, West Sussex

Library of Congress Cataloging-in-Publication Data

Slay, Ben, 1958-
The Polish economy : crisis, reform, and transformation / Ben Slay.
p. cm.
Includes bibliographical references and index.
ISBN 978-0-691-63600-9
1. Poland—Economic conditions—1980- 2. Poland—Economic policy—1981- 3. Post-communism—Poland. I. Title.
HC340.3.S59 1994
338.9438—dc20 93-44823

Portions of chapters 3 and 4 are adapted from two chapters I contributed to *Capitalist Goals, Socialist Past: The Rise of the Private Sector in Command Economies,* ed. P. L. Patterson, 1993, by permission of Westview Press, Boulder, Colorado, and from my articles "The Banking Crisis and Economic Reform in Poland" and "Evolution of Industrial Policy in Poland," originally published in *Radio Free Europe/Radio Liberty Research Report* (June 5, 1992, and Jan. 8, 1993), by permission of the RFE/RL Research Institute.

This book has been composed in Galliard ITC

Princeton University Press books are printed on acid-free paper and meet the guidelines for permanence and durability of the Committee on Production Guidelines for Book Longevity of the Council on Library Resources

Printed in the United States of America

1 2 3 4 5 6 7 8 9 10

TO AMY, LIZA, AND BEVERLY

Contents

Tables

List of Acronyms

THE FOLLOWING acronyms for the names of organizations and some other terms appear in the text. When the acronym stands for a Polish name or term, the English translation is given parenthetically.

CEFTA—Central European Free Trade Association, Agreement, or Area

CMEA—Council for Mutual Economic Assistance

EC—European Community

FOZZ—Fundusz Obsługiwania Zadłużenia Zagranicznego (Fund for Servicing the Foreign Debt)

FTO—Foreign Trade Organization

GATT—General Agreement on Tariffs and Trade

GPE—Government Economic Program

IMF—International Monetary Fund

KLD—Kongres Liberalno-Demokratyczny (Liberal Democratic Congress)

KOR—Komitet Obrony Robotniczej (Worker Defense Committee)

KPN—Konfederacja Polski Niepodległej (Confederation for an Independent Poland)

KSRS—Konferencje Samorządu Robotniczego (Workers' Self-Management Conferences)

NBP—Narodowy Bank Polski (National Bank of Poland)

OECD—Organization for Economic Cooperation and Development

OPZZ—Ogólnokrajowe Prezydium Związków Zawodowych (National Trade Union Federation)

PC—Porozumienie Centrum (Center Alliance)

PL—Porozumienie Ludowe (Peasant Alliance)

PPR—Polska Partia Robotnicza (Polish Workers' Party)

PPS—Polska Partia Socjalistyczna (Polish Socialist Party)

PSL—Polskie Stronnictwo Ludowe (Polish Peasant Party)

PZPR—Polish United Workers' Party

ROAD—Ruch Obrony Alternatyw Demokratycznych (Citizens' Movement for Democratic Alternatives)

SAD—Standard Administrative Document

SDRP—Socjalna Demokracja Rzeczpospolitej Polski (Social Democracy of the Republic of Poland)

SLD—Sojusz Lewicy Demokratycznej (Democratic Left Alliance)

UD—Unia Democratyczna (Democratic Union)

WOG—Wielka Organizacja Gospodarcza (Large Economic Organization)

ZChN—Zjednoczenie Chrześcijańsko-Narodowe (Christian National Union)

ZUS—Zakłady Ubezpieczenia Społecznego (State Insurance Office)

A Chronology of the Transition, 1989–1993

APRIL 1989—After months of roundtable negotiations, leaders of the Polish United Workers' Party (PZPR) and the outlawed Solidarity trade union movement announce Solidarity's legalization and agree on a framework for political democratization.

JUNE 1989—Parliamentary elections are held, in which the PZPR is defeated by Solidarity candidates in the contests for open seats. A hung parliament results.

AUGUST 1989—Solidarity leader Lech Wałęsa engineers a behind-the-scenes transfer of power from the cabinet of Prime Minister Mieczysław Rakowski to a coalition government headed by Solidarity activist Tadeusz Mazowiecki.

SEPTEMBER 1989—The Mazowiecki government, with Leszek Balcerowicz as deputy prime minister and minister of finance, is confirmed by the Sejm.

JANUARY 1990—The implementation of the Balcerowicz Plan for economic transformation begins, with the support of the International Monetary Fund and the World Bank.

MAY 1990—Wałęsa calls for a "war at the top" of the Solidarity movement, and begins his campaign for the presidency. Tension between the Wałęsa and Mazowiecki camps weakens the Mazowiecki government and foreshadows the split and subsequent disintegration of Solidarity.

JULY 1990—Landmark privatization legislation, creating the Ministry of Ownership Transformation and authorizing the re-creation of the Warsaw stock market, is passed by the Sejm.

NOVEMBER 1990—Mazowiecki finishes third in the first round of the presidential elections, behind Wałęsa and political unknown Stanisław Tymiński. The Mazowiecki government announces its resignation.

DECEMBER 1990—Wałęsa is elected president of Poland. A new government under the direction of Prime Minister Jan Krzysztof Bielecki is formed, with Balcerowicz remaining as deputy prime minister and minister of finance.

JANUARY 1991—Poland switches to world price accounting and hard currency financing in its trade with the Soviet Union and other members of the Council for Mutual Economic Assistance. Declines in trade with Poland's southern and eastern neighbors accelerate, as do increases in the OECD countries' share of Poland's trade.

APRIL 1991—An agreement to forgive approximately half of Poland's international debt, largely held by the Paris Club of OECD governments, is announced.

JUNE 1991—The "privatization offensive," including a mass privatization program based on the free distribution of shares in national investment funds, is announced.

SEPTEMBER 1991—Aid from the International Monetary Fund is suspended due to Poland's rising budget deficit and above-forecast inflation levels.

OCTOBER 1991—Twenty-nine parties, none of which received more than 13 percent of the popular vote, are elected to the Sejm in Poland's first freely-contested parliamentary elections since 1928.

DECEMBER 1991—A five-party coalition approves the government of Prime Minister Jan Olszewski, over the oppposition of President Wałęsa.

MARCH 1992—Economic recovery begins, led by strong increases in industrial production.

MAY 1992—Finance Minister Andrzej Olechowski resigns in protest over the Sejm's inability to maintain fiscal discipline.

JUNE 1992—The Olszewski government loses a vote of confidence, precipated by its decision to release secret police files on parliamentary deputies.

JULY 1992—A seven-party parliamentary coalition approves a new government headed by Prime Minister Hanna Suchocka. During the next year legislation authorizing the mass privatization program and debt consolidation is passed.

MAY 1993—The Suchocka government loses a vote of confidence sponsored by the Solidarity trade union. Wałęsa dissolves parliament, and new elections are scheduled for September.

SEPTEMBER 1993—The Democratic Left Alliance (SLD) and the Polish Peasant Party (PSL), descendants of the pre-1990 political system, win the parliamentary elections and gain an absolute majority in both the Sejm and Senate.

OCTOBER 1993—The government of Prime Minister Waldemar Pawlak receives parliamentary confirmation.

Preface

THE ORIGINS of this book can be traced to early 1989, when the idea of explaining how Poland had become "one of socialism's economic basket cases" was first proposed to me. At that time, the roundtable discussions that were to change the future of Poland and, subsequently, help shatter what used to be called the Soviet bloc, were just beginning. Since I (and everyone else) had virtually no idea of the momentous changes the next years would bring, this book was originally conceived as a study of the political economy of the Polish crisis and as an explanation of how the crisis had pushed the communist regime into considering progressively more radical reforms. As such, the historical roots of the Polish crisis, many of which predated the establishment of People's Poland, had to play a central role in the analysis.

The whirlwind events of the next three years demonstrated the final inadequacy of attempts at reforming the Soviet-style economy in Poland and elsewhere. Economic transformation became the key to understanding Polish political economy and the focus of the book shifted accordingly. By the time the final version of the manuscript was completed, in mid-1993, only two of the book's five chapters were directly concerned with the historical roots of today's "Polish question" and only one dealt with the events preceding the rise of Solidarity in 1980. Although the description of the historical context remained, the emphasis had shifted to the post-1989 economic transformation and its accompanying political developments. The fluid dynamics of the changes in Poland were therefore reflected in the twists and turns of this manuscript's development.

I have benefited in preparing this book from the help of many specialists and institutions within Poland, in other Central European countries, and in the United States. While I cannot hope to formally express my gratitude to all who deserve it, I would like to especially thank Andrzej and Zosia Ananicz, Josef Brada, Wojciech Bieńkowski, Keith Crane, David Das, Kálmán Mizsei, Krzysztof Obłój, Robert Rządca, and Louisa Vinton for their assistance, comments, and guidance over the years. I would like to express gratitude for the research support afforded me by the Radio Free Europe/Radio Liberty Research Institute in Munich, and to the many excellent specialists there who helped me better understand the problems and opportunities facing the region to which Poland belongs. I would also like to thank Bates College, and especially my colleagues in Russian and East European studies, for their support during the preparation of this manuscript. Finally, while the book benefited significantly from referees' comments, I must emphasize that all conclusions and any remaining errors are my own.

The Polish Economy

Introduction

ECONOMIC CRISIS, reform, and transformation in Poland entered the 1990s linked together. The Polish economy began the decade in much the same condition as it had started the 1980s—with balance-of-payments tensions, declining production and incomes, rising inflation, a decreasing share of world trade, an ever-widening technological gap vis-à-vis the capitalist West, and deterioration in such quality-of-life measures as environmental quality, housing availability, and life expectancy. As in the early 1980s, the 1990s began with the widespread realization that Poland's economic problems had reached critical levels and that solving them required major policy and institutional changes.

However, the 1980s were a decade of *reform*, in which attempts at improving economic performance were made within the economic and political framework of Soviet-style socialism. By contrast, the 1990s began as a decade of economic *transformation*, in which the framework of state socialism was explicitly abandoned in favor of market capitalism and political democracy. However, while radically alleviating some aspects of Poland's crisis, such as pervasive shortages and poor external creditworthiness, the transformation that began during 1989–1990 introduced new elements of crisis, including the appearance of double-digit unemployment, the collapse of entire branches of industry, and the failure of postcommunist elites to develop stable, effective political institutions.

In addition to being a decade of economic malaise, the 1980s saw the rise, fall, and rebirth of the Solidarity trade union, the Soviet bloc's first large-scale opposition movement. Solidarity's creation, in August 1980, had its roots in Poland's economic collapse of 1979–1982, during which time national income produced[1] declined in real terms by 24 percent, prices increased by almost 200 percent, the volume of exports and imports registered double-digit declines (imports by more than 30 percent), and gross investment fell a staggering 60 percent.[2] The Polish economy experienced a recovery of sorts after 1982, but by the start of the recession that began in 1989, national income produced, gross investment, and imports from Western countries had still not regained their 1979 levels. Retail prices, which increased more than tenfold during the 1980s, increased fifteenfold with the price liberalization introduced in 1989–1990.

Economic difficulties are common to virtually all the postcommunist economies. In contrast to some of its neighbors, however, Poland's economic crisis is closely linked to important aspects of Poland's historical and political development. A number of factors—a long history of resistance to foreign oppression, firmly rooted Roman Catholicism, strong cultural ties to Western Europe and the United States, and anti-Russian sentiments, as well as the brutality with which the communist Polish People's Republic was established during the period 1948 to 1953—prevented the acceptance of Soviet-style socialism by the Polish body politic. During its forty-year rule (1948–1989), the Polish United Workers' Party (PZPR) came to be regarded by ever-widening circles of Polish society as illegitimate, as was evident in the ignominious defeat the PZPR suffered at the hands of Solidarity in the June 1989 parliamentary elections. The roots of the communists' failure to create stable political and economic institutions, as well as the tendencies toward crisis that dominated People's Poland, lie in large measure in Poland's historical experience.

Indeed, crisis has been a constant theme of Polish historiography. Long before the establishment of the People's Republic, Poland's borders, socioeconomic institutions, sovereignty, and statehood were in regular flux and crisis. Before 1918 the "Polish question" that vexed the Russian, German, and Austrian empires concerned Polish prospects for reattaining statehood and the implications for the stability of the European order. The Polish Second Republic of 1918–1939 was marked by a crisis of economic underdevelopment and incomplete (though not unimpressive) progress in the construction of a viable modern nation-state. Polish history would suggest that the passing of the People's Republic in 1989 should not be taken to mean that the crisis is over. Instead, as postcommunist Poland changes, the Polish crisis may also be undergoing change, reflecting the new realities and conditions in which Poland finds itself.

Turning points in Polish political development occurred in 1956, 1968, 1970–1971, 1976, 1980–1981 and 1988–1989. In these years the tensions generated by the PZPR's unpopular rule and widespread dissatisfaction with lagging economic performance burst into the open in the form of protests, strikes and, in the 1980s, mass movements against Soviet-style socialism per se. The ruling elite responded to these protests by promising reforms, first in the economic system, and later in the political system as well. Once the storms had passed, however, the PZPR either abandoned its reform programs or let its attention be diverted to other matters. Poland's postwar history is littered with unsuccessful attempts at economic reform (1957–1958,[3] 1963–1965, 1969–1970, 1973–1975, and 1982–1988).

As the Polish sociologist Jadwiga Staniszkis has pointed out, promises of economic and political reforms served as a "systemic shock absorber," helping the political elite to weather the storms that lashed at the ship of People's Poland. Because they were treated as crisis-management instruments, reforms failed to address the underlying causes of the crisis and helped set the stage for the next eruption. In the process, the concept of reform as a method of improving the functioning of the economy and the polity lost much of its credibility in Polish society. This credibility gap was one of the factors behind the PZPR's decision in 1988–1989 to risk expanding the reform process beyond the point at which its monopoly on political power could be assured.

Economic reform was thus simultaneously a cause and a consequence of the cycles of crisis in Poland's postwar economic and political development. Economic and political difficulties persuaded the PZPR to attempt economic reforms; but, once introduced, the reforms exacerbated other problems (inflation, the credibility gap) and contributed to the development of the next phase of the crisis. These cycles were manifested in frequent explosions of protest, the "reform strategies" pursued by the PZPR after an explosion, the abandonment or weakening of reform initiatives, and the subsequent reaccumulation of social and political tensions leading to the next explosion. The extent to which the post-1989 transformation of Poland's economic and political systems constitutes a decisive break with this cyclical pattern, as opposed to a new phase in its development, remains to be seen.

Poland's long experience with economic and political reforms also provides a rich history useful in analyzing other countries' reform prospects. This experience illustrates the economic, political, and social barriers to economic reform as well as the links between political and economic reform. It also serves as an example of the difficulties inherent in trying to reform a Soviet-style economy, and why a transformation into capitalism may be regarded as the only solution to the economic crisis, even if the initial effects of the transformation may exacerbate economic problems. The difficulties encountered in the transformation of Polish socialism into capitalism cannot really be understood in isolation from the previous, largely unsuccessful attempts by the PZPR at "improving" socialism through reform.

The PZPR's inability to effectively reform the Polish economy led to its collapse and to the creation of the Solidarity-led coalition government in August 1989. The electorate's overwhelming rejection of the old system, the failures of previous reform attempts, and the country's dire economic situation convinced the new government of Prime Minister Tadeusz Mazowiecki to attempt the transition from socialism to capitalism. In so doing, Poland took a leap into the unknown. While a transition from capitalism to socialism can be analyzed in the historical experience of many countries (the Soviet Union, the Eastern European countries, and China, to name a few), there were at that time no well-established cases, or even fully developed threories, of the opposite, a conversion from socialism to capitalism. Yet this is precisely what has been attempted in Poland since January 1, 1990, and in other postcommunist countries since then. The outcome of this experiment is therefore of more than academic interest. In addition to its impact on the Polish economy, the course of this transformation has important implications for independent states of the former USSR and the other Central and Eastern European countries, as well as for East-West relations and the future of Europe.

The problems posed by this transformation are immense. The Polish economy during the 1980s was squeezed by balance-of-payments tensions, the depreciation of its capital stock, rising inflation, pervasive shortages, and falling living standards. Before 1990 Poland had no real capital markets or market-based financial institutions. Knowledge of Western financial and accounting practices was minimal. Industrial structures were highly concentrated, with many products produced by a single firm. The private sector was dominated by small-scale producers and was corrupted by regulatory agencies and its ties to the PZPR *nomenklatura*. Finally, the PZPR lost control of monetary and fiscal policies in 1988–1989 as a result of concessions it made to Solidarity and its last-ditch efforts to secure its position before the June 1989 elections. The resulting monetary explosion led to triple-digit inflation in 1989 and the apparent inevitability of hyperinflation in 1990. In addition to effecting a transition from socialism to capitalism, the Mazowiecki government also had to administer a painful dose of macroeconomic austerity, precisely the kind of program the PZPR had been unable to enforce during its rule.

Macroeconomic stabilization from 1990 to 1992 proved successful in terms of reducing inflation, and significant progress was made in liberalizing domestic and external activity and in improving Poland's external creditworthiness. But the new government's fiscal and monetary policies were accompanied by deep cuts in real incomes and output, and by elections in November and December 1990 and October 1991 whose results seemed to partially undermine what had been accomplished. While the private sector grew rapidly during the years 1990 to 1992, programs for the rapid privatization of large state enterprises were a spectacular failure. And despite the beginnings of an economic recovery in 1992, the rapid growth of the budget deficit, a decline in enterprise profitability, and a gathering crisis in the banking system and other financial institutions posed the threat of a financial meltdown. But in spite of these problems, Poland had clearly emerged as a pioneer in the postcommunist economic transition and its experience seemed broadly applicable to other countries in the region.

An interdisciplinary synthesis of the political economy of the Polish transformation and the historical, political, and economic factors that condition it is developed in the pages that follow. Extensive use is made of primary Polish sources as well as Western sources. Chapter 1 describes Polish political economy before 1980, the year Solidarity appeared. Roughly half the chapter is devoted to the legacy of Poland's presocialist economic and political traditions, with special emphasis on the legacies of the partitions, the record of the interwar period, the devastation of the Second World War, the multisectoral economy that emerged between 1945 and 1948, and the establishment of Soviet-style socialism from 1948 to 1953. The remainder of Chapter 1 analyzes economic development from 1948 to 1980, the period after the establishment of socialism but before the appearance of Solidarity. Special attention is given to the economic and political causes and consequences of the developments of 1956, 1968, 1970–1971, and 1976, and to Poland's pre-1980 record of economic performance. The economic reforms attempted in the 1950s, 1960s, and 1970s are examined, with emphasis on developments during the periods 1956–1958 and 1973–1975.

Chapter 2 examines the causes and consequences of the economic collapse of 1979–1982, including Poland's external disequilibrium, economic policy decisions, and the secular causes of the collapse, and investigates the reforms of economic and political institutions and policies that occurred in the 1980s. The Solidarity movement of 1980–1981 and the martial law period of 1982–1983 are discussed in terms of their effects on economic performance and reform. The strengths and weaknesses of the first and second stages of the economic reforms introduced during the years 1982 to 1988 are examined, as well as the factors behind the partial economic recovery of that period. The evolution of political reforms during the 1980s and their connection to the economic reform process are also analyzed, together with environmental devastation, the second economy, and other issues that gained in significance during the 1980s. Chapter 2 ends with a description of the economic and political events leading up to Solidarity's rise to power in August 1989.

Chapters 3 and 4 analyze the problems and prospects for transforming socialism into capitalism in Poland. Chapter 3 focuses on the successes, failures, and political implications of the program for economic transformation pursued during the years 1990 to 1992. The analysis focuses on macroeconomic stabilization, improvements in foreign-trade performance, privatization, and the politics of the transition. Chapter 4 provides a snapshot view of important sectors of the Polish economy at the end of 1992 and early 1993, more than two years after the start of the transition, in order to examine the extent of the changes produced by the transformation. The emphasis is placed largely on the economics of the transition, since the Polish economy had by 1993 become increasingly independent of the political system.

The lessons of this most recent "Polish experiment" for other postcommunist economies in transition are considered in Chapter 5. To be sure, the advantages Poland possessed at the start of the transition limited the relevance of the Polish experience for other countries. Still, Poland showed that a heavily indebted postcommunist economy may be effectively pulled back from the brink of hyperinflation and reoriented away from trade with the (former) socialist world, and that it can effect dramatic increases in the private share of economic activity and experience the beginnings of recovery within two or three years. As such, the Polish experience can be read as a hopeful one for the countries of the former Soviet Union, Central Europe, and the Balkans.

CHAPTER I

The Polish Crisis and Polish Socialism

THE RISE of the Solidarity movement during 1980–1981, and the collapse of Soviet-style socialism in Poland after 1989, can be ascribed to many factors. The institutional inefficiencies of central planning and command management were certainly major causes, as was popular dissatisfaction with decades of misrule by the Polish United Workers' Party (PZPR).[1] The economic policies pursued during the 1970s, which dramatically increased Poland's external indebtedness, also played an important role. These factors do not tell the whole story, however. Poland's economic and political institutions did not differ dramatically from those of other Soviet bloc countries, and Poland was only one of dozens of developing countries caught in the international debt trap during the 1980s.

Although by the late 1980s socialism was in crisis throughout the Soviet bloc, communist rule collapsed first in Poland. This was not a coincidence: Soviet-style socialism in Poland was in a state of crisis virtually from its inception in the late 1940s. The tensions afflicting People's Poland can in turn be linked to elements of Poland's historical experience before the postwar period. They can in part be ascribed to developments during the Second World War (1939–1945), the interwar period (1918–1939), and less directly to the era of the partitions (1795–1918), in which the Polish state essentially disappeared from the map of Europe. While these factors did not deterministically produce the collapse of Polish socialism, they form the historical context within which the rise and fall of People's Poland and the following transition to capitalist democracy are best understood.

THE POLISH-LITHUANIAN COMMONWEALTH AND THE PARTITIONS

During the Middle Ages the Polish Commonwealth was the Eastern bastion of Roman Catholicism. The Commonwealth was integrated with the rest of Europe through the Church, commerce, and dynastic intermarriage. For much of its history the Commonwealth was one of the largest, wealthiest, and most powerful European states. While few economic statistics from this period exist today, it is well accepted that economic development in agriculture, finance, mining, timber, and trade was relatively advanced. This was especially true in the years of the Polish-Lithuanian Commonwealth, also known as Poland's First Republic, following Poland's constitutional union with Lithuania in 1569.

The Commonwealth possessed relatively well developed traditions of civil society and gave broad political rights to the nobility, a group that included both landed magnates—who possessed vast landholdings, controlled rural life and stood at the apex of the Commonwealth—and the much larger and poorer (often landless) noble classes. The King or Queen was actually elected by the nobility as a whole. This function illustrated the nobility's passionate opposition to regal restrictions on its privileges. Legislation in the nobility's Sejm (parliament) was based on the principle of unanimity; a single nobleman could frustrate the will not only of the sovereign but also of the rest of the nobility through exercising his *liberum veto*. In the later years of the Commonwealth, the nobility, frequently acting at the behest of influential magnates, were often able to deny the sovereign the human, financial, and military resources necessary to rule effectively. From 1717 to 1773, for example, when the Commonwealth was larger in area and population than either France or Spain, it had no central treasury and a standing army of only 12,000 soldiers (Davies 1984, 1:511–513).

In many ways, the nobility's "golden freedom" served the Commonwealth well. It prevented the development of royalist absolutism, it attracted the allegiance of the nobility from a variety of lands between the Baltic and Black seas, and the Commonwealth's relative socioethnic tolerance provided a haven for Jews and others fleeing persecution in more authoritarian neighboring states. In fact, the Commonwealth's ability to loosely confederate a wide variety of national and religious groups[2] can be regarded as one of its greatest successes. However, the constraints that the "golden freedom" imposed on the central government's ability to take decisive action in the face of external threat ultimately proved to be the Commonwealth's ruin.

The royal elections and the prerogative of a single nobleman to bring the machinery of state to a halt provided foreign powers with numerous opportunities to intervene in the Commonwealth's internal affairs. The rise of the Russian, Austrian, and Prussian empires was accompanied (and made possible) by their manipulation of strife and intrigue among the Polish-Lithuanian nobility. Attempts at reforming the political mechanisms that jeopardized the Commonwealth's interests were frustrated by foreign powers interested in the Republic's demise. Internal strife and a series of wars, the most devastating of which were with Sweden, loosened the Polish-Lithuanian hold on the Ukraine and the Baltic seacoast during the seventeenth century. These defeats weakened the Commonwealth's ability to defend itself against the designs of the Russian and Prussian empires. In 1772, 1793, and 1795 Russia, Prussia, and Austria subjected Poland-Lithuania to three partitions. Attempts at internal reform, such as the promulgation of the constitution of 3 May 1791, only stiffened imperial resolve to settle what became known as the "Polish question" more firmly. In 1795, the third partition essentially obliterated Poland from the map of Europe.

Polish history from 1795 to 1918 is thus a history of a people that began acquiring national consciousness while being divided between the Russian, Prussian (German), and Austrian empires. Poles in the German partition enjoyed the most advantageous socioeconomic circumstances; they benefited from the rapid German industrialization of the nineteenth century and until German unification, in 1871, experienced only moderate cultural germanification. By 1914, economic development had progressed furthest in the German regions, and many Poles migrated from the Austrian and Russian partitions to the German provinces of Silesia and Posen (Poznań) in search of opportunity.

In contrast to the German partition, where the scope of political and cultural autonomy was reduced during the course of the nineteenth century, Polish reformers in Galicja in the Austrian Empire were able to broaden the scope of local Polish control in the latter half of the nineteenth century, especially after the creation of the dual Austro-Hungarian Monarchy in 1867. Cracow attained a leading position in scientific and ecclesiastical affairs. However, as Polish culture prospered in the Austrian partition, economic development stagnated. According to a contemporary (1887) observer,

> rural overpopulation in Galicja had outstripped that in all other parts of Europe, and was approaching levels prevalent in China and India. . . . some 50,000 people were dying each year as a result of near starvation conditions. . . . As compared with the standard of living in England at that time, the average Galician produced only one-quarter of the quantity of basic foodstuffs, ate less than one-half of the standard English diet, possessed only one-ninth of the Englishman's propertied wealth, and received barely one-eleventh of the English farmer's return on his land; yet he paid twice as high a proportion of his income in taxes. (Davies 1984, 2:145)

Grinding poverty in Galicja helped produce a number of bloody peasant revolts and exacerbated tensions between Poles, Ukrainians, Ruthenians,

Jews, and other ethnic and religious groups. It also produced large migrations of Polish peasants to the German partition, to other German and European states, and, in the nineteenth century, to the Americas.

Poles in the Russian empire faced political oppression from the tsarist autocracy, russification campaigns focusing on Polish culture and Catholicism, and often stifling imperial controls over economic life. The suppression of Polish politics and culture was strongest in the Russian partition, especially following the death of Tsar Alexander I, in 1825. The assertion of tsarist absolutism by Nicholas I ("the gendarme of Europe") and his successors in turn incited the Poles to open rebellion in 1830–1831 and 1863. Both uprisings were brutally suppressed. On the other hand, because of their close proximity to Europe at the Russian empire's western edge, protective tariffs, and a high level of economic development relative to the rest of the Russian empire, Polish cities like Warsaw and Łódź became important commercial and industrial centers. The abolition of serfdom, in 1861, was followed by a more lenient attitude toward private enterprise, and the Polish lands in the Russian partition experienced agricultural and industrial revolutions of sorts, especially during the last decades of the nineteenth century.

Despite these differences, Poles in the three empires shared a number of experiences. The power of the landed magnates and the nobility was reduced and economic life became subject to firmer central state control. When the agricultural and industrial revolutions began to take hold in the nineteenth century, the degree of state direction was greater than in Britain or the United States, and probably greater than would have been the case if the relatively decentralized Polish-Lithuanian Commonwealth had been preserved. Because of this, when economic modernization came to Poland it was often directed by state institutions that regarded Polishness with indifference or hostility.

More specifically, economic development in the lands of the former Commonwealth was distorted by the borders now crisscrossing it. The partitions turned much of the Polish territories into borderlands in each of the three empires that were relatively vulnerable to military attack. This vulnerability made the imperial authorities reluctant to locate important industries or transportation and communication facilities in the Polish lands. The lack of political sovereignty affected the economic sphere, since policies that failed to promote (and at times persecuted) Polish businesses were also obstacles to economic development. The division of Poland into thirds reduced the size of Polish markets within each partition relative to their pre-1772 size. This made capturing economies of scale more difficult for entrepreneurs wanting to service the Polish community within each partition. Large-scale economic ventures were often conducted with non-Polish capital, often under imperial guidance or control. The borders dissecting what had been the First Republic provided Poles with greater opportunities for enrichment through smuggling, arbitrage, and speculation than would otherwise have been the case. Entrepreneurship, as it developed during the partitions, thus contained large measures of conspiracy and corruption.

Politically, Poles during the nineteenth and early twentieth centuries faced the dilemma of reconciling their increasingly well defined Polish national consciousness with their citizenship in one of the partitioning states. Polish nationalism in its modern form[3] thus began to take shape at a time when the Polish state in which Poles could be Polish citizens was either dysfunctional or nonexistent. The conflict between Polish nationalism and non-Polish citizenship forced individuals to adopt one of three postures: loyalism, conciliation, or insurrection (Davies 1984, 2:29–60).

Loyalists essentially adopted the world view of their overlord, (re)casting their ethnic identity to correspond to their Russian/German/Austrian citizenship. Insurrectionists thus branded the loyalists as collaborators and traitors, while the authorities regarded loyalists as models for russification or germanification. Insurrectionists, by contrast, viewed themselves as Poles first and foremost, and generally refused to acknowledge the finality of either their non-Polish citizenship or the destruction of the Polish state. In the context of emerging nations in the nineteenth-century empires, this romantic nationalism made the insurrectionist a revolutionary who often rejected as collaboration all forms of compromise with or participation in official political life. Insurrectionism in turn provoked a harsh reaction from the authorities, who, especially in the Russian partition, often punished the population to a degree quite disproportionate to its support for the insurrectionists' programs and methods.

Conciliators occupied the center. While sharing many of the insurrectionists' goals of independence and self-determination, the conciliators adopted more moderate, pragmatic programs for attaining them, emphasizing cooperation with the authorities when it served national ends. In taking the long view, the conciliators hoped to salvage as much of Polish nationhood as possible, both before and after Poland's eventual release from imperial bondage. Conciliation was responsible for much of the socioeconomic progress made during the partitions, especially in such areas as education.

These world views made a deep imprint on Poland's national consciousness and had important implications for Polish political and economic life after the recovery of statehood in 1918. The legacy of insurrectionism, which was linked to certain elements of the nobility's prepartition "golden freedom," hindered the development of a democratic political culture based on moderation, conciliation, and compromise. The loyalist tradition tended to equate dissent and opposition with conspiracy and sedition. These polarizing tendencies were reinforced by the crucible of the Nazi and Soviet occupations during the Second World War and by Poland's postwar subjugation to the Soviet Union.

These historical trends did not by themselves determine the path of Poland's economic and political development, of course. Nor were they unique to Poland, since the national consciousness of other Central and Eastern European nations developed under broadly similar circumstances in the late nineteenth and early twentieth centuries. Still, these trends did structure the historical context in which modern Poland emerged. The tensions evident in this structure, especially in the effects of the loss of statehood on Poland's economic development and in the political culture that formed during the awakening of modern Polish national identity, are important in understanding post-1918 developments.

The Rise and Fall of the Second Republic

Poland reemerged as a nation-state in 1918 with the collapse of the Russian, German, and Austrian Empires at the end of the First World War; its exact borders and population were determined by a series of military campaigns, treaties, and plebiscites from 1918 to 1921. The war and its aftermath had devastating economic consequences for Poland. More than 80 percent of the land area subsequently included in the Second Republic had been contested during the war and destructive battles were fought on more than 20 percent of what became Polish territory. Confiscation and expropriation by passing armies of everything from foodstuffs to industrial plant and equipment was common.[4] According to one estimate, 11 percent of Polish assets, 18 percent of its housing stock, more than 1.5 million farm buildings, and one third of the country's livestock were destroyed in the war (Taylor 1952, 12). More than one million Poles are thought to have perished, and 3.6 million were involved in migrations during the period 1914–1918 (Kostrowicka and Przeciszewski 1989, 36–37).

The Second Republic was the phoenix that arose from these ashes. Despite the fact that it possessed only 35 percent of the territory included within the 1772 frontiers (Taylor 1952, 4), the Second Republic was the sixth largest European state in area. It was decidedly multiethnic: according to the 1921 census,[5] national and ethnic minorities (primarily Ukrainians, Jews, Belarussians, and Germans) constituted approximately 30 percent of the general population and over 60 percent of the population in some of Poland's Eastern districts. More than one million ethnic Poles remained outside the new borders, primarily in Germany. The Polish economy in 1921 was overwhelmingly agricultural: 74 percent of the population lived in villages and 53 percent were classified as peasants (27 percent were classified as workers, 11 percent as small entrepreneurs, and 5 percent as intellectuals). The magnates continued to dominate the countryside, with 0.3 percent of the population owning more than 40 percent of the land (ibid., 33–34); the nobility's position was only marginally affected by the land reform of 1925 (Davies 1984, 2:410). Overpopulation and poverty haunted poorer farmers, many of whose farms were too small to be efficiently mechanized. Not surprisingly, peasant strikes and rural unrest were common in the Second Republic.

The economic problems facing interwar Poland were immense. In addition to organizing the recovery from wartime destruction, the leaders of the Second Republic had to create a national economy for a Polish state that had been nonexistent for 123 years. A sense of common statehood had to be forged, not only among Poles but among a variety of other nationals who had formerly been citizens of the three empires. The economic links connecting Poland to Vienna, Moscow, and Berlin—ties that had been central to nineteenth-century industrial and agricultural development—had been weakened or broken. Three different systems of law and administration, tariffs and taxation, and credit and finance, not to mention separate currencies, had to be integrated and standardized. External support for Poland from the Western powers was soon overshadowed by German and Soviet irredentism, which played on the fears of Poland's German and Slavic minorities and heightened antagonisms between these groups and the Polish majority. Most sources of domestic Polish capital had been destroyed during the war; most large-scale capital was owned by foreign interests, primarily French, German, and American (Taylor 1952, 60). Given the relatively small size of the Polish economy and its former dependence on the partitioning empires, extensive trade with neighboring countries had to be a key element of a successful economic program. However, tensions between Poland, Germany, and the USSR made such cooperation virtually impossible, as seen, for example, in the German "Tariff War" of 1926–1934.[6] The Polish economy was thus reconstituted in a state of crisis and faced serious questions about its viability.

Evaluating the Second Republic's economic performance is a difficult and controversial task. Comprehensive, good-quality statistics from the interwar period, methodologically comparable with post-1945 data (which are themselves quite problematic), are rare. Tremendous problems of economic reconstruction and integration, as well as Poland's vulnerability to pan-European economic developments such as the German hyperinflation of the 1920s and the Great Depression of the 1930s, complicate the interpretation of quantitative performance measures. A balanced accounting is also hindered by the fact that the Second Republic was vilified by the propagandists of the postwar People's Republic and idealized by some elements of the anticommunist opposition. In general, though, two points about the interwar Polish economy can be fairly made: (1) While different economic policies were pursued by different governments, creating national economic institutions remained of paramount importance throughout the period; (2) the role of the state in the Polish economy was significant, regardless of the parties in government.

The inflation of the early 1920s was the predictable result of wartime and postwar dislocation, of inflation imported from neighboring countries (especially Germany), and of policy decisions by Polish governments attempting to create a unified national economy without the appropriate institutional or policy structures. This is most apparent in fiscal policy, where tax revenues covered as little as 10 percent of government expenditures from 1919 to 1923 (Davies 1984, 2:415). The central government's budget was not brought into balance until 1926, eight years after the country's rebirth. Yearly inflation rates are estimated to have ranged from 395 percent in 1921 to 35,715 percent in the hyperinflationary year of 1923 (Morawski 1989, 258).

The hyperinflation of 1923 was followed by reforms implemented in 1924 by Prime Minister and Treasury Minister Władysław Grabski. These included the creation of an independent central bank, tax reform, and the introduction of a new currency, the *zloty*, 30 percent of which was to be backed by gold and foreign exchange. Grabski's reforms helped create financial institutions compatible with an international economy then attempting to return to the gold standard and prewar currency stability. Combined with more restrictive fiscal policies (the government budget was kept in surplus from 1926 to 1929), Grabski's reforms improved Poland's external creditworthiness and convinced Western governments to reschedule loans made during 1918. This helped Poland attract new foreign loans after 1926. These reforms were followed by the industrial expansion of 1923–

1929,[7] symbolized by the opening of the port in the Baltic town of Gdynia in 1927.

While Grabski's reforms represented a relatively orthodox, laissez-faire approach to macroeconomic and trade policies, they took place within a framework of state-directed institution-building intended to speed recovery from wartime devastation and to ensure national control over finance (state banks dominated throughout the entire interwar period), education, and social-welfare policy. Even the anti-inflationary emphasis on creating a strong currency through tight money policies and backing the zloty with gold was viewed as support for an important symbol of Polish statehood.

The policy orthodoxy represented by Grabski's reforms did not survive the Great Depression that began in 1929. Poland was one of the few European countries that did not abandon the gold standard during the Depression: Great Britain and the United States went off gold in 1931 and 1934, respectively. Instead, austerity policies were followed, to support the zloty and to maintain Poland's international appeal as a repository for liquid assets. (This was seen as necessary in order to provide the government with funds to service the foreign debt.) While these policies allowed Poland to maintain its external creditworthiness, they contributed to reductions in output, rising unemployment, strikes, and social unrest. These effects were especially severe during the first years of the Depression: industrial production declined by about 27 percent and industrial employment by around 35 percent from 1929 to 1933 (Drożdowski 1963, 11–13).

In addition to weakening the economic basis of the laissez-faire macroeconomic and financial policies of the 1920s, the dislocation produced by the Depression was widely perceived as jeopardizing the progress made after 1918 in establishing Poland's national economy. The combination of the austerity policies pursued during the first years of the Depression, the discrediting of laissez-faire throughout Europe, the rise of the cartels, and growing social tensions produced an institutional shift toward greater state regulation, interventionism, and planning during the late 1930s. This shift is associated with another series of reforms, begun in 1936 by Eugeniusz Kwiatkowski, Deputy Prime Minister and Treasury Minister. Although public institutions were already playing important roles in such areas as education and social-welfare policy, Kwiatkowski believed that the state had to more actively compensate for the weaknesses of the Polish private sector. Kwiatkowski's vision was of a mixed economy consisting of strong private and cooperative sectors; a state sector dominant in such areas as infrastructure and industries of strategic, geopolitical, and military significance, as well as in education and social welfare; and state institutions to regulate the private sector and coordinate interdependent public and private activities.

Kwiatkowski supervised the construction of Poland's first "State Plan" and established the Bureau of Economic Planning to design and implement it. (A loan of 2.6 billion francs from the French government, reflecting in part the French concern over the militarism of Hitler's Germany, helped finance the plan.) He promoted the planning and development of the "central industrial region" in Southeastern Poland, in which the Polish state owned and managed metallurgical, mining, and armaments firms. In general, Kwiatkowski took a more *dirigiste* approach to macroeconomic policy, foreign trade, industrial development, and finance than his predecessors. The central bank lost much of its autonomy vis-à-vis the government during this time, and controls over foreign exchange transactions were tightened significantly. Moreover, in addition to the expanded role of national and regional economic planning mentioned above, the state had by 1939 acquired the lion's share of ownership in key industrial sectors[8] and finance, as well as maintaining monopolies over the lottery and the sale of alcohol, tobacco, salt, and matches. The renunciation of laissez-faire was widely seen at the time as a success (Davies 1984; Taylor 1952), since it coincided with the resumption of economic growth during the second half of the 1930s.[9]

Did the new institutions and policies resolve the economic crisis confronting Poland in 1918? In one sense, the answer is clearly yes. The leaders of the Second Republic were able to create a viable nation-state and national economy out of fractious peoples previously belonging to three different empires. The country survived hyperinflation and depression without the catastrophic political consequences that befell Weimar Germany, and important progress was made in heavy industry, mining, military production, finance, education, culture, and elsewhere. To the extent that the economic crisis in 1918 challenged the viability of the Polish state and national economy, the Second Republic met the challenge.

On the other hand, the Polish economy in 1939 remained overwhelmingly rural. Relatively little progress had been made either in lightening the burden that overpopulated, undercapitalized, and inefficient peasant agriculture imposed on industrial development or, more specifically, in reducing the share of the labor force absorbed by agriculture.[10] Many peasant families were pushed to the brink of subsistence; markets for manufactured goods in rural areas collapsed; declining real (and nominal) wages created disincentives to invest in labor-saving modern technologies; and stock-market activity and capital formation in the private sector slowed significantly. Unemployment in both urban and rural areas remained a serious problem until the late 1930s. While Poland's economic performance during the interwar period was not inconsistent with the performance of many other European economies during this period, the Second Republic looks rather anemic compared to the industrial dynamism of the Soviet economy, as well as that of Nazi Germany during this period.[11]

Poland's economic problems were also reflected in the country's political life. Although the Second Republic did not collapse into the totalitarianism that afflicted Poland's neighbors during the interwar period, the democratic institutions established between 1918 and 1921 did give way to authoritarianism. Józef Piłsudski, the leader of the military and diplomatic campaigns associated with the restoration of independence during this period, launched a coup d'état in May 1926 that effectively spelled the end of parliamentary democracy in interwar Poland. The *Sanacja* governments that ruled under Piłsudski's supervision and after his death, in 1935, dominated the Sejm and the political parties, forcing the country's pluralistic aspirations to be rechannelled into more nationalistic, corporatist, and authoritarian modes of articulation. Tensions between the Polish majority and the Ukrainian, German, Jewish, and other ethnic minorities worsened during the interwar period, especially after Piłsudski's death.

To its defenders, the Second Republic's success in forging a viable nation-state and national economy outweighs its failures, which are often ascribed to the 123 years of foreign domination, Poland's difficult geopolitical situation during the interwar period, the brevity of the Republic's twenty-year existence, and misfortunes (such as the Great Depression) beyond the country's control. The economic progress made during the interwar period, the fact that the political system did not collapse into totalitarianism, and the preservation of many individual liberties—all are taken as evidence of the basic correctness of capitalism for interwar Poland. The Second Republic's critics, especially defenders of the People's Republic (1945–1990), stress the Republic's lack of industrial dynamism, the poverty of the urban and rural masses, Polish entrepreneurs' dependence on foreign capital and technology, the persecution of national minorities, and the country's inability to effectively marshal its internal resources in the face of external threats. Interwar Poland's capitalist economic institutions were often blamed for these failures during the communist period.

The Second Republic was obliterated during the Second World War (1939–1945). As a consequence of seven years of brutal fighting and resistance to Nazi and Soviet military occupation, Poland's population was reduced by a third, from 34,849 at the end of 1938 to 23,930 in February 1946 (*Polska 1918–1988* 1989, 9). Six million citizens of the Second Republic perished during the war, most of whom (5.4 million) died in concentration camps, public executions, and guerrilla resistance rather than in standard military campaigns. Warsaw was razed to the ground on Hitler's orders after the ill-fated Warsaw uprising of August–September 1944. The Nazi and Soviet occupations destroyed the Polish financial system and expropriated or destroyed most of the country's liquid assets. According to one estimate, 38 percent of the country's prewar (1938) national wealth had been destroyed by 1945 (Secomski 1950, 12). Retail prices increased more than 100-fold from 1939 to 1945 (Montias 1962, 69). Agriculture was largely devastated by the war and most of the population was quickly reduced to living at subsistence levels.[12] The Soviet armies that "liberated" Poland in 1944–1945 plundered everything from livestock to factories, including the entire electrified Silesian railroad network (Davies 1984, 2:481).

The war's impact on Polish society was similarly devastating. Once again, Polishness per se was persecuted. Poles performed slave labor for German and Russian overlords and were again faced with the dilemma of choosing between loyalism, conciliation, and insurrection. Economic success—indeed, survival—often depended on black marketeering, speculation, connections, and bribery. The unhappy lessons of the partitions, which had been partially unlearned during the Second Republic—unyielding patriotism/nationalism, unwillingness to compromise, deception as a prerequisite for economic survival, and resistance to many forms of state authority—were reinforced during the war. On the other hand, the widespread and heroic resistance to the Nazi and Soviet occupations illustrated the sacrifices that many Poles were willing to make for Poland. This reinforced the more noble qualities of perseverance, personal dignity, and honor in the face of official oppression—traits which were to reappear in the democratic opposition's struggle against communism after the war.

Because the war largely obliterated the Jewry, the intelligentsia, and much of the propertied classes, the peasantry and the working class became by default the two dominant social groups in postwar Poland. The Catholic Church also found its relative position strengthened by the war, since the Church was one of the few institutions in which Polishness could be expressed during the occupation. The Church's wartime role as "the guardian of Polish nationhood" helped moderate the anticlericalism present in many groups' attitudes toward the Church during the interwar period.

The war also produced far-reaching geographic and demographic changes in Poland. As a result of agreements at the Teheran, Yalta, and Potsdam summit conferences in 1944 and 1945, 178,220 square kilometers of Polish territory east of the Bug River were ceded to the Soviet Union. In return, Poland received 101,200 square kilometers of former German territory in the north and west, much of which had not been inhabited by Poles for hundreds of years. In all, Poland moved some 150 miles west and lost about 20 percent of its prewar area. The war's end also produced dramatic migrations from east to west. From 1944 to 1949 approximately 2.3 million Germans left or were expelled from Polish territories new and old. (Most made their way to what was to become the Federal Republic–West Germany). Approximately 1.5 million Poles and other ethnic groups chose to emigrate to Poland rather than stay in territories that had been included in the Soviet Union (*Polska 1918–1988* 1989, 10). Poland in 1945 not only found itself without its prewar Jewish population, but the German minority had been largely expelled and most of the Ukrainian, Belarussian, and Lithuanian citizens of the Second Republic now found themselves in the Soviet Union. For the first time in its history, Poland was a homogeneous, almost exclusively Roman-Catholic and Polish state.

The Establishment of Socialism

Although the end of the Second World War consigned Poland to the Soviet sphere of influence, the establishment of the pro-Soviet People's Republic was neither immediate nor simple. A number of factors, including the initial Soviet desire to maintain amicable relations with the Western powers, the electoral procedures agreed upon at the Yalta and Potsdam conferences, and strong opposition to sovietization within Poland, prevented the Soviet Union from moving faster. The weakness of the pro-Soviet left in Poland was also important, since the Communist movement in Poland prior to 1945 had generally been weak or nonexistent.

The Soviet liberation of Poland in 1944–1945 meant new life for the few Polish Communists who survived Stalin's purges during the 1930s and the war. The period between 1945 and 1947 was marked by acrimonious attempts at compromise between the government-in-exile in London and the Soviet-sponsored Polish Committee of National Liberation, which was dominated by the newly created Polish Workers' Party (PPR). Despite political antagonisms within the coalition government, there was broad agreement concerning the need for a prominent state role in the economy. This reflected the legacy of the Kwiatkowski period and the urgent need for recovery from war damage and for restoration of a Polish national economy. During the period 1945–1947, therefore, the coalition government introduced land reform; (re)nationalized the banking system, transportation, communications, and much of industry; instituted price controls in an attempt to prevent hyperinflation; and took on the burden of social welfare. These activities were conducted within the indicative-planning framework of the "Three Year Plan for Reconstruction" of 1947–1949. The nationalizations were not directed primarily at Poland's propertied classes (which had largely fled or been liquidated during the war) but were instead intended to ensure Polish control over what were regarded as Polish assets. Given the prewar traditions of state intervention and planning, as well as the pan-European rise of socialism and social democracy in the immediate postwar years, the reappearance of the Polish state's formidable prewar economic role was probably inevitable.

The Polish economy during the years 1945 to 1947 was decidedly multisectoral, with cooperative and private (largely nonindustrial) firms functioning alongside state enterprises. This multisectorality resulted less from a grand design than from the spontaneous reappearance of prewar private and cooperative firms, a plethora of unstable regulatory, tax, and ownership policies, and a wildly speculative socioeconomic environment in which the authority of the Polish state had yet to be definitively reasserted. This was especially true in the territories acquired from Germany. In any case, most of the targets in the Three Year Plan were achieved and inflation was brought under control after 1948.

The economic policies implemented following the PPR's fraudulent victory in the January 1947 elections marked the end of this postwar interregnum. Questions about the role of the private and cooperative sectors were quickly settled with Stalinist resolve. The declaration by Minister of Industry and Trade Hilary Minc in May 1947 that "We have won the battle over production, and we shall attempt to win the battle over trade" symbolized the PPR's determination to impose the Soviet model. Pricing, taxation, and regulatory policies were turned against private entrepreneurs, who increasingly found themselves at a disadvantage to the state sector. Entrepreneurs who violated the stiffened and often contradictory regulations were subject to prohibitive fines, five-year jail sentences, and confiscation of property without compensation. Similarly, the cooperative sector was increasingly etatized: small cooperatives were forcibly amalgamated into larger units whose management was selected by the PPR. The campaign to collectivize private agriculture was stepped up in the countryside, reversing the decentralizing trend begun by the 1946 land reform.

Not surprisingly, the number of legal private trading and service establishments declined precipitously after 1947. Many went bankrupt, others went underground. The authorities generally declined to replace these private firms with state enterprises, concentrating instead on the development of heavy industry, an area in which the private sector had been poorly represented. Although statistics from this period are of notoriously poor quality, Aaslund (1985) estimates that the number of legal private firms in Poland declined by 41 percent between 1947 and 1953, while employment in the private sector registered a 61 percent drop (p. 232). Average enterprise size and the share of state ownership increased, since small-scale industrial firms often proved to be of little use to the PZPR's new central planning apparatus, which lacked the administrative flexibility, personnel, and inclination to manage them effectively. According to a Planning Commission estimate, approximately 10,000 nationalized small industrial shops stood empty in 1951–1952 (ibid., 49) and only 6,500–7,000 private nonagricultural establishments were legally functioning at this time (ibid., 235).

Equally important was the corruption of the private sector, both illegal activities conducted by otherwise legal firms and the growth of organizations that were entirely illegal. As Aaslund put it,

> The conditions were almost ideal for the creation of an underground economy. The number of regulations was very large, so they could neither be followed nor effectively supervised. They were frequently altered, and the announcement of new regulations was often late. Regulations were seldom clear, often inconsistent, and impossible to comply with. They lacked support from tradition and public opinion. . . . Penalties were very severe, but were not an effective deterrent in a time of extensive violation of the multiplicity of laws. (Ibid., 52)

The fruits of corruption were shared by the regulatory organs policing the private sector, in the form of bribes and payoffs, and by the state firms that illegally supplied private entrepreneurs with inputs at high prices. The high demand for privately produced goods and services generally unavailable in the official economy; the extra costs of risk, uncertainty, and corruption associated with illegal production; and the absence of competition among sellers—all this produced rapacious private entrepreneurs whose penchant for high prices and short-term profits fit the regime's portrayal of the private sector as a nest of blood-sucking bandits.

In keeping with the Soviet model, planning was centralized in the hands of the State Commission for Economic Planning and became compulsory and comprehensive. (By contrast, before 1948, planning targets were assigned to public enterprises only in certain key sectors such as coal mining;

planning in general had an indicative character.) The number of industrial ministries swelled from one in 1948 to six in 1949 and ten in 1954, reflecting the increasing bureaucratization of economic decision making. Rapid growth of heavy industry through increased investment and slower consumption growth became the focus of the "Six Year Plan" of 1950–1955. Investment in agriculture, trade, services, and light industry was thus sacrificed to the development of heavy industry. Political control over the economy was exercised by the party *nomenklatura*, through its appointment of managers, planning officials, and trade-union leaders. Trade flows were reoriented away from Western trading partners toward the USSR and the Council for Mutual Economic Assistance (CMEA), created in 1949. Zloty convertibility was not reestablished. In 1947 Poland refused aid from the Marshall Plan aid and withdrew from the International Monetary Fund.

At the same time, political options were narrowed. The unwilling Polish Socialist Party (PPS) was forced to merge with the PPR, creating the PZPR. The other political parties were either liquidated or subordinated to the PZPR, and the Catholic Church and other autonomous social institutions were attacked and frequently subverted. Within the PZPR, the dominance of the pro-Moscow faction, led by First Secretary Bolesław Bierut, was established over the "national communist" faction of Władysław Gomułka. Bierut replaced Gomułka as First Secretary in 1948, and Gomułka was subsequently imprisoned. Political and ideological conformity was imposed through Stalinist terror. Although for a time anti-communist forces offered armed resistance to the Stalinist juggernaut, they were no match for Polish and Soviet security forces. By 1948, Poland's fate had been sealed.

Despite this, it is important to note that the Polish rendition of Stalinism was milder than the versions introduced in other Eastern European countries after 1947. The noncommunist PPS, the Peasant Party (*Stronnictwo Ludowe*), and the Democratic Party (*Zjednoczone Stronnictwo Demokratyczne*) were spared complete annihilation; Gomułka and Cardinal Stefan Wyszyński were imprisoned but not executed; peasants who resisted collectivization were not deported or resettled;[13] intellectuals were denied freedom of expression but not persecuted; and relatively tight controls over the secret police were maintained after 1947. Poland's historical traditions of individual liberties, civil society and resistance to foreign oppression thus helped prevent the worst excesses of Stalinism. Whereas Stalinism was able to create a social basis for its perpetuation in the USSR, Romania, and other Soviet bloc countries, in Poland it did not long outlast Stalin's death in 1953.

Ironically, the imposition of Stalinism in Poland was accompanied by economic growth and recovery.[14] The postwar rebuilding program and the

PZPR's emphasis on forced industrialization allowed Polish national income to grow (in real terms) by more than 76 percent from 1947 to 1950, according to the official statistics. Gross agricultural and industrial production more than doubled from 1946 to 1950. This growth spurt was accompanied by a decline in agriculture's share of national income, which fell from 70 percent to 60.3 percent from 1946 to 1950. This decline reflected the start of a significant reallocation of labor and other resources away from agriculture to industry. Trade (in nominal terms) with both capitalist and socialist countries more than quadrupled. Open unemployment was eradicated and central control over pricing prevented the appearance of overt inflation.[15] Even allowing for official exaggeration, these data are not unimpressive, especially when compared to statistics from the period 1921–1926, after the First World War.

On the other hand, official statistics also illustrate the downside of this initial effort at forced industrialization. The consumption share of national income declined relative to the investment share, with the result that living standards grew more slowly than production. Relatively slow growth in the production of consumer goods, together with price controls, resulted in chronic shortages and poor-quality products. Although the investment share of national income increased by 35 percent from 1947 to 1950, this increase was spread unevenly across the economy: the share of investment devoted to agriculture registered a 61 percent decline, for example, while the share absorbed by industry more than doubled. Although reliable data on labor and capital productivity for this time period are generally unavailable, it is widely accepted that this rapid industrialization and economic growth resulted largely from marshaling under- or unemployed labor reserves, recovery from wartime damage and, later, the relatively slow growth in living standards, rather than increases in factory productivity, improved education, or technological changes.[16] Stanisław Gomułka (1986), for example, estimates that 85 percent of Poland's economic growth from 1947 to 1953 was attributable to postwar reconstruction alone (pp. 159–160). The Soviet model may have produced an initial measure of industrial dynamism and economic security in Poland, but this was not matched by a comparable rise in living standards.

Most important, the period 1946 to 1950 marked the beginning of Poland's isolation from Western sources of capital, technology, consumer goods, and managerial know-how—essentials that could not be provided by the CMEA. Although Poland's economy became more modern, urban, and industrialized during this time, it also became inefficient, trade-averse, resource-intensive, and shortage-prone, dependent on the Soviet export market and importing Soviet raw materials. Moreover, the end of World War II ushered in a period of rapid economic growth throughout Europe and the international economy. As Table 1.1 shows, Polish growth statistics look less impressive relative to other countries, both capitalist and socialist.

While the initial progress of the 1950s seemed to address the Second Republic's problems of underdevelopment, the institutions that accompanied this "progress" also created new, more formidable and ultimately unsustainable pressures and tensions. The illegitimacy of the People's Republic in the eyes of the population, the hostility with which its relationship to the USSR was viewed, the communist regime's suppression of civil and human rights and its attacks on Catholicism and other elements of Polish culture—all this created tremendous resistance to communism, resistance that could not be bought off indefinitely with the diminishing returns of forced industrialization.

Since socialism came to be associated with domination by the Soviet Union, much of Polish society felt itself toiling again under a Russian overlord. Choosing between insurrectionism, loyalism, and conciliation again became an omnipresent feature of political life, resulting in divided loyalties, mutual hostilities, emigration, "internal exile," and much wasted energy that could have been devoted to the common good. This undoubtedly had a profoundly negative impact upon work incentives, labor discipline, and productivity. The black markets that were inevitable adjuncts to Soviet-style socialism also presented Poles with vast new opportunities for personal enrichment through smuggling, bribery, and other forms of corruption, further weakening the economic culture acquired during the Second Republic and unlearned during the Second World War. On the other hand, traditional qualities of resistance, personal dignity, and honor in the face of oppression, reinforced during the Nazi and Soviet occupations, lent themselves to widespread (initially passive) opposition to the new order, causing continual problems for the PZPR.

In the thirty years between the consolidation of Soviet-style socialism in Poland (1950) and the appearance of the Solidarity opposition movement (1980), these tensions produced a number of distinct political crises in which the PZPR's hold on Polish political life weakened noticeably. In addition to demonstrating the PZPR's political weakness, the events of 1956, 1968, 1970–1971, and 1976 produced a series of economic policy mistakes in the 1970s that created first a pronounced economic crisis in the 1980s and then, after 1989, the collapse of Polish socialism. It is to these developments that we now turn.

TABLE 1.1
National Income Per Capita for Selected Countries, 1938 and 1975

	1938	*1975*
Poland	100	100
Hungary	95	96
Italy	106	126
Japan	137	181
Soviet Union	123	139

Source: Jezierski and Petz 1988, 435.

STALINISM AND THE POLISH OCTOBER

The period 1945–1955 ended in a political crisis in which a national uprising against the ruling PZPR and the occupying Soviet military forces was only narrowly averted. The crisis also produced Poland's first serious discussion of (and a less serious attempt at) reforming its Soviet-type economy. Although economic factors were probably not the most important cause of the crisis, they did play an important role in creating the socioeconomic tensions that formed the backdrop to the events of 1956.

Poland's traditions of anti-Russian sentiment and resistance to foreign oppression generated immense pressures on the communist regime and made Stalinism an untenable long-term proposition. Stalin's death, in March 1953, was followed by a thaw in the USSR and Poland in which voices of dissent (usually Marxist) were permitted. In 1954–1955 the thaw developed into a full-fledged de-Stalinization campaign culminating in Soviet Premier Khrushchev's secret speech denouncing Stalin at the twentieth congress of the Soviet Communist Party, in February 1956. Combined with the news from Moscow, attacks on Stalinism at home proved to be more than the PZPR leadership could handle. The death of First Secretary Bolesław Bierut (possibly by suicide) during the Soviet party conference in Moscow plunged the PZPR into turmoil; the party rank and file, the Sejm, and Polish society in general were increasingly demanding the decentralization and democratization of political and intellectual life. This ferment also reinvigorated the PZPR's "national communist" faction loyal to former First Secretary Władysław Gomułka, who had been imprisoned in 1948.

These political developments occurred against a backdrop of slowing economic growth, declining real wages, increasing shortage pressures, overextended investments, and the chronic underfulfillment of the overambitious Six Year Plan of 1950–1955, especially in agriculture and construction. The attack on the private sector begun in 1947 had reduced supplies of consumer goods and foodstuffs. 1953 was the peak year in socialist Poland's first investment cycle: the share of gross investment in national income used (in 1971 prices) reached 19 percent in 1953, up from 12 percent in 1948. Despite this investment boom, yearly growth of national income used fell from 30 to 6 percent during this period (Moskwa, Socha, and Wilkin 1981, 211–213). Consumers' purchasing power therefore increasingly exceeded the economy's capacity to supply consumer goods, despite the confiscatory monetary reform of 1950 and the reintroduction of food rationing in 1951 and again in 1954–1955. Although the plan called for 50 to 60 percent increases in real wages from 1950 to 1955, they actually declined in 1951–1952 and did not regain their 1949 levels until 1956 (Montias 1962, 63). Internationally, Poland's share of world imports and exports declined by 8.6 and 4.9 percent, respectively, during the Six Year Plan (Feiwel 1971, 1:708), while the share of Polish trade with socialist countries increased at the expense of trade with advanced capitalist countries. Not surprisingly, the Polish Economics Association, at its June 1956 conference, took advantage of the more open political environment to criticize the country's economic performance and demand "corrections" in the "economic model."

After Stalin's death, Bierut and his associates moved to reduce the economic pressures on the regime. The share of national income used that was devoted to investment fell from 19 to 15 percent between 1953 and 1956; more resources were allocated to agriculture and consumer-goods production; the fall in real wages was arrested; the pace of agricultural collectivization in the countryside was slowed; a special Economic Council of blue-ribbon economists, including Oskar Lange, Michał Kalecki, Włodzimierz Brus, and others, was appointed to advise the Council of Ministers on possible changes in the economic "model." But it was too little too late. 53 people were killed when riots broke out in Poznań during the June 1956 trade fair, and unrest spread to other cities. Collective farms spontaneously dissolved (collectivization was officially halted in July 1956), workers' councils took control of key state enterprises, and the PZPR's authority began to collapse. A national uprising, and the bloody Soviet repression which would inevitably have followed, were barely avoided by Gomułka's ascension to power, in October 1956.

Gomułka assumed the mantle of leadership with an enormous degree of popular support. In addition to having been imprisoned for his lack of subservience to Moscow in 1948, Gomułka had faced down Khrushchev and avoided a national catastrophe. Moreover, in the months following the "Polish October," Gomułka convinced the Soviets to allow the Polish government and the PZPR more autonomy in domestic policy, to call home the Soviet members of the Polish Council of Ministers (such as Soviet General Konstantin Rokossowski, the Polish Minister of Defense from 1945 to 1956), and to offer compensation for Soviet plundering of the Polish economy during the Stalinist period. The aftermath of the Polish October therefore seemed an ideal time in which to attempt far-reaching reforms of the Soviet-type economic and political systems.

However, the Economic Council did not question the superiority of socialism over capitalism and found fault only in the unsophisticated and "voluntaristic" nature of the Six Year Plan. The Council sought instead to improve central planning through increasing the role of markets and prices within the planning process; it did not advocate replacing the plan with the market. State enterprises were to become less bureaucratic, more participatory, and more "genuinely socialistic"—not more entrepreneurial. Although the significance of prices was to increase, there was general agreement within the Council that the price-setting role of the market should be secondary to that of the state. Central direction of the macroeconomy through determination of the investment-consumption split and the growth rate were viewed as essential. So was the need for direct central control over enterprise investment activity and in cases in which manipulation of prices failed to produce the desired result (i.e., when autonomous enterprise decisions were inconsistent with the central plan). Crucially, the Council did not call for the abolition of mandatory enterprise plans and administrative supply allocation, only for limiting their scope. (The degree to which the retention of these features of the traditional system would reduce the effectiveness of reforms in other areas of the economy was not then appreciated even by reform economists [Zielinski 1978].) Above all, there was no call for denationalizing state enterprises or property; the Council's attitude toward the private sector ranged from indifferent to hostile.[17]

The years 1957 to 1960 saw a period of "counter-reform." The PZPR's authority was reasserted and the thaw that had begun after Stalin's death came to an end. The workers' councils that had appeared spontaneously in 1956 had by 1958 been incorporated into "Workers' Self-Management Conferences" (KSRs) controlled by the PZPR and the official trade unions. Censorship restrictions were tightened; the critical student journal *Po Prostu* was closed in the fall of 1957. The orthodox emphasis on investment over consumption returned: the share of national income used that was devoted to investment began a twenty-year increase in 1957. The Economic Council was dissolved after some of its proposals were implemented, but the retention of mandatory plan targets and central materials allocation and the preservation of gross output as the de facto indicator of enterprise success rendered the changes that were introduced virtually meaningless. And although the private sector's share of employment (relative to the state and cooperative sectors' shares) increased from 1956 to 1958, it then declined steadily through 1963 (Aaslund 1985, 230).

Of all the changes during 1954–1956, only the decollectivization of agriculture survived the counter-reforms. By December 1956, only 1.4 percent of the country's farmland was tilled by collectives, down from 11.2 percent in June of the same year; compulsory deliveries of some farm products to the state were abolished in late 1956 (Montias 1962, 272, 314). But even here there was backsliding, as the development of state (as opposed to collective) farms was emphasized after 1959. So although 1956 marked the end of the PZPR's application of class struggle to the countryside, it did not signify an acceptance of private farming.

By the early 1960s the reform process had come full circle and the pre-1956 status quo had been essentially reestablished. This circle constituted communist Poland's first "reform cycle"; similar cycles were evident during the 1970s and 1980s in Poland as well as in other socialist countries.[18] During periods of intense crisis, when the sociopolitical pressures on the regime became too great, the PZPR would promise and sometimes attempt to implement economic and political reforms. Once the threat had passed, however, the imperative of reform waned and would be lost in the crush of other concerns. Promises of reform thus served as a "systemic shock absorber" (Staniszkis 1984). Thus, Gomułka's ascension to power in October 1956 was both made possible by, and in itself reinforced, widespread expectations of reform; these expectations allowed Gomułka to strengthen the party's position in Poland, which helped to assuage Soviet concerns about the PZPR's political control.[19] Once the crisis at hand had passed, many promised reforms were forgotten; others (such as economic reforms) were implemented in a half-hearted, ineffective manner; and spontaneous changes that had already occurred (such as the introduction of workers' councils) were formally or informally reversed.

This instrumental treatment of reform (visible also in the "normalization" that followed the events of 1970–1971 and 1980–1981) would in turn help pave the way for the next political crisis, since temporizing on reform further reduced the PZPR's standing with Polish society. For this reason, the effectiveness of the "shock absorber" function of reform also declined over time, since promises of reform became less credible with each successive political crisis. In this way, reform became an element of the more fundamental crisis afflicting the People's Republic.

From October to December: The Gomułka Years

Economic policy after 1958 returned to the orthodox priorities, now realized in a somewhat more pragmatic fashion. As Table 1.2 shows, yearly increases in national income produced (in 1977 prices) averaged approximately 3 percent during 1955–1960 (the first Five Year Plan), 7 percent during 1960–1965 (the second Five Year Plan) and 6.5 percent during 1965–1970 (the third Five Year Plan). While these rates placed Poland near the bottom of the CMEA countries in terms of economic growth, they were still respectable by international standards, especially during the 1960s. The share of the labor force engaged in agriculture continued to fall, while the share of industrial production and construction in national income continued to grow. Yearly increases in real wages for workers in the "socialized" (state and cooperative) sectors averaged 4 percent between 1955 and 1970. The ratio of foreign trade to national income increased, as did Poland's share of world imports and exports.

Table 1.2
Selected Indicators of Economic Development, 1955–1970

	1955	*1960*	*1965*	*1970*
National income produced (NMP) (1970 = 100)	40.4	55.5	74.9	100.0
Gross industrial production (1970 = 100)	28.2	44.8	67.0	100.0
Gross agricultural production (1970–1975 = 100)	57.2	68.8	79.0	100.0
Percentage of labor force engaged in:				
Agriculture	48.2	43.3	39.1	34.3
Industry and construction	30.8	32.0	34.3	36.4
Share of NMP produced by:				
Agriculture	42.3	34.5	29.7	22.7
Industry and construction	37.8	44.8	49.1	55.7

Note: All data are in constant prices.

Sources: Rocznik Statystyczny 1989, xxxii, xxxviii, and *Rocznik Statystyczny: Przemysł* 1988, xxxviii.

On the other hand, even the official statistics indicated that rates of labor and capital productivity growth fell throughout this period, as shown in Table 1.3. Declining capital productivity meant that progressively larger shares of national income had to be devoted to investment in order to maintain economic growth rates; declining labor productivity growth meant that increases in employment often had to exceed planned rates in order to provide enterprises with the requisite labor force. Investment's share of national income used rose from under 15 percent in 1956 to 23 percent in 1970 (Moskwa, Socha, and Wilkin, 1981, 212), and the growth of consumption continued to lag behind that of national income. Maintaining balance on consumer goods markets in the face of rising rates of investment and above-plan labor force growth therefore required slow growth in real wages. Yearly growth in real wages for all workers averaged only 1.8 percent between 1960 and 1970 (Brus 1983, 29), indicating a virtual stagnation in living standards. Despite this slow growth, shortage pressures continued to be a problem. Although foreign trade played a larger role in the Polish economy under Gomułka, this was mainly the result of increases in trade with the USSR and the other socialist countries. So although the industrialization drive begun in the late 1940s continued in the Gomułka era, it took an ever-increasing toll on the Polish economy.

The absence of Stalinist discipline (the destruction of which Gomułka himself helped engineer) within the PZPR meant that Gomułka was unable to prevent the growth of divisive factions within the party. This factionalism reflected Poland's regional heterogeneity, the pluralism of the country's political traditions, and the PZPR's latent weakness. Following the destruction of the Stalinist wing after the events of 1956, the party consisted of three main factions: (1) Liberal Marxist reformers, represented by such "revisionists" as philosopher Leszek Kołakowski and student leader Jacek Kuroń, who believed that the PZPR and socialism could be reformed and democratized from within; (2) an antireform, populist-nationalist group called "the partisans," associated with the Minister of the Interior, Mieczysław Moczar; and (3) "pragmatic" technocrats (typified by Edward Gierek, the party boss from Silesia) who advocated "modernizing" the political and economic systems through "professional expertise and sound management" as an alternative to liberalizing reform (Bielasiak 1983, 14). No faction called for far-reaching economic reform; at issue was the desirability of reform within the polity and the state administration, not in the economy. In contrast to reform proposals then being developed in Czechoslovakia and Hungary, discussions of economic reform discussions within Poland essentially marked time during the 1960s. In such a situation, the

TABLE 1.3
Trends in Labor and Capital Productivity, 1947–1968

	Growth Rate of Labor Productivity[a]	*Capital Productivity*[b]
1948	26.6	—
1949	13.8	—
1950	10.0	—
1951	4.8	—
1952	5.1	0.571
1953	8.2	
1954	9.3	0.516
1955	7.1	
1956	4.8	0.497
1957	6.9	
1958	6.5	0.376
1959	4.6	
1960	6.4	0.387
1961	7.7	
1962	0.3	0.254
1963	3.3	
1964	5.9	0.308
1965	5.1	
1966	4.3	—
1967	2.6	—
1968	6.4	—

Note: Investment in the service sector is excluded.

[a]Defined as "national income produced per worker in material production" (Feiwel 1971, 1:681). Labor productivity in the service sector is excluded.

[b]Defined as "increases in gross national product per zloty of gross productive investment" (Feiwel 1971, 1:626). Data are two-year averages, so that the entry for 1964, for example, denotes the average figure for 1964-1965.

PZPR would have been incapable of undertaking serious reforms even if it had wanted to.

Such a delicate political equilibrium could last only as long as the factions chose not to challenge it directly. However, in 1964 an open letter critical of the regime, sponsored by the party's liberal wing, demonstrated the revisionists' growing disaffection from the leadership, and by 1967 Kołakowski and other liberals had been expelled. The decision in January 1968 to cancel a Warsaw performance of Mickiewicz's play *Dziady* (Forefathers) because of its anti-Russian overtones led to protests by students and confrontation between the regime and the intelligentsia. As the protests spread and Gomułka's position deteriorated, the "partisan" faction tried to turn the confrontation to its advantage by attacking the party leadership for its alleged lack of patriotism and respect for national ideals. The partisans' campaign "deteriorated into an anti-Jewish, anti-'Muscovite,' antirevisionist and antiliberal witch hunt" (ibid., 15), which led to the persecution and exile of some of Poland's best economists, including Brus. Gomułka, with the help of the "pragmatic" faction, was able to defeat the partisan campaign. The unexpected result of these intrigues was that the pragmatists were able to push their agenda, calling for administrative and economic modernization and rationalization, to the fore.

Despite these intraparty schisms and Gomułka's general distaste for reform, coalitions of reform economists, pragmatists, and revisionists succeeded on two occasions during the 1960s in pushing mild proposals for economic reform to the top of the political agenda. These proposals were linked to the country's disappointing macroeconomic performance and inspired by the wave of economic reform that swept through the Soviet bloc in the early and middle 1960s. Although the Economic Council's reform theses of 1956–1958 were not translated into practice, the belief that economic performance could be improved by abolishing the worst features of the traditional system did make its way into official policy. The second Five Year Plan (1961–1965), for example, was based on the assumption that the economic mechanism could be "improved" in order to make the transition from "extensive" economic growth (based on quantitative increases in inputs) to "intensive" economic growth (based on increases in resource productivity). The economy's failure to make this transition (the second Five Year Plan was underfulfilled in many areas) also legitimized the search for new reform ideas, if not their implementation.

The PZPR's fourth congress, in June 1964, and the Central Committee's fourth plenum, in July 1965, called for the introduction of concrete economic reform steps during the years 1965–1967. Special attention was to be paid to state enterprise incentives and autonomy: profitability was to supplement gross output as the key indicator of enterprise performance. Some changes were also introduced in the intermediate layer (i.e., between enterprises and ministries), where industrial associations (*zjednoczenia*) were created. The regulatory environment for private artisans was liberalized in 1965–1966. Once again, however, the key elements of the traditional system were not attacked: mandatory enterprise output targets were retained and administrative supply allocation was preserved. The measures introduced in 1964–1965 were neither comprehensive nor internally consistent, and rather bore the appearance of sloganistic tinkering.[20] Intraparty divisions and resistance by the party and state bureaucracies to the reform's principles effectively prevented the implementation of even these minor changes.

In any case, the significance of these attempts at reform lies not in their impact on the economy but in their connection to the political events of 1968 and 1970–1971. The second reform under Gomułka was introduced after the events of March 1968 and bore the stamp of the ascending pragmatic faction. The PZPR's fifth congress, in November 1968, authorized the establishment of "a comprehensive and internally consistent system of planning and management" in order to permit the country to follow a "selective growth strategy." In practice, the reform, attempted in 1969–1970, took on an anti-consumer tone. The pragmatists' slogans of "economic rationalization" and "a new system of incentives" were implemented in a restrictive wage policy, a shift in consumer-goods production away from foodstuffs toward luxury items, and a renewed attack on the private sector. In 1970–1971, for example, the number of private firms active in industry, handicrafts, and retail trade declined by 6 to 8 percent (Aaslund 1985, 86). In such a situation, maintaining equilibrium (or preventing further deterioration) on consumer-goods markets required increasing the relative price of foodstuffs. In a display of incredibly poor political judgment, the Gomułka regime instituted major increases in food prices on December 12, 1970, just a few days before the Christmas holidays. The price increases sparked strikes and demonstrations in the Baltic city of Gdańsk and then in other cities. The authorities used police, security, and military forces to "pacify" the Baltic coast as Poland once again erupted in political crisis. The results of unleashing the repressive apparatus of the "workers' state" upon striking workers traumatized the party and the country. When the guns fell silent some three hundred people, mostly civilians, were dead. Gomułka resigned in disgrace on December 20, eclipsing what should have been a proud achievement: only two weeks earlier he had signed a treaty with West Germany recognizing Poland's western borders.

The legacies of the Gomułka era were far-reaching. Though the events of 1956 and the Polish-German rapprochement of 1970 increased Poland's de facto sovereignty, the wave of popular support that brought Gomułka to power in 1956 was squandered without producing major systemic change. The hopes raised in 1956 for a democratic and prosperous "Polish road to socialism" had come to nothing. In addition to further discrediting itself in the eyes of Polish society, the PZPR had also purged its most liberal members. Moreover, economic reform had become linked in public opinion to unpopular price increases, a connection that was to come back to haunt future attempts at reform. And, because the new government was forced to rescind the price rises introduced in December 1970, workers in heavy industry learned that by adopting an uncompromising (almost insurrectionist) pose, they could prevent macroeconomic adjustment and even bring down the government.

Gierek's "New Development Strategy" and the WOG Reform

It fell to Edward Gierek, the party boss from Katowice and new leader of the PZPR, to pick up the pieces. The PZPR was in a difficult situation. In addition to finding some way of extinguishing the fires of rebellion burning along the Baltic coast, the party also had to fashion a credible program of social reconciliation. Reform would have to be a key element of any such program, and reforms of political and economic institutions were duly promised by the new leadership.

Gierek adopted a less imperial style than his predecessors, as if to show that his concern for the country's problems was the same as the average citizen's. (Gierek's background as a coal miner was emphasized, casting him as a friend of the "common man.") Shortly after assuming power, Gierek visited the shipyards in Szczecin and Gdańsk, the nerve centers for the striking factories along the Baltic Coast, and convinced the workers to suspend their strikes. After several more such meetings, including one in February at the Rosa Luxemburg textile factory in Łódź in which Gierek agreed to rescind the price increases that had begun the conflagration and to hold food prices constant for five years, the workers agreed to end the strikes. The Gierek leadership thus gained some time—time that could have been used to design a program of reform and reconciliation.

Initially, "the new regime radiated confidence and optimism. Free discussion, and a spirit of experimentation were in the air" (Davies 1984, 2:626). The promotion of "class struggle" was abandoned by the PZPR in favor of the slogan "moral-political unity of the nation." Censorship restrictions were relaxed and the weekly *Polityka*, under the editorship of party liberal Mieczysław Rakowski, became a forum for criticizing corruption and ineptitude in the state (and, less frequently, the party) bureaucracy. Reconciliation was sought with the Catholic Church, the intelligentsia, and other social groups. Perhaps most important, Gierek essentially forswore the use of violence against Polish society. Gierek's common touch, his interwar and wartime experience as a coal miner in France and Belgium, his reported fluency in French, and the fact that he was the first Eastern European communist leader not to have been trained in Moscow—all these qualities lent some credence to the belief that the PZPR had turned over a new leaf. The government's decision to open the borders and allow Poles to travel more easily to Western countries also increased Gierek's popularity. While this approach was not calculated to endear Gierek to the Brezhnev leadership in the USSR, Gierek's success in restoring the PZPR's "leading role," as well as Soviet distaste for his more nationalistic rivals, like Moczar, seemed to make Gierek's program acceptable to the Soviets.

Gierek proposed a "New Development Strategy," based on rapid increases in living standards, consumerism, and increased integration into the international economy, as the answer to Poland's economic troubles. Gierek's program thus sought to attack the regime's key economic problems—slow growth in living standards and economic backwardness (relative to the West)—by taking advantage of Poland's new position in the international arena. Reductions in East-West tensions and the flowering of *détente* in the early 1970s offered promising new financial and technological opportunities for Poland, while increased independence from the Soviet Union softened the constraints on Polish economic diplomacy. Combined with the political reconciliation with Polish society, to be achieved through the PZPR's more moderate, rational, and modern policies, the New Development Strategy would allow the party and society to work together to "build a second Poland."

The key to this strategy was obtaining Western imports of investment goods (to modernize Polish industry and agriculture) and consumer goods (to improve living standards and work incentives). Because these imports would tax Poland's meager export capacity, they would have to be purchased largely on credit provided by Western banks and governments. Once the imported capital and technology was in place, Poland's modernized factories and farms would be able to increase exports to the West, thus earning the hard currency required to pay off the debts incurred by the imports. This "import-led" growth strategy became the foundation of the fourth Five Year Plan (1971–1975).

Such a development strategy was not inherently unreasonable, since other developing countries (such as South Korea) have parlayed similar strategies into favorable economic results. Because this program promised to integrate Poland into the international economy, it did place a premium on the efficient allocation of imported investment goods and on improving hard-currency export performance. These prerequisites would require far-reaching economic reforms. A commission of party and state officials, the Szydlak Committee, was established in 1971 and charged with developing reforms to "modernize" the economic system.

The so-called WOG reform began in January 1973. "WOG" is the Polish acronym for *wielka organizacja gospodarcza*, or "large economic organization."[21] As the term suggests, the essence of the WOG reform of 1973–1975 was administrative, not economic. It was based on the premise that changes in the organizational structure of the state's administration and enterprises would be sufficient to increase economic efficiency. In part, this attitude reflected the technocratic orientation of the less doctrinaire officials promoted by Gierek and his leadership, as well as the belief that transforming state enterprises into "socialist corporations" was the key to modernization and increased efficiency.

The crux of the reform was the subordination of state enterprises to vertically and horizontally integrated WOGs. While WOGs varied in size, some included as many as 40 or 50 firms and employed tens of thousands of workers (Wanless 1980, 34). WOGs were to replace state enterprises as plan executants (i.e., recipients of plan targets and inputs) and to treat their firms as divisions within a large corporation. In this sense, the WOG reform was a centralizing reform, as enterprises lost legal authority to the WOGs. On the other hand, the operative role of the industrial branch ministries was to be considerably reduced, to permit the Planning Commission and other central organs to influence the WOGs directly; since some authority was to pass from the industrial ministries to the WOGs, the WOG reform could also be regarded as a decentralizing reform. Paring down the size of the industrial ministries was meant not only to reduce these organs' perennial interference in production matters; it would also allow the central organs to use "parametric" or "indirect" financial instruments (prices, taxes, and other financial norms) to influence the WOGs. Since entire branches of production were to be concentrated in a single WOG, the assignment of supply responsibilities to individual WOGs was supposed to simplify supply relationships and reduce shortage pressures. All this, it was hoped, would facilitate a transition away from traditional centralized methods of determining enterprise production and supply plans. Research and development institutes, service departments, transportation equipment depots, and foreign-trade offices were also to be relocated in WOGs in order to reduce barriers to the diffusion of new technologies, make the WOGs economically self-sufficient, allow them to establish direct contacts with foreign suppliers and customers, and to improve the quality of products and services.

The financial instruments that were to replace, or at least supplement, the traditional obligatory output and supply plans, would constitute an "integrated economic-financial system." The key elements of this system were these: (1) Value added and net profit, the indicators used to evaluate performance and to which the salaries of workers and managers were linked; (2) new taxes on labor and capital, to encourage producers to economize on their use of these resources; (3) permission for WOGs to retain a share of their profits in order to finance decentralized investments; and (4) price reforms that allowed WOGs to set the prices for newly-introduced products (to encourage product development) and linked domestic producer prices more closely to world-market prices.

Although the desire to replace the direct, central determination of enterprise output and supply plans was implicit in the emphasis on the transition to "indirect" financial instruments, this principle was inconsistent with the increased organizational concentration the WOGs represented. Even without branch ministries, expecting WOGs to effectively coordinate production and supply decisions without mandatory plan targets and central input allocation was unrealistic—unless efficiently functioning market prices and institutions to guide those decisions could be created. This the reformers were unwilling to do. Instead, the WOG reform clung to the belief that administrative manipulation of (often inconsistent) financial instruments affecting net (rather than gross) financial measures of enterprise performance would be sufficient to evoke the desired changes in enterprise behavior. In the event, this belief turned out to be mistaken. Inconsistencies between different financial instruments were never insignificant enough to convince the center to drop the mandatory plan targets.

In addition to this inconsistency within the reform blueprint, a number of problems arose during the reform's implementation. The branch ministries resisted being "pared down to size" and were largely able to maintain their traditional role in setting plan targets and allocating supplies. This helped prevent the transition to indirect central management via financial instruments. While the branch ministries' survival resulted in part from the Gierek leadership's desire to centralize economic and political power at the expense of regional authorities, it also reflected tensions inherent in trying to make the behavior of state enterprises conform to central intentions without explicit central direction. The branch ministries were seen as best able to provide this direction; so, rather than devolve the branch ministries' operative functions to the WOGs, the reform simply added another layer to the economic administration—the WOGs themselves. Because of their size and the resources at their disposal, the WOGs in turn became powerful lobbies in their own right.

The inconsistency with which the reform was implemented in different sectors was also a major problem. The chemical industry was virtually unique, in that it was the only sector in which WOGs were established throughout the industry, ultimately absorbing most state enterprises. In other sectors, membership in the WOGs was largely voluntary. Some firms within a given industry or branch were therefore subordinated to a WOG and functioned (more or less) according to the logic of the reform, while in the other firms the old system was still in effect. The definition of "value added" that was used to determine performance varied among WOGs, with the result that "each WOG adopted whichever method happened to place least strain on their accounting system at the time the new system was introduced" (Wanless 1989, 43).

Given these problems, it is hardly surprising that many other planned changes were not introduced and that the ones that were had effects somewhat different from what was intended. For example, state enterprises and WOGs repackaged old products as new ones, which allowed them to increase prices (and thus profits), value added, wage and bonus payments, employment, and investment spending. This built a new inflationary bias into enterprise behavior. The branch ministries and other central organs responded to this phenomenon with new restrictions on the activities of WOGs and enterprises, further complicating an already muddy situation. Producer prices were never really liberalized, owing to inflationary pressures and to the fact that official increases in the prices of consumer goods were ruled out for political reasons.

External factors also constrained the effectiveness of the WOG reform. The ascendancy of the conservative Brezhnev leadership in the Soviet Union made economic reform an increasingly risky political proposition in Eastern Europe during the 1970s. Gierek's ability to consolidate the PZPR's position between 1971 and 1973 also removed some of the urgency of economic reform. Perhaps most important, the success of the New Development Strategy in receiving Western credits seemed to offer larger, more immediate economic benefits.

The macroeconomic and foreign trade components of the New Development Strategy dominated the reform from 1971 to 1975; in effect, expanded commercial relations with the West acted as a substitute for reform. An unprecedented investment boom took place under Gierek: investment in 1975 was 124 percent above its 1970 level (in real terms) and investment's share of national income used rose to 32 percent in 1975, up from 22 percent in 1971 (Moskwa, Socha, and Wilkin 1981, 212). This investment boom did not result solely from the leadership's economic strategy; it also reflected the bargaining power of the WOGs, which lobbied successfully for new investment projects and were able to obtain western imports without close central oversight. The boom took investment spending far above planned levels: whereas the fourth Five Year Plan called for investment to increase at a yearly rate of 7.7 percent, the actual rate averaged out at nearly 14 percent and in 1972 rose to 23 percent (Brus 1983, 38). Although it led to a rapid infusion of Western investment goods and technology, the investment boom was unsustainable; it also had important negative side effects on Poland's inflation rate and balance of payments.

The investment boom, coupled with fixed prices for most consumer goods, caused rapid increases in purchasing power: real wages increased by an average of 6.8 percent per year between 1971 and 1975 (Poznański 1986, 459). Production initially spurted ahead to absorb this surge in spending: yearly growth in national income produced (in real terms) averaged 9.5 percent in the same period, while the average yearly growth rate in consumption (in real terms) exceeded 17.5 percent (*Rocznik Statystyczny* 1989, xxxii, xxxiv). Even agricultural performance improved: gross agricultural product increased by 22 percent from 1970 to 1974 (Korbonski 1981, 276), helped by increased investment in agriculture, the regime's final abandonment of compulsory deliveries, and favorable weather. This allowed Gierek's "propaganda of success" to portray the new leadership as well on its way to "building a second Poland."

Increased imports of Western consumer and investment goods were the underpinnings of this boom. The value of imports from nonsocialist countries nearly quadrupled between 1971 and 1975 (compared to a twofold increase in the value of imports from socialist countries), well below the growth in the value of exports, which more than doubled during this time. Consequently, Poland's balance of trade with the nonsocialist countries, which had recorded a surplus of 451.2 million dewiza zloty in 1971, had by 1975 reached a deficit of 8.9 million dewiza zloty. Poland's net foreign debt to the West therefore increased from $1.2 billion to $7.6 billion between 1971 and 1975 (Poznański 1986, 461).

Initially, this increase in Poland's debt burden seemed a reasonable price to pay for the prosperity it produced. The rich natural resource base of coal, ores, and other minerals made Poland appear to be a good credit risk to Western lenders, especially after the "oil shock" of 1973 led to rapid increases in world-market prices of minerals and fuels. Poland's previous record of debt repayment had been exemplary and Western governments saw political advantage in supporting Gierek's attempts at liberalization at home and increased autonomy from the USSR. The recession of 1974–1975 in the capitalist world also left international financial institutions with billions of unrecycled petrodollars for which Western borrowers could not be found. Poland and other socialist countries were thus able to obtain credit on very favorable terms.

The initial successes in the economic arena allowed Gierek to further consolidate his political position. Working-class opposition to the regime receded in the aura of prosperity and isolated strikes could be bought off by promises of higher wages. By the end of 1971 Gierek had removed from the PZPR leadership not only most of Gomułka's supporters, but Moczar and his henchmen as well. In their place Gierek installed a new breed of *apparatchik*. Younger, better-educated, more sophisticated and less ideological technocrats and managers replaced Gomułka's hidebound ideologues. However, while the new *apparatchiks* may have been better educated than their predecessors, they were not necessarily more professional or more scrupulous; growing corruption and cynicism within the party and the state administration accompanied the rise of these new careerists. The Western consumer goods and currencies flowing into Poland in the 1970s brought with them new opportunities for private gain at public expense. The number of managerial positions in economic and social life subject to the *nomenklatura* personnel system expanded dramatically during the 1970s, thus increasing the party's role in dividing the spoils of power (Smolar 1983). This swelling of cynical opportunism did not go unnoticed by the public.

The Gierek regime and its corrupt *nomenklatura* were so blinded by the initial successes of the New Development Strategy that the long-term implications of its weaknesses, even signs of impending danger, were generally ignored. Investment projects and licenses for foreign technology were forced on reluctant firms by the central authorities as the investment boom lost all sense of proportion. The realization that Poland's westernized industrial and agricultural base would, far into the future, demand a steady stream of raw materials, components, semi-finished products, and spare parts imported for hard currency seems not to have sunk in. Brus (1983) argued that

> when the massive expansion got underway, no apparent provision was made for an adverse turn in events beyond the leadership's control, such as changes in Western markets or poor weather. . . . The country was led into a state of euphoria, with sycophants among economists proclaiming as outdated and defeatist many interrelationships and constraints that were, in fact, vital. (p. 38)

The Collapse of the New Development Strategy

Just as the roots of Gierek's political good fortune lay in the economic victories of the New Development Strategy, the reappearance of economic tensions in 1975–1976 heralded the return of political problems. The investment boom and the increases in purchasing power it generated by 1975 were clearly exceeding the economy's ability to absorb them. Prices, which had remained fairly constant in 1971–1972, began an upward drift in 1973 despite the presence of price controls; retail prices increased by about 10 percent from 1973 to 1975. Bad harvests in 1975 and 1976 made matters worse: gross agricultural production declined by about 3 percent during that time (see Table 1.4). Imported foodstuffs helped push Poland's merchandise trade deficit to $3 billion and increased hard-currency indebtedness by $2.8 billion in 1975 and by another $3.6 billion a year later; By 1976, Poland's net hard-currency debt had reached $11.2 billion. The ratio of debt-service payments to hard-currency export earnings—a measure of the burden that debt repayment was imposing on the Polish economy—increased from 12.4 percent in 1971 to 34.4 percent in 1976, until one out of every three dollars earned through export had to be used to service the foreign debt. (A one-in-four ratio is considered safe.) The debt-servicing burden began to crowd out imports of consumer goods and the semi-finished products, components, and spare parts necessary to finish import-dependent investment projects and to keep new factories running once they had come on line. This growth in external indebtedness was unsustainable, and sooner or later would have to be corrected.

The "economic maneuver" announced in 1976 was an attempt at correction: growth in investment and consumption spending was to be reduced in order to slow the growth of imports and increase exports. This proved to be difficult. The recession of 1974–1975 had reduced the demand for Polish exports. Hard-currency imports proved difficult to reduce, owing to higher energy costs after the 1973 "oil shock" and the dependence of the New Development Strategy's investment program on imports. Although investment's share of national income (less net exports) declined from 32 to 29 percent from 1975 to 1976 (Moskwa, Socha, and Wilkin 1981, 212), further reductions in investment spending would have meant freezing millions of dollars of imports in unfinished investment projects. Since the regime no longer felt bound by Gierek's 1971 promise to keep food prices constant for five years, the government decided in 1976 to reduce consumption by raising the prices of meat and other foodstuffs.

TABLE 1.4
Macroeconomic and External Trends, 1975–1980

	1975	*1976*	*1977*	*1978*	*1979*	*1980*
National income produced (% change)	9.0	6.8	5.0	3.0	−2.3	−6.0
Gross investment (% change)	10.7	1.0	3.1	2.1	−7.9	−12.3
Consumption (% change)	—	7.8	5.7	0.8	2.4	1.2
Gross agricultural production (% change)	−2.1	−1.1	1.4	4.1	−1.5	−10.7
Retail price inflation	—	4.0	4.5	8.4	7.4	8.5
Imports from non-socialist countries (% change)	12.2	11.4	−10.1	−2.0	−4.5	−7.2
Exports to non-socialist countries (% change)	5.8	12.3	4.0	2.9	2.1	5.0
Convertible currency merchandise trade balance ($ billions)	−3.0	−2.8	−1.8	−1.5	−1.9	−0.7
Net western debt ($ billions)	7.6	11.2	14.3	16.9	20.7	23.5
Debt service ratio (percentage)	26.3	34.4	45.6	60.8	75.0	83.2

Sources: Rocznik Statystyczny 1989, xxxii, xxxiv, xxxviii, xliv, *Rocznik Statystyczny: Handel Zagraniczny* 1989, 8; Poznański 1986, 461.
Note: Data in rows 1–4, 6, and 7 are in constant prices.

The price increases provoked the same vociferous public disapproval that had greeted Gomułka's ill-fated price increases in 1970. Strikes, demonstrations, and riots again broke out, this time centered in the city of Radom and in Ursus, an industrial suburb of Warsaw, and were met by police retaliation. The regime quickly rescinded the price increases, but arrested the strike leaders (whom they termed "hooligans" and "firebrands") and put them on trial. In so doing, the government set in motion a series of events that would lead to the creation of the Solidarity movement four years later. Furthermore, Polish workers had again used the strike weapon to veto a macroeconomic stabilization program.

The regime's inability to raise food prices and slow consumption further complicated the task of drafting an effective stabilization program. As Table 1.4 shows, the regime reacted to the events of 1976 by slowing investment growth to a crawl. Imports from nonsocialist countries began falling in 1977, but hard-currency exports continued to increase, with the result that Poland's deficit in hard-currency trade fell by 50 percent from 1975 to 1978. Despite the cancellation of the 1976 food price increases, inflation was used to try to keep demand in line with supply. According to official statistics, the rate of open inflation from 1976 to 1980 (6.6 percent on average) was more than double the 1971–1975 rate, and the actual rate for 1976–1980 was almost certainly much higher. The spread of "hidden inflation," caused by the WOGs' repackaging of existing products as new ones, was particularly galling to consumers.

As investment and imports fell, imported capital was increasingly frozen in unfinished investment projects (and, in some cases, lost permanently). By 1980, some 821 billion zloty had been frozen in these projects, a figure representing the equivalent of about 50 percent of national income produced for that year (Brus 1983, 39). The failure of these investment projects to come on line meant that they were unable to supply other firms with inputs called for in the plan, which set off ripple effects downstream. The import-led investment boom had so opened the Polish economy that, according to a 1981 government study, a one-zloty decrease in imports resulted in a decline in industrial production of 2–2.5 zloty (Lubowski 1981). Completed projects were often much less efficient than planners had anticipated, owing to poor investment decisions made during the investment boom. The metallurgical complex of Huta Katowice, in Gierek's home district, became a symbol of the New Development Strategy's catastrophic bungling, of uneconomical white elephants that wasted millions of dollars of imported machinery and technology. Simultaneously, international lenders increasingly doubted the wisdom of feeding Poland's propensity to import Western consumer and investment goods on credit. All this was magnified by bad harvests in 1979 and 1980 and by the second "oil shock," in 1979.

This "import-led detonator" slowed the growth in national income and export production, pushing Poland's ratio of debt-service payments to exports to 83.2 percent in 1980. As output growth slowed, so too did consumption, exacerbating inflationary and shortage pressures and reducing work incentives. These negative processes fed on one another and led Poland to the brink of economic collapse. National income produced began to fall in 1979; by the time its decline was finally arrested in 1982, output had fallen by 25 percent.

While many under-developed capitalist countries (especially in Latin America) also became caught in the debt trap during this period, the excessive pace of the 1971–1975 investment drive and the failure to reform the investment and foreign-trade mechanisms must bear a large share of the blame for Poland's fate. Enterprise managers (and their superiors), with no fear of bankruptcy, did not have to worry about the consequences of poor investment decisions or inept use of imported machinery or licenses. Introducing the New Development Strategy into an unreformed Polish economy was thus a recipe for disaster. However, instead of turning to more radical reforms as the storm clouds gathered, the Gierek leadership moved to recentralize economic authority after 1976. The stage was set for an economic catastrophe.

The Democratic Opposition and the Birth of Solidarity

The second half of the 1970s saw the development of an organized, democratic opposition movement in Poland. The rise of the opposition reflected a number of factors. These included the more liberal political environment of the Gierek era, the regime's emphasis on improved relations with Western nations (apparent in Poland's signing of the Helsinki human rights accords in 1975), and the spread of information technologies that promoted clandestine publishing activities, as well as the economic problems of the late 1970s. While opposition movements also stirred in the Soviet Union and other Eastern European countries during the 1970s, their development was particularly rapid and significant in Poland.

The regime's prosecution of workers active in the events of 1976 in Radom and Ursus catalyzed the Polish opposition movement. Shortly after the workers were put on trial, a group of fourteen intellectuals announced the formation of the "Worker Defense Committee" (KOR) to provide legal and material assistance to the imprisoned workers and their families. KOR's significance was at least fourfold (Lipski 1985). First, KOR underscored the PZPR's domestic weakness by calling international attention to the party's persecution of worker activists. Second, KOR brought together representatives of a wide variety of noncommunist political ideologies. Its most important element consisted of former communists who had renounced the PZPR and Soviet-style socialism; this group included Jacek Kuroń and Adam Michnik, leaders in the student rebellion of March 1968. Prominent social democrats like the economist Edward Lipiński were also represented, as were liberal members of the Catholic intelligentsia. The heterogeneity of these political viewpoints underscored the pluralistic nature of the opposition.

Third, KOR helped forge an alliance between the working class, which had been behind the turmoil of 1970 and 1976, and the intelligentsia, which was now almost completely alienated from the PZPR. In aiding the leaders of the 1976 strikes, KOR helped establish common political organizations and strategies and increased the sophistication of working-class opposition to the regime. Fourth, and perhaps most important, KOR operated in a largely public and open manner. KOR used the Western press and exploited the regime's unwillingness to risk damaging relations with Western countries by cracking down on the opposition. In the process, it set the example of "self-organization" that became a hallmark of the Polish opposition. By acting in an open and democratic fashion, KOR in effect said to Polish society, "If you want to live in an open, democratic society, form organizations that function in an open, democratic manner." In a sense, KOR constituted a new form of conciliatory opposition to the official system, one that offered the potential of negotiation and compromise rather than insurrection.

KOR's message grew more infectious with the passing of time. By 1980 numerous other unofficial political groups had appeared, and the growth of underground printing and publishing networks was beginning to exceed the capacity of a government crackdown to destroy them. The opposition also derived valuable logistical and moral support from the Catholic Church and received an important boost from Pope John Paul's triumphant return to his homeland in June 1979. The democratic opposition's growing appeal to working-class opposition, human rights activism, Roman Catholicism, and Polish nationalism stood in increasingly strong contrast with the Gierek leadership, which was identified with loyalism vis-à-vis the USSR, corruption and mismanagement in the economy, and authoritarianism in the polity.

Popular ferment, growing support for the opposition and the Church, and increasing economic tensions all played on one another, heightening the disarray within the party. Gierek's authority weakened as the PZPR vacillated between confrontation and compromise with the opposition. On July 1, 1980, the government announced a series of gradual price increases of varying degrees for different parts of the country. But "what might perhaps have worked ten years earlier did not work now" (Bielasiak 1981, 23), and strikes again broke out. The government responded by attempting to settle isolated strikes with promises of higher wages. This tactic only encouraged other factories to go on strike. Meanwhile, the population's increased purchasing power worsened economic conditions and created more worker unrest.

By August 1980 Poland was gripped in a major wave of strikes, the nerve center of which became the Lenin Shipyards in Gdańsk. This time, the workers leading the strikes (and their KOR advisors) found the PZPR's emissaries to be unconvincing and refused to be bought off by promises of higher wages. Instead, the Gdańsk strike committee, led by an electrician named Lech Wałęsa, demanded political concessions, including the right to form a trade union independent of party control. With its back to the wall, the government had no choice but to agree to the workers' demands. On August 31 the Polish government signed a series of accords guaranteeing, among other things, the right to form an independent trade union with access to the official media, and the right to strike. Far-reaching economic and political reforms were promised, in order to "bring the country out of the crisis." The period of "national renewal" (*odnowa*) had begun.

Although the new Solidarity trade union promised to respect the PZPR's "leading role" and not to function as a political party, the break in the PZPR's thirty-year monopoly on official political activity was obvious. In effect, the Gierek leadership had indicated that in order to make the party more acceptable to Polish society, it was willing to at least consider the possibility of a more pluralistic polity. Not surprisingly, the Gdańsk accords generated deep concern in the USSR and Poland's other neighbors, as well as gestures of support from the West.

Some Poles saw in the birth of Solidarity the hope that the events of 1956 would replay themselves, this time with a happier ending. According to this scenario, Polish society would stand behind a reformist PZPR leadership and force the Soviet Union to realize that it had no alternative but to accept the changes occurring in Poland, as long as the PZPR retained its "leading role" and Poland remained within the Soviet bloc. Indeed, in August 1980 the Soviet Union could only have viewed the possibility of military intervention in Poland with extreme distaste: Soviet diplomatic efforts were focused on keeping American Pershing missiles out of Western Europe and the Red Army was becoming mired in a hopeless war in Afghanistan—circumstances that argued strongly against the military option in Poland. It therefore seemed possible that the basic causes of what had become widely known as "the Polish crisis"—systemic illegitimacy and dysfunctionality—could be addressed in a meaningful way.

Events quickly disabused the optimists of these hopes. By 1980 the overwhelming majority of Polish society had lost faith in the PZPR and viewed the vision of "democratic socialism" ambiguously offered by the PZPR as neither probable nor desirable. The PZPR in turn was anything but united behind its "reformist" leadership: Gierek was unceremoniously sacked as party leader less than ten days after the Gdańsk accords were signed. Most important, Soviet control over the PZPR and the Polish army and security forces had strengthened since 1956. In the months that followed the creation of Solidarity it became clear that the PZPR had neither the ability nor the desire to realize the vision of Poland's future implied by the Gdańsk accords.

Although it reflected problems that had afflicted the People's Republic throughout its existence, the political crisis of 1980 was qualitatively different from the crises of 1956, 1968, 1970–1971 and 1976. The Polish economy in 1980–1981 was collapsing—an unprecedented occurrence among the post-1945 socialist economies. From 1979 to 1982 national income produced declined by 25 percent, inflation reached triple digits, and Poland became unable to service its debts. Some sectors, such as housing construction, had not fully recovered from this collapse ten years later.

While Gierek's New Development Strategy bore a large share of the blame for this state of affairs, it had also introduced important qualitative changes into the Polish economy. Perhaps most important of these was the expansion of the dollar economy, as a result of which Poland became increasingly integrated into the international economy. The combination of hard-currency credits obtained by the Polish government and the influx of hard-currency incomes earned by Poles working abroad not only "dollarized" the illegal economy and financed its expansion, it also led to the development of the official dollar economy. The networks of state-owned PEWEX and Baltona dollar stores expanded dramatically during the 1970s as the government attempted to attract the population's dollar spending. By the late 1970s cars, apartments, and consumer durables, as well as many foodstuffs and alcoholic beverages, were sold in the state dollar stores. Polish citizens were allowed to open hard-currency bank accounts as well. By the end of the decade, many (perhaps most) private sales of real estate, cars, and consumer durables were transacted in dollars. Both the official and second economies in Poland had become addicted to hard currency.

The events of August 1980 proclaimed the final bankruptcy of Soviet-style socialism in Poland. The "social credit" that Gierek had earned in the early 1970s had gone the way of Gomułka's credit of 1956. Even the PZPR admitted that fundamental economic and political changes were necessary. The question was, Could the PZPR institute such changes? And would the Soviet Union permit them?

CHAPTER II

Crisis and Reform in the 1980s

THE 1980s were more than the decade of Poland's economic collapse. Two sets of economic reforms (the so-called first and second stages) were attempted between 1981 and 1988, reforms that tested the boundaries of the Soviet-style economy. The martial-law crackdown on Solidarity in December 1981 was followed by a controlled attempt at gradual political reform from above, dubbed "normalization" by the PZPR leadership. The 1980s were also a decade rich in irony. Political and economic reforms that would have been inconceivable in the 1970s were introduced in the 1980s, but instead of improving economic performance and democratizing the political system they contributed to the ultimate collapse of Soviet-style socialism in Poland. In the process, the decade of reform made an important contribution to the creation of the socioeconomic infrastructure necessary for a market economy to function. Not only did the final bankruptcy of Soviet-style socialism in Poland, as well as the final attempts at reforming it, occur in the 1980s: by the end of the decade, the imperative of *transforming* authoritarian socialism into democratic capitalism had become widely accepted.

MARTIAL LAW AND THE "FIRST STAGE" OF ECONOMIC REFORM

The declaration of martial law on December 13, 1981, brought the 1980–1981 renewal period to an unfortunate conclusion. The PZPR, under the leadership of General Wojciech Jaruzelski, certainly bore a large share of the blame for this tragedy; but the PZPR's failure to live up to the 1980 Gdańsk accords that legalized the Solidarity trade union was hardly the only cause. The PZPR faced a multitude of impossibly contradictory choices in 1980–1981. Politically, Solidarity and Western governments called on the party to live up to and implement the Gdańsk accords, while the Soviet Union regarded Solidarity's existence as a threat to its geopolitical interests and demanded Solidarity's subordination to the Soviet interpretation of the PZPR's "leading role." On the economic front, the party was caught between social demands for higher living standards and the expectations of

Western creditors that Poland's foreign debt be serviced. Even a party with a solid political base and a strong popular mandate would have found this situation difficult. For the PZPR, whose political base was weak and which possessed neither a genuine willingness nor the authority to share power, the situation was untenable.

The conflicting forces buffeting the PZPR were apparent in the Gdańsk accords themselves. In addition to acceding to the strikers' political demands—including the right to form an independent trade union, the right to strike, access by non-PZPR institutions (initially Solidarity and the Roman Catholic Church) to the state-run media, and the participation of independent social groups in official reform discussions—the party also agreed to economic demands that could only exacerbate the hopeless economic situation of 1980. These demands included shortening the work week to five days, limiting exports to those products in surplus on the domestic market, tightening controls on price increases in both the public and private sectors, increasing the minimum wage and retirement pensions, lowering the mandatory retirement age, and introducing three-year paid maternity leaves. The combination of the population's increased purchasing power and the reductions in aggregate supply caused by these measures further fueled inflationary fires that were already burning out of control and increased balance-of-payments pressures. The discussions of economic reform called for in the Gdańsk accords were thus overshadowed from the start by the deterioration in internal and external balance that the accords helped produce. Furthermore, Solidarity's unwillingness to challenge Poland's relationship with the Soviet Union, an implicit sine qua non of the Gdańsk agreements, removed from discussion many of the Soviet-style economic and political institutions that were ultimately responsible for Poland's political and economic crises.

The party leadership's first response in this hopeless situation was to sack Gierek. Details of the corruption and economic mismanagement of the Gierek years were made public in an attempt to blame the former leader for the mess in which the country found itself. However, since the PZPR's new leaders, like former Interior Minister Stanisław Kania (the new First Secretary) and General Jaruzelski, had held important positions during the Gierek era, these tactics did little to encourage confidence in the new leadership. In the months that followed, the PZPR struggled to prevent an open split between liberals favoring cooperation with Solidarity and conservatives advocating a crackdown, and to turn back calls for internal democratization from its rank and file. Unable to act decisively, the PZPR temporized and backtracked on its implementation of the Gdańsk accords. Efforts to design a credible program for political reconciliation and economic recovery languished, and the economic situation continued to deteriorate.

The accords' economic postulates, the recession that had begun in 1979, and the PZPR's inability to design a viable program of economic stabilization and reform proved to be a disastrous combination. As Table 2.1 shows, the economic downturn that began in 1979 accelerated in 1980–1981. National income produced (in real terms) declined by 23.6 percent from 1979 to 1982; investment fell by 44.9 percent and consumption by 2.0 percent. These declines were driven by a catastrophic 54 percent fall in the volume of the hard-currency imports on which the Polish economy had come to depend and were accompanied by a 169-percent increase in retail prices (as measured officially). Perhaps most disquieting was the controversial "inflationary overhang"—the difference between the population's money holdings and the nominal value of the goods available in the official economy.[1] Combined with the PZPR's lack of credibility in Polish society, internal pressure from Solidarity and external pressure from the USSR and Poland's Western creditors created an environment for the design and implementation of economic reforms unprecedented in the Soviet bloc.

On the plus side, Solidarity, as a potentially pro-reform actor, filled a role that had been missing from the previous reform attempts: an institutional guarantor of hopes for pluralistic political evolution and social control over the reform process. Given the depth of the economic problems on the one hand and the strengths of the passions aroused during the 1980–1981 renewal on the other, a reform program that harnessed these passions while simultaneously addressing Polish society's hopes for a better future would have had the best chances of success. As a Solidarity activist told me in 1983, "We would be willing to tighten our belts, to accept lower living standards for a long time, maybe ten years, if we believed that, eventually, the economy will really improve, and that this crisis will be put behind us permanently."

Nevertheless, Solidarity plainly did not have the answers to the country's reform dilemmas. In fact, the Solidarity movement in 1980–1981 represented a plethora of socio-economic interests that rarely spoke with a single voice on economic issues, with the exception of vociferous objections to price increases. In fact, during most of the 1980–1981 period Solidarity refused to develop a comprehensive economic program, probably to avoid being drawn into a hopeless argument. Only in 1981 did Solidarity come out in favor of a reform program based on worker self-management, but largely because of its political features.

The other major plus of the 1980–1981 period was that the official

TABLE 2.1
The Economic Collapse of 1979–1982

	1979	*1980*	*1981*	*1982*
Gross national product (% change)	−1.9	−2.6	−5.3	−0.6
National income produced (% change)	−2.3	−6.0	−12.0	−5.5
Gross investment (% change)	−7.9	−12.3	−22.3	−12.1
Consumption (% change)	2.4	1.2	−5.2	−12.3
Gross agricultural production (% change)	−1.5	−10.7	−3.8	−2.8
Retail price inflation (%)	7.4	8.5	18.4	109.4
Imports from non-socialist countries (% change)	−4.5	−7.2	−31.5	−24.2
Exports to non-socialist countries (% change)	2.1	5.0	−22.1	0.9
Net western debt ($ billions)	20.7	23.5	25.5	25.4

Sources: Rocznik Statystyczny 1989, XXXII, XXXIV, XXXVIII, XLIV, XLVI; *Rocznik Statystyczny: Handel Zagraniczny* 1988, 8; Fallenbuchl 1989, 103; Poznański 1986, 461.

Note: Data in rows 1–5, 7, and 8 are in constant prices.

economic reform debate was accompanied by a great deal of open, professional analysis and public discussion (Krawczyk 1981). This had three important effects on the economic reform process in Poland. First, it pushed the official Committee for Economic Reform further in the direction of radical reform than would otherwise have been the case. Second, it increased support for reform among Polish economists and, more generally, the intelligentsia. Third, and most important, the unofficial component of the 1980–1981 reform debate marked a crucial step in the evolution of reformist thought throughout the 1980s. In particular, the unofficial reform blueprint produced in 1981 by a group of young economists working under the direction of Leszek Balcerowicz at Warsaw's Central School of Planning and Statistics initiated a decade of informal work on reform projects (Balcerowicz et al. 1981). Following Solidarity's ascension to power in 1989, this group provided the initial conceptual basis and the personnel for Poland's transition from socialism to capitalism in 1990–1991.

The PZPR's disarray in 1980–1981 led the government, first under Kania and then under Jaruzelski, to adopt a conservative attitude toward economic reform in which primary emphasis was placed on maintaining control over the official reform debate. The size and clumsiness of the official Committee for Economic Reform were consequences of this attitude. The committee was a leviathan of 500 members with 14 separate working groups that took more than a year to produce the official reform blueprint (*Kierunki reformy gospodarczej* 1981). This official reticence stood in sharp contrast with the more radical plan completed by Balcerowicz's group in November 1980, as well as the other, unofficial, reform projects proposed in 1981 (Krawczyk).

An additional aspect of the sociopolitical confusion into which the first stage was introduced deserves special emphasis. Because of the economic collapse, the breaking of cooperative links formed with Western suppliers and customers during the 1970s, and frequent administrative reorganizations, by late 1981 the institutional relationships of the traditional economic mechanism were in a state of disarray. As a result, the reform was not introduced into a stable, integrated institutional network capable of "rejecting transplants" that upset its organizational equilibrium (Zielinski 1978). Instead, the first stage of economic reform was introduced into a "systemic vacuum" (Fallenbuchl 1982) in which neither the traditional nor the reformed economic mechanism had a clear institutional mandate. The question was, Would this institutional confusion promote the implementation of the new mechanism or the regeneration of the old?

This unique situation produced an interesting reform blueprint (*Kierunki reformy gospodarczej*), which served as the basis for the first stage of the economic reforms introduced largely between 1981 and 1983. In its emphasis on market principles this document was quite radical compared to previous Polish reform blueprints and official reform programs developed in other Soviet bloc nations. It declared that the root cause of the economic collapse could be found in the country's political system and recognized the need to democratize the planning and policy-making mechanisms. However, the blueprint was not without its internal inconsistencies and loose ends. Most important of these was the fact that although market relations were to replace obligatory output plans and administrative input rationing for state enterprises within the planning process, the blueprint did not provide institutional guarantees ensuring that its principles would be translated into behavioral change in the central administration and the PZPR apparatus.[2] Neither the renunciation of central planning nor a reconsideration of private ownership was envisioned.

The heart of the first stage's reform design was captured by the "Three S's" slogan—self-reliance and self-financing of enterprises and self-management by workers. Enterprise managers and workers' councils (to which the managers were supposed to be accountable) were to design their own production plans and arrange their own supply and distribution networks without obligatory physical targets from the central authorities. Managerial and worker incentive systems were to be linked to yearly enterprise profitability. The compliance of enterprises with the central plan was to be influenced through financial instruments whose magnitudes would be determined both administratively and by market forces; this element implied major changes in the role and scope of central planning. Direct-planning targets for enterprises could be issued only to meet CMEA trade obligations, for national defense production, or for national emergencies. Approximately 75 percent of total investment was to be decentralized to the enterprise level, while 25 percent would be devoted to completing the unfinished central investment projects left over from the 1970s.

Major reform of the central administration was called for, including a reduction in the number of industrial branch ministries—from ten to one or two—and significant reductions in staffing and budget for the new ministry(s). A newly created Supply Bureau would assume the branch ministries' responsibilities for providing enterprises with centrally rationed inputs. The traditional intermediate-layer organs (*zjednoczenia*) were to be replaced by largely voluntary producer associations (*zrzeszenia*) formed by, and ultimately responsible to, the enterprises themselves. In addition to reducing the branch ministries' ability to micromanage the enterprises, these changes were meant to diminish the central administration's traditional branch orientation (and thus to strengthen its ability to function in an economy-wide, parametric manner) as well as to reduce the significance of branch-oriented, closed-door lobbying.

Since private farmers supplied the bulk of Poland's agricultural output, agricultural reform was directed primarily at reducing instability and uncertainty for farmers (Cook 1984; Mazurkiewicz 1982). Private farmers were guaranteed in perpetuity a secure position in Polish agriculture, as well as income parity with urban dwellers and equal access to agricultural capital and credit. The "Three S's" were to be applied to state farms and agricultural cooperatives, with emphasis on replacing the intermediate-layer organs with self-governing producer associations more responsive to farmers' needs. The ministries of Agriculture and Food Production were also merged. Finally, a Bureau of Economic Reform was created to oversee the reform's implementation; its head, who was accorded the title of minister, was Władysław Baka, chairman of the Economic Reform Commission that had designed the reform blueprint.

A number of factors constrained the effectiveness of the first stage of economic reform designed in 1980–1981. Some applied almost universally to attempts at economic reform in socialist countries. These included:

The lack of competitive-market and entrepreneurial traditions.

Industrial-policy decisions made before the 1980s, favoring such sectors as shipbuilding, mining, and energy production, that created favored sectors with strong lobbies able to perpetuate industrial structures incompatible with emphases upon enterprise self-financing and profitability.

The lack of hard currency, which prevented the appearance of anything more than symbolic import competition.

Conflicts inherent in trying to reconcile greater enterprise autonomy and an emphasis on profitability with the bureaucratic nature of CMEA trade.

The desire to prevent enterprise bankruptcy and the appearance of open unemployment.[3]

It is difficult to exaggerate the impact of the nineteen months of martial law (from December 13, 1981, to July 22, 1983) that paralleled the early days of reform in 1982 (Fallenbuchl 1984). The declaration of martial law and the government's subsequent war on Solidarity and other independent organizations decoupled economic reform from the forces of political reform and renewal. Martial law came to be widely perceived as the most recent instance of the PZPR's desire to preserve its political position at the country's expense. In destroying Solidarity's ability to act as a cohesive national political force, the Jaruzelski regime removed a potentially powerful pro-reform actor from the stage. Many economists active in the reform process either refused to participate in its implementation or left the country after the introduction of martial law. Already damaged by the failure to reform the central administration (one of the few institutions on which the PZPR could rely for unqualified support), economic reform was further discredited in the eyes of the public by the triple-digit price increases for many consumer products introduced in early 1982—foodstuff prices were raised by 160 percent during January and February 1982, for example (Mieszczańkowski 1987, 1).

Since economic reform had became widely associated with price increases imposed at gunpoint, the political opposition was able to present the regime's reform program to Polish society as something fundamentally undemocratic and undesirable, something "they" were doing to "us" that "we" would stop if "they" could be gotten rid of. Having been driven underground by the state security apparatus, the political opposition had little reason not to pander to such sentiment. The economic sanctions imposed by Western governments and financial institutions after martial law was instituted also reinforced the "us against them" mentality. The Western response to martial law also deprived the Polish government of the financial support that could have eased the transition to the reformed system.

In purely economic terms, the shortage conditions and negative growth trends prevailing at the start of reform implementation guaranteed frequent and painful conflicts between reform imperatives (such as changes in the enterprise financial system necessary to make the self-financing and self-reliance slogans a reality) and other policy imperatives concerning inflation and excessive growth in wages and enterprise liquidity. The resulting "compromise" solutions to these dilemmas, many of which were sanctioned as "temporary measures" by the reform blueprint, often sacrificed the spirit of the reform. Examples of this include the PFAZ wage-fund tax and a sharply progressive tax on enterprise sales receipts (replaced by a proportional tax in 1983), both of which were authorized by decree by Council of Ministers on November 30, 1981.[4] A tax in 1987 on enterprise sales, ostensibly imposed to siphon off "excess" enterprise liquidity to help finance the repayment of Poland's foreign debt, was another case of what the Polish press dubbed "excessive fiscalism."

Unfinished investment projects remaining from the boom of the 1970s were also a major constraint on the reform. These projects presented Polish planners with a painful choice: either devote the bulk of the country's incremental capital to finishing these projects, thus reducing the resources for industrial modernization and restructuring, or lose the capital frozen in these projects indefinitely. The authorities by and large chose the former of these two evils; from 1986 to 1988 up to 85 percent of investment capital was still devoted to completing projects begun in the previous decade. While investment authority may have been decentralized on paper, confiscatory taxation and extensive subsidy programs ensured that enterprise liquidity was channeled toward construction firms engaged in the completion of unfinished central investments.

Other compromise solutions sanctioned by the reform blueprint included the "temporary" retention of direct planning for the production of goods regarded as "critically important" to the national economy, as well as the central allocation of imported raw materials and hard currency. Although free prices (*ceny umowne*) set at equilibrium levels were the long-run goal of price policy, some prices (e.g., for foodstuffs, children's clothing, and other consumer products) would continue to be set administratively (*ceny urzędowe*); others would be subject to ceilings (*ceny regulowane*).

These compromises in reform instruments required corresponding compromises in respect of the institutions that would administer these instruments. The decision in July 1981 to reduce the number of industrial branch ministries to five, rather than the one or two specified by the reform blueprint, was perhaps the greatest institutional compromise, since it effectively preserved the traditional branch structures within the central economic administration. The retention of the unreformed instruments and institutions inevitably caused friction with other elements of the reform program. This friction worked largely to the detriment of reform during and after the martial-law period of 1982–1983, since many of these "temporary," "compromise" solutions remained in effect for years, often in expanded form.

On the other hand, martial law offered the PZPR a certain escape from the hopeless predicament in which it found itself in 1980–1981. General Jaruzelski's putsch weakened the workers' veto power over unpopular stabilization programs—a power they had successfully exercised in 1970–1971, 1976, and again in 1980–1981—thus restoring price increases for consumer goods, as well as macroeconomic adjustment, to the realm of the politically possible. Through its militarization of coal production and other key sectors, by late 1982 the government was able to halt the downward spiral in energy and raw-materials production, and subsequently the decline in hard-currency exports, hard-currency imports, and industrial production.

Rather than junking reform, as the Husak leadership did in Czechoslovakia after Soviet tanks ended Alexander Dubček's "Prague Spring" in 1968, the Jaruzelski government also took a number of significant pro-reform steps in 1981–1982. Tax and legal regulations affecting small state-sector and private manufacturing firms were liberalized in 1981. The "Three S's" were introduced into the management of state farms in July 1981. Later that month the Councils of Ministers and State reduced the number of branch ministries. In late September the Sejm passed two key laws on enterprise autonomy and self-management. November saw the decision to abolish (as of January 1, 1982) the traditional intermediate-level organizations, the *zjednoczenia*. Nine more pieces of legislation were approved by the Sejm in February 1982, reforming the foreign trade mechanism, the enterprise financial and system, and the price, tax, and banking systems, and opening the central-planning process to greater consultation with interest groups and outside experts (Baka 1982).

The first stage of economic reform consisted essentially of a flurry of legislation combined with military discipline. As a method of quelling labor unrest and protests against price increases, it was an effective combination. Progress was made toward restoring internal equilibrium in 1982, and the legal foundations for a new economic mechanism for state enterprises was created. The tension between partial economic decentralization and economic and political militarization could not be defused indefinitely, however. The imperative of implementing economic reform and restoring order in the economy had played a key role in Jaruzelski's original justification for declaring martial law. Once martial law had effectively destroyed Solidarity's ability to challenge the government's programs, the Jaruzelski regime came under strong pressure to fulfill the second half of the implicit bargain—to solve, or at least reduce the severity of, the economic crisis. Consequently, the government's willingness to implement massive price increases and to resist the ensuing demands for higher wages (especially in such priority sectors as mining, metallurgy, and shipbuilding) weakened noticeably after 1982. After falling in 1982, real wages remained roughly constant in 1983 and registered yearly increases from 1984 to 1986.[5]

On December 30, 1981, a decree of the Council of Ministers suspended the reform's self-management component.[6] In addition to giving the reform a more managerial orientation, the suspension further deepened Polish workers' cynicism and mistrust toward economic reform and removed another important player from the pro-reform camp. The decree also transferred responsibility for central supply allocation to the Council of Ministers' Economic Committee, a super-central agent of branch ministerial interests, rather than to the Supply Bureau that had been created in October 1981 expressly for that purpose (Jermakowicz and Krawczyk 1985, 158). These moves helped rescue the branch ministries from the precarious position in which they found themselves in late 1981, having only barely avoided in July their amalgamation into the single industrial ministry called for in the reform blueprint. Although in January 1982 the branch ministries were reduced in number from ten to five and absorbed large cuts in budgeting and staffing, by the end of 1985 the industrial ministries had increased their employment by more than 10 percent over 1982 levels (Piesiewicz 1987). Before the workers councils' "reactivization" in late 1982 and 1983, the branch ministries managed to ensure that both the obligatory and (ostensibly) voluntary producers' associations (*zrzeszenia*) were formed according to the ministries' own self-serving criteria. Consequently, the number and composition of both types of associations came to closely resemble those of the *zjednoczenia* they replaced (Ancerowicz and Cylwik 1984; Cylwik 1984).

In addition to reaffirming the central administration's branch structure, this decree also sanctioned the reintroduction of direct-planning instruments, in the form of "operational programs." These programs' roots lay in a special "Anti-Crisis Task Force" formed by the branch ministries in July 1981. This force was intended to guarantee, by direct-planning methods, the production and distribution of foodstuffs, articles of personal hygiene, and other staple items in short supply. The Supply Bureau established in October was supposed to assume this function through the creation and supervision of special "operational programs" with narrowly defined goals and mandates. The programs were to be administered by officials appointed by and accountable to the Supply Bureau.

The decree of December 30 transferred responsibility for the operational programs' design and execution to the branch ministries. The number of programs expanded from six in 1981 to nine and then 14 in 1982. According to various estimates, 70 product groups, comprising 60 percent of industrial production in 1982, were included in these programs; 85 product groups were on central input balances administered by the branch ministries, the Planning Commission, and the Supply Bureau (Bogus and Kasperkiewicz 1983; Fallenbuchl 1982; Jermakowicz 1983). Although enterprise participation was ostensibly voluntary, these programs offered firms supplies that were otherwise unobtainable. Not surprisingly, up to 80 percent of state enterprises expressed an interest in participating in at least one operational program (Jermakowicz and Krawczyk 1985).

The rationing of "scarce" inputs by the branch ministries and other central organs was not limited to products included in the operational programs. In fact, the number of inputs subjected to sub-central rationing increased in 1983, despite the fact that the reform blueprint called for the abolition of such practices by the end of that year (Mieszczańkowski 1987, 4). The branch ministries were also instrumental in placing state enterprises on a list of "firms of key importance to the national economy" that were exempted from the reform's principles. The number of firms on this list expanded from 200 in 1981 to 1,372 (out of 6,372) in 1984 (Holland 1988, 136; Kasten 1986, 67–101; Pełnomocnik rządu ds. 1985, 6–7).

In this way the industrial ministries not only avoided abolition, they recreated the intermediate layer largely according to their own designs, reassumed de facto supply responsibilities for the enterprises subordinated to them, and were authorized to design and implement the operational programs, the essence of which was the direct planing of enterprise output and supply decisions. The institutional chaos into which the first stage was introduced, once the field had been cleared of Solidarity and the workers' councils (which otherwise would have had to confirm their enterprises' participation in the operational programs and "voluntary" *zrzeszenia*), promoted the regeneration of traditional economic institutions and instruments. The flurry of reform legislation introduced between 1981 and 1983 was unable to prevent the resurrection of the old system.

Numerous changes called for in the 1981 reform blueprint were not implemented during the first stage. These included the abolition of the branch ministries and, more generally, reform of the central administration; the establishment of an antimonopoly agency; the de facto decentralization of investment decisions; and the commercialization of the banking system. Following the flurry of legislative activity in 1981 and 1982, only two other important reform measures were introduced before 1986: legislation authorizing bankruptcy procedures for state enterprises, and the partial decentralization of enterprise wage determination (Jacukowicz 1986; Smuga 1986).

The reappearance of compulsory enterprise plan targets and the central allocation of inputs was accompanied by a reduction in the significance of market prices in the state sector. As of January 1 1982, the shares of free (unregulated), regulated (free but subject to a ceiling), and administrative (i.e., administratively determined) prices were approximately 50, 15, and 35 percent respectively; by September 1982, the ratio had slipped to 39, 15, and 46 percent, respectively—an 11 percent shift from the free to the administrative category (Jermakowicz 1983, 17). This slippage was accompanied by loud campaigns in the press and local PZPR organs against "excessive" price increases. In 1982 the Council of Ministers enacted a policy under which factors "external" to state enterprises (i.e., demand conditions) were prohibited from playing a role in price determination in the administrative and regulated pricing spheres; in 1983 the prohibition was extended to the free price category. Since only "justified" costs were regarded as legitimate price-determining factors, these regulations considerably reduced the economic significance of the free price category and guaranteed that virtually all prices would retain their traditional cost-plus character. The relevance of free prices was further reduced by a five-month freeze on all price increases during the second half of 1983, and by another freeze on free prices for consumer goods during part of 1984. Instead of being market determined, prices remained first and foremost a bargaining issue with the Price Bureau and, indirectly, other central organs.

These weaknesses in market forces were accompanied by increased industrial concentration in a number of sectors. Not only did the antimonopoly policy called for in the reform blueprint fail to appear, but government decisions actually increased the number of monopolies or near monopolies. At the central level, the maintenance of central input rationing perpetuated the monopolistic control of the branch ministries' trading organs. At the enterprise level, the five-year charters for many of the branch-oriented obligatory producer associations, which enterprises had been forced to join in 1982, expired in 1985 and 1986. This led to numerous attempts by the branch ministries to preserve control by amalgamating the firms under their purview into larger multiplant enterprises (*wspólnoty*) or national concerns (*gwarectwa*). Concentration pressures were particularly strong in the Mining and Energy Ministry, which by 1986 had established a number of supraenterprise concerns that dramatically reduced the autonomy of the subordinated enterprises. The Metallurgical and Machine Tool Ministry attempted to form a national concern in the steel industry during 1985 but was only partially successful, largely because of opposition from the workers' councils of the affected enterprises, as well as from outside experts.[7]

In terms of foreign trade, the blueprint for the first stage of reform contained the following elements:

As a corollary to increased enterprise autonomy, firms were authorized to apply to conduct foreign-trade activities independent of the Foreign Trade Ministry and its agents, the foreign trading organizations (FTOs). This was intended to encourage competition among FTOs and to allow enterprises to interact directly with foreign firms.

The close link between the ministry and the FTOs was to be broken, in order to encourage the FTOs to behave more like commercial organizations. The ministry was reduced in size and reorganized, in order to reduce its control over operational decisions made by FTOs and producing enterprises and to redirect its focus to macro-trade and industrial-policy issues.

The majority of FTOs were transformed into joint-stock companies whose shares were held by the FTOs' major domestic clients as well as by the ministry. This was intended to better integrate production and trade activities, improve domestic firms' information about world markets, and promote enterprise investment in export-oriented projects.

Commands and administrative instruments in foreign-trade management were to be replaced by financial instruments. In particular, different commercial and tourist exchange rates were to be replaced by a unified "submarginal" exchange rate, guaranteeing the profitability of at least 75 percent of Poland's exports. This would allow closer linkage between domestic and world-market prices, especially for raw materials and primary products. Deviations in domestic prices by more than 5 percent from world-market prices were to trigger compensating revaluation of the exchange rate.

Joint ventures and other forms of cooperation between Polish and foreign firms were to be encouraged. Cooperation was sought with firms from Western and CMEA countries.

Exporting enterprises were permitted to retain a certain portion of their hard-currency export receipts in order to finance hard-currency imports.

Central rationing of foreign exchange was to be supplemented by loans and auctions of convertible currencies conducted by the Foreign Trade Bank.

The final two reform steps were intended to create an internal market for convertible currencies (Rymarczyk 1985). As a whole, these changes were supposed to lead to zloty convertibility at some unspecified future date. The most immediate concern, however, was improving the country's hard-currency export performance and debt-servicing capabilities.

The problems afflicting reform in the domestic economy also affected foreign trade. The goal of loosening the Foreign Trade Ministry's structural controls over the FTOs and the producing enterprises was not realized in practice. The core of the structural reform—transforming the FTOs into independent, commercial joint-stock companies—had few positive consequences, and a number of undesirable side effects. The Foreign Trade Ministry was still the majority shareholder in the new joint-stock companies, a position that afforded the ministry almost as much leverage over the new FTOs as it had exerted over the old. This leverage was commonly used to prevent domestic firms from exercising their choice among "competing" FTOs, as was intended by the reform legislation (Rymarczyk 1985). Shortage conditions and inflationary pressures played havoc with pricing and exchange-rate policies, overvaluing the zloty and exacerbating difficulties in linking domestic to world-market prices. Although a unified exchange rate was formally introduced in 1982, the goal of sub-marginality was honored mostly in the breach. Despite numerous devaluations (the official dollar-zloty exchange rate fell from 80 to 502.5 zloty per dollar between 1982 and 1988), the goal of using world-market prices to help rationalize the domestic price system remained elusive. Instead, domestic prices for tradeables played a catch-up game with world-market prices: successive devaluations would widen the gap between world-market and domestic prices, and the correction principle would be applied too gradually to make up the difference between devaluations. The resulting shortages provided a justification for the maintenance of the traditional central rationing and price-correction programs administered by the Foreign Trade Ministry, and the resurgent branch ministries and their agents. Enterprise export incentives continued to be weak, since inflationary pressures remained strong and virtually everything produced by Polish firms could be sold at home.

The attempt at establishing an internal hard-currency market during the first stage of reform was essentially reduced to the introduction of foreign-exchange accounts for exporting enterprises. Hard-currency auctions administered by the Foreign Trade Bank played an insignificant role in allocating foreign exchange; less than 1 percent of the hard-currency stock was allocated through auctions from 1982 to 1986 (Boffito 1988; Tarnowski 1987). Enterprises with foreign-exchange retention accounts were not permitted to participate in the auctions or to sell their export receipts to other firms, although they were allowed to use them as payment for services rendered.

Enterprise foreign-exchange accounts were established in 1982, primarily as a result of pressure applied by large enterprises. The percentage of total hard-currency imports financed by these accounts never rose above 30.2 percent (1985), and the percentage of export revenues retained by enterprises was held to 20 percent (Boffito 1987; Mizsei 1986a; Rymarczyk 1985; Slay 1988). The percentage of export receipts retained by enterprises was generally determined according to sector- and enterprise-specific criteria, and purchases made with these funds were often subjected to administrative controls and delays.[8]

Although the Council of Ministers had issued regulations in 1976 permitting Poles living abroad to invest in small-scale manufacturing within Poland, as of January 1982 only 144 production licenses had actually been granted to these *polonia* firms. The economic collapse of 1979–1982 brought a change of attitude, and the Sejm liberalized the 1976 law during the summer of 1982. The specter of empty shelves in Polish stores caught the attention of potential investors: 374 licenses were granted in 1982 and 190 more in 1983. By mid-1985 the figure stood at 736, not including the 436 applications for licenses that had been denied (Loch 1986).

The Polish authorities were initially so desperate for increased consumer-goods production that the *polonia* firms were given a three-year income-tax holiday, although other tax liabilities remained in force. By 1984 these firms accounted for 9.8 percent of total output in small-scale manufacturing; *firma polonijna* had become synonymous in the mind of many Polish consumers with the West, better quality, and higher prices.

As the economic situation began to improve, however, and as the *polonia* firms' activities encountered criticism from defenders of the primacy of state industry, the firms' regulatory environment became more uncertain. In July 1983 three modifications to the 1982 regulations were introduced: (1) The income tax exemption was made conditional on the reinvestment of one-third of the profits in the firm; (2) the *polonia* enterprises were required to sell 50 percent of their export receipts to the state treasury at the official exchange rate; and (3) the post-exemption tax rate on gross income was increased by more than 50 percent. In addition, the minimum investment requirement was raised in January 1985 to $100,000. As a result of the expiration of the tax holiday in 1985 and the above-mentioned (and other) disincentives, the *polonia* firms' share of total exports began to decline in 1984 decreased and between mid-1985 and early 1986 their number decreased. This was not the type of track record likely to inspire confidence in potential large-scale investors. As Plesiński (1987) noted about the *polonia* firms, "The economic benefits of their activities turned out to be incomparably smaller than the propaganda and psychological damage resulting from the policy instability they have faced."

The first stage of reform scarcely addressed trade with other CMEA members. The Foreign Trade Ministry continued to issue mandatory import quotas and export targets for both traditional FTOs and the joint-stock FTOs, which were supposed to be free of direct ministerial supervision (Rymarczyk 1985). While the FTOs were not, in most cases, supposed to issue production orders to enterprises in order to fulfill CMEA export obligations, during the first stage precious little changed in this area. Although the reform did envision the introduction of competitive bidding procedures in import allocation, they were applied only in hard-currency import allocation, not for CMEA imports, and on an insignificant scale (Zarzycki 1985). The sole innovation in CMEA foreign trade was the creation, in 1985, of enterprise transferable ruble retention accounts. Since, however, transferable rubles did not allow their possessors to make claims on other CMEA countries' currencies or products, the significance of these accounts was marginal. Joint ventures with firms from other CMEA countries, primarily the USSR, Hungary, Czechoslovakia, and Bulgaria, were also attempted, especially in 1986 and 1987. Because of their small numbers (approximately two dozen in 1987), and since these ventures were established by the traditional CMEA mechanism, it is difficult to ascribe much significance to them (*Polish Economy in the External Environment* 1988, 64).

The "Second Stage" of Economic Reform: 1986–1988

By the autumn of 1985, prospects for economic reform in Poland did not look very promising. The "first stage" legislation of 1981–1982 had created a new financial system for state enterprises, increased the importance of financial instruments, and partially reformed the intermediate layer; but the reassertion of the branch ministries' dominance, the rapid increases in money wages, the continued subsidization of large and inefficient firms, and increased structural concentration all violated the spirit (and frequently the letter) of the 1980–1981 blueprint. Prime Minister Zbigniew Messner's announcement in November 1985 that the reform's implementation had been essentially completed, as well as the subordination of the government's Economic Reform Bureau and the secretariat of the Economic Reform Commission to the Planning Commission, seemed to signal the end of the reformers' hopes.

To the surprise of many observers, however, the PZPR leadership's commitment to reform became firmer in 1986. In June and July the tenth party congress called for a "second stage" in the economic reform and authorized the consideration of proposals that had been beyond the realm of the politically possible since December 1981. A number of factors seem to have played a role in this turnaround, including the Gorbachev leadership's adoption of an ambitious reform program at the twenty-seventh Soviet party congress, in February 1986; Poland's readmission to the International Monetary Fund and World Bank in the spring of 1986, implying possible improvement in relations with Western creditors; and the failure to fulfill the 1986 plan for hard-currency exports, as well as the general recognition that many of the temporary factors specific to the post-1982 economic recovery had largely played out and that future economic growth would have to come from increases in efficiency and factor productivity.

A number of reform steps were taken in 1986 and 1987, including the passage of legislation authorizing large-scale joint ventures with Western firms, creating an Export Development Bank to promote foreign trade and joint ventures, and establishing an Anti-Monopoly Bureau to prevent further increases in industrial concentration. More general questions about the nature of the second stage remained unanswered until March 1987, when the PZPR Central Committee's third plenum approved a set of 174 theses drafted by the Economic Reform Commission (*Tezy w sprawie drugiego etapu* 1987). The theses roundly criticized the shortcomings of the first stage of reform and set out a more coherent, far-reaching vision of a market socialist economy than was evident in the first stage. The basic principles of the second stage, as set forth in the theses, were:

Establishment of the economic preconditions necessary for markets to function, including market equilibration, reduction of restrictions on free prices, reduction of rationing as well as of other barriers to resource reallocation between enterprises and sectors, and strict observance of the principle of enterprise self-finance, including the liquidation of unprofitable enterprises.

Emphasis on "socialist entrepreneurship" based on industrial deconcentration, antitrust policy, the creation of new enterprises, and relaxed restrictions on cooperation between enterprises with different forms of ownership.

Completion of the reform of the central administration begun in 1981–1982.

Support for worker and local government self-management.

Popular opposition to price increases for consumer goods made the tenet on market equilibrium particularly problematic; three variant solutions for achieving internal equilibrium were initially proposed. The first variant called for equilibration in the course of a single year through a series of massive price increases; the second proposed introducing price increases over a two- or three-year period; the third envisioned stretching the increases out over a longer period of time. These options were subsequently reduced to a choice between the "immediate" introduction of massive price increases in early 1988 and their more "gradual" introduction over a period of several years. This question was at the heart of the referendum on economic reform submitted to Polish voters on November 29, 1987 (see discussion below).

Reform of the central economic administration was approved by the Sejm in October 1987. Three of the four industrial branch ministries were combined into a single Ministry of Industry, and other ministries and offices were consolidated as well.[9] Two other important pro-reform steps were also sanctioned by the Sejm: (1) The number of state enterprises on the list of "firms of essential importance to the national economy" was reduced from 1,391 to 347 (Szwarc 1987); and (2) the National Bank and other banks were added to the list of sub-central and territorial organs authorized to create new state enterprises (Kowalska 1987).

The reform of the central authorities was by no means a complete victory for the pro-reform forces, however. Most of the branch ministries' supervisory functions were retained by the Ministry of Industry and the Ministry was empowered to take drastic administrative actions vis-à-vis the firms subordinated to it. Moreover, despite the formal abolition of the branch ministries, the Ministry of Industry and the other new ministries quickly developed branch-oriented internal structures. Also disquieting was the creation of two nationwide concerns (*wspólnoty*) in the coalmining and energy sectors (*Węgiel Kamienny* and *Energetyka i Węgiel Brunatny*), an arrangement that effectively snuffed out the last remnants of enterprise autonomy in these branches. (The *Wspólnota Węgla Kamiennego* subsumed 48 enterprises and employed more than 600,000 workers.) The subordinated enterprises had their yearly plans approved by the *wspólnota*'s director general and the Minister of Industry was authorized to impose compulsory plan targets on the *wspólnota* (Kowalska 1987). This arrangement was a throwback to the WOG reform of the 1970s, except that enterprise membership in the WOG had been largely voluntary.

The Implementation Program that followed the Reform Commission's theses called for three further institutional changes intended to facilitate the introduction of tighter monetary and credit policies: (1) The commercialization of the banking system, (2) reductions in subsidies to unprofitable enterprises, and (3) the creation of a bond market, as well as (eventually) a stock market. (*Program realizacyjny* 1987, 46–47):

The second stage also reflected the desire to more effectively reform the foreign-trade mechanism. Its most important steps were to be the following:

The Foreign Trade Ministry's control over trade was further loosened. FTO ownership regulations were again liberalized, allowing the Ministry's ownership share to fall below 51 percent (except for products of "central importance to the national economy"). Virtually all state enterprises became able to purchase shares in FTOs. As part of the reform of the central administration, the Ministry was again reorganized (becoming the Ministry for International Economic Cooperation) and absorbed further cuts in budget and staffing.

A number of changes were intended to expand the enterprise foreign-exchange retention system. Reducing the variability of different retention rates, as well as granting exporting enterprises ownership rights to the funds in their accounts, may have been the most beneficial changes; restrictions on interenterprise hard-currency transfers were also loosened. However, these changes were accompanied, in 1987, by some steps backward as well, including (1) reducing by 20 percent the percentage of export revenues retained; (2) requiring enterprises to purchase the hard currency in "their" accounts, and at the official exchange rate; and (3) requiring that these purchases take place within the first three months of the time of deposit (otherwise, the enterprise could lose the right of purchase).

A more "active" exchange-rate policy was pursued, aimed at tightening the link between domestic and world-market prices. The zloty was devalued against the dollar by approximately 40 percent in nominal terms (around 15 percent in real terms) during late 1986 and early 1987, allowing closer adherence to the sub-marginal exchange-rate policy after the second half of 1987.[10] 1988 saw further liberalization of import and export prices, reductions in the number of centrally rationed imports, and the introduction of stronger tax incentives to export for enterprises.

The 1986 legislation authorizing large-scale joint ventures between Polish and Western firms was significantly liberalized in December 1988. In addition to simplifying the licensing and administration of joint ventures and relaxing the requirement that at least 50 percent of the capital invested in any joint project be owned by the Polish government, companion legislation passed in December 1988 permitted all economic organizations, regardless of ownership, to engage in any legal business activity.

The first step in commercializing the banking system was taken on November 1, 1987, when the PKO savings bank became independent of the

National Bank of Poland (NBP). During the course of 1988, independent commercial banks were carved out of the NBP's divisions; enterprises were to have the right to select the bank of their choice. In contrast with the traditional direct control over monetary aggregates, the creation of indirect monetary-policy instruments to be applied by the NBP, such as equilibrium interest rates and reserve requirements, was also envisioned, as was the creation of a network of banks to service enterprise hard-currency import and export requirements. The sale of bonds to private citizens as well as to other state enterprises was to provide an additional source of enterprise finance.[11]

In light of the controversial sociopolitical implications of enterprise self-financing, the dramatic reduction in subsidies, and the attendant price increases envisioned during the second stage, the Messner government put the issue before the voters in the form of a referendum, held November 29, 1987, on the pace of the second stage's implementation. (A companion referendum on the desirability of "far-reaching political reforms" was also held.) While two-thirds of those who cast ballots voted in favor of both proposals, the voter turnout failed to exceed the legally-mandated 50 percent minimum, thus invalidating the results. This low turnout (even compared to the previous elections, in June 1984 and November 1985) was perceived as a victory for the political opposition, which had called for an electoral boycott. Correctly perceiving the depth of popular disaffection with economic reform, Solidarity realized that a low turnout would both invalidate the election results and hand the government an embarrassing defeat. The opposition's strategy was aided by the vagueness with which the referenda were worded.

In any case, the referendum results did not prevent the Messner government from raising prices. Although the government decided to phase in a 110 percent increase in food prices over three years, increases of 140 to 200 percent in rents, heating, and fuel costs were implemented as scheduled during the first quarter of 1988. These increases caused a firestorm of protest and demands for compensating wage increases. The protests boiled over into a wave of strikes in April and May 1988 that threatened the political stability on which the PZPR's reform strategy rested. Many of the strikes, such as those at the Lenin Shipyards in Gdańsk and the Lenin Steel Works in Nowa Huta, had strong political overtones, including demands for legalizing Solidarity.

The government bought off the strikers by continuing the pattern, begun earlier in the year, of dramatic, above-plan increases in nominal wages. Not surprisingly, real incomes (as statistically measured) increased by 13.8 percent in 1988, following two years of relatively small (2.4 and 1.4 percent) increases (*Rocznik Statystyczny* 1991, 194). By the end of the year, the goal of restoring internal balance through market equilibration and enterprise self-financing was further from realization than it had been at the start of the year. Although the Messner government managed to weather the spring strike wave, a second, more widespread, wave shook the country in August 1988 and forced the government's resignation; its downfall was accompanied by sharp criticism of the second stage's implementation. Messner was replaced as prime minister by Mieczysław Rakowski, the former editor of the liberal weekly *Polityka*, in September 1988.

In some respects, the second stage of economic reform was a failure. In economic terms, the second stage injected strong new inflationary pressures, as well as a fresh measure of organizational flux, into the Polish economy. Politically, it led to the resignation of Zbigniew Messner's government and destroyed the political stability so painfully restored by martial law. On the other hand, important institutional changes were made in the central administration, the banking system, foreign trade, joint ventures, and elsewhere. A dialogue with Western governments, the International Monetary Fund, and the World Bank was reestablished. And the failure of the second stage convincingly demonstrated the futility of attempting far-reaching economic reforms without seeking some sort of accommodation with the political opposition.

In any case, the reform trend intensified under the Rakowski government. In December 1988 the Sejm approved important legislation promoting the rapid development of the private sector and liberalizing key provisions in the 1986 law on joint ventures. The black-market trade in foreign currencies was legalized in March 1989, increasing zloty convertibility for Polish households. Subsidies and price controls on food and many inputs were reduced or abolished during Rakowski's tenure. Furthermore, despite attempts to close the Gdańsk shipyards, the center of Solidarity activism, the Rakowski government practiced progressively more liberal internal political policies.

Political Reform during the Second Stage

The second stage of economic reform was accompanied by political reform pursued more broadly than at any previous time in People's Poland. During the second half of the 1980s the PZPR capitalized on the relatively liberal political atmosphere cultivated after the 1983 conclusion of martial law to create a more decentralized, pluralistic political mechanism within the framework of PZPR hegemony. The "normalization" of the post-martial-law period gave way to a more active agenda of political reform in which far-reaching *institutional* changes were proposed and ultimately implemented.

Initially, political reform was probably not regarded by the PZPR leadership as an end in itself, but rather as a means to the ends of improved economic performance and reduced socioeconomic tensions. As Staniszkis put it, political reform was "simply an attempt by the power elite to avoid the traps it set for itself in the process of creating a totalitarian society" (Staniszkis 1984, 248).[12] Political reform in Poland also dovetailed neatly with Mikhail Gorbachev's *perestroika* in the USSR and with demands by Western governments that improved economic relations be preceded by internal liberalization. The inclusive slogan "Everyone who is not against us is with us," associated first with the Kádár regime in post-1956 Hungary and then with the Gierek leadership in the early 1970s, was replaced by another, more expansive, compromise theme that might be stated, "Criticism of the system and proposals for reform are permissible by anyone not actively trying to overthrow the system."

The political reforms accompanying the second stage of economic reform evolved out of the Jaruzelski regime's strategy of "normalizing" state-society relations after martial law. Restrictions on self-management activities were partially lifted in late 1982 and 1983, and by 1987 workers' councils (of varying degrees of effectiveness) had been established in approximately 70 percent of state enterprises.[13] Semi-autonomous anti-Solidarity trade unions, without the right to strike, were established within the framework of the National Trade Union Conference (OPZZ). Censorship restrictions became progressively more liberal after 1983, and the regime relaxed its (largely futile) persecution of the burgeoning underground publishing networks. A major amnesty for political prisoners was announced in September 1986; persecution of the self-management movement waned during the second half of the 1980s; increased emphasis was placed on safeguarding individual rights and liberties, under the designation "socialist legality" (e.g., the 1984 trial and conviction of the police officials accused of murdering the pro-Solidarity priest Jerzy Popiełuszko).

These changes indicated that the PZPR had come to accept the permanent presence of organized opposition groups and activities. The development of underground publishing networks during the 1980s significantly eroded the party's monopoly on information and forced the official media to adopt a more open and sophisticated information policy that downplayed ideological indoctrination. Faced with these developments, the PZPR probably concluded that the political costs of eliminating these groups or dramatically curtailing their activities were likely to exceed the political benefits of such a crackdown.[14] The party remained willing, however, to permit unfettered participation in the political process by the groups whose views frequently appeared in the underground press, at least until 1989.

"Electoral democracy" was a major political reform theme during the 1980s. The PZPR became increasingly willing to allow national and local legislative bodies to take a more active role in policy-making, since representatives of these organs subscribed to the principle of "loyal opposition" and bore some kind of electoral relationship to society at large. Legislation introduced in February 1984 liberalized Poland's electoral laws, creating a system of single- and multi-candidate legislative and local government districts. Because many seats could now be contested, this system encouraged a certain measure of competition among office-seekers in the multiple-candidate districts. At the same time, top government and party officials were pre-selected and placed on a "national list" of unopposed candidates, in order to facilitate continuity in government and prevent embarrassing electoral surprises for the regime. Although PZPR membership was not a formal requirement for candidacy, party control over the elections was exercised fairly effectively. Candidates were required to accept the political platform of the Patriotic Movement for National Renewal (a PZPR-sponsored umbrella group created during martial law), and the nomination processes in individual electoral districts were frequently manipulated by the party to prevent the selection of "undesirable" candidates.

Despite these PZPR controls over the electoral process, the more direct relationship that many parliamentary and local government officials "enjoyed" with the electorate forced officeholders to pay closer attention to public opinion. This had a direct effect on economic reform and policy. For example, in October 1986, after the Sejm voiced strong objections, the Messner government removed a series of amendments from parliamentary consideration that would have gutted the legal foundations of the first stage of economic reform. And in September 1988, after months of heated parliamentary criticism over the government's handling of the economy, reform, and labor relations, the government lost a vote of confidence in the Sejm and resigned.

The Roundtable Agreements

The waves of strikes in August 1988 that precipitated the collapse of the Messner government also convinced the PZPR to reopen negotiations with

Solidarity. Further attempts at compromise were made in December 1988 and January 1989, when, following the PZPR Central Committee's tenth plenum, the Rakowski government offered Solidarity a series of power-sharing deals. The first proposal, for 30 to 40 percent of the seats in the Sejm (*The Economist*, February 4–10 1989, 46), was followed in February by a dramatic agreement to open the electoral process to members of the political opposition, permit the formation of noncommunist political parties, and relegalize Solidarity. Roundtable discussions between government and opposition leaders were held on such topics as political structures, the economy, trade union issues, health care, the media, and the environment. The Roundtable Agreements, dealing with the most pressing political and economic issues facing the country, were formally signed on April 5, 1989. The PZPR had come a full circle from its December 1981 declaration of martial law.[15]

Despite the threat they posed to the PZPR's political position, the Roundtable Agreements seemed to offer three distinct advantages. Since reconciliation with Solidarity had been a key precondition for improved economic relations with the European Community and the United States, the Jaruzelski regime hoped the agreements would lead to an infusion of new credits. The PZPR also hoped that Solidarity would be less dangerous as a junior partner, within the government and appealing for order, than as an underground "thousand-headed monster" inciting Poles to resistance. Finally, the PZPR hoped to entrust Solidarity with responsibility for economic policy and thus tar the opposition with some of the blame for the country's economic mess.[16]

Despite virulent opposition from PZPR hardliners, the Roundtable Agreements seemed to pose no immediate threat to the PZPR's position. An election date was set for June 1989—too early, it seemed, for Solidarity to mount an effective electoral campaign. Constitutional amendments were approved, creating a second legislative chamber (the Senate) alongside the Sejm, and establishing a presidency authorized to dissolve the parliament and call new elections. Although elections to the Senate were said to be completely "free," the Roundtable Agreements specified that candidates of the PZPR and its allies, the previously subservient Polish Peasant and Democratic parties, would fill 65 percent of the seats in the Sejm, while Solidarity would be competing with other independent groupings for the remaining 35 percent. Moreover, the presidency was obviously destined to be filled by General Jaruzelski. No matter what happened, it seemed that the PZPR and its allies would be able to govern by controlling the presidency and the Sejm, the key lower house of parliament. In return, Solidarity was relegalized and its leaders were promised that the next national elections (to be held within four years) would be genuinely democratic. The Roundtable Agreements could thus be seen as a coup for the PZPR. Lech Wałęsa, Solidarity's leader, described the Roundtable Agreements at that time as "the terrible price we have to pay in order to get our union back" (Weschler 1989, 64). A number of Solidarity leaders accused Wałęsa of "selling out" to the communists, called for an electoral boycott, and withdrew their recognition of Wałęsa's leadership of Solidarity.[17]

Despite this rigged electoral system, the June elections gave a stunning defeat to the PZPR. Solidarity candidates won 260 of the 261 contested parliamentary seats, while Jaruzelski, Rakowski, and other PZPR leaders running unopposed on the "national list" failed to receive enough votes for their election to be valid. After 45 years of Soviet-imposed communist rule, Polish voters used the first quasi-free elections to register an overwhelming vote of no confidence in the PZPR. The end result was humiliation for the PZPR and a hung parliament.

The PZPR leadership spent June and July of 1989 trying to put together a new government. On August 2 General Jaruzelski nominated Interior Minister Czesław Kiszczak to be the next prime minister, but the Solidarity bloc in parliament was able to prevent Kiszczak from forming a government. At the same time, Solidarity's weak position in the Sejm (where only 35 percent of the seats had been contested) ruled out a pure Solidarity government—even if the USSR were to go along and Solidarity itself were ready and willing to take on the burden of governance.[18] Both the PZPR and Solidarity were thus divided and uncertain about the future. Meanwhile, passions edged closer to the boil when food prices were liberalized on August 1.

The stalemate was broken by Wałęsa and his advisers who, behind the back of Solidarity's parliamentary delegation, entered into secret negotiations with the PZPR's allies, the Peasant and Democratic parties. Fearing that continued alliance with the PZPR would spell political disaster, the other parties agreed to support a Solidarity-led coalition government. By promising that the PZPR would maintain control over the ministries of Defense and the Interior, Wałęsa secured approval for his coup d'état from the Soviet ambassador and then from General Jaruzelski. The deal was then presented to Solidarity's parliamentary delegation and the PZPR rank and file as a fait accompli. Both were outraged, but neither could do anything about it. Three Solidarity candidates for prime minister were then submitted to General Jaruzelski, who selected Tadeusz Mazowiecki, the most moderate, to form the new government. The PZPR's 45-year reign had ended, and the region's first noncommunist head of government had been installed. Neither Poland nor the Soviet bloc would ever be the same.[19]

The Private Sector in the 1980s

The degree to which reforms in the state enterprise sector during the 1980s were accompanied by sustained growth in the private sector's share of the Polish economy is unclear.[20] While the significance of private activity certainly grew during the 1980s, especially in the second half of the decade, data and methodological issues complicate discussions of the extent and implications of that growth. This issue is important, in that perceptions of private enterprise in the post-1989 transition to capitalism often hinge on whether the 1980s prepared the private sector for a takeoff. At issue are essentially three problems:

The quality of the official statistics per se (see Table 2.2) is in doubt.[21]

Data on the private sector refer only to *legal* private-sector activities. Inclusion of illegal activities and unregistered activities carried out by legal private firms would certainly increase the private sector's share of output and employment (although whether this would affect its growth trend is unclear).

The definition of national income produced excludes most of the service sector, where the private sector had been relatively well represented and where much of its growth during the 1980s is thought to have occurred. Official data on sectoral shares during the 1980s are measured relative to national income produced.

According to official data for 1980–1989, the private sector's share of national income produced remained relatively constant (see Table 2.2). Although the private sector's share of total employment did increase during this period, and the share of the labor force devoted to nonagricultural private activities more than doubled (see Table 2.3), the relatively rapid growth of the private labor force implies that labor productivity in the private sector grew less rapidly than in the socialized sector. Rostowski estimates that the share of the population's money income generated by private economic activity in 1986 could have been as high as 45.2 percent (Rostowski 1989, 195). While this figure certainly seems large relative to its equivalent for, say, 1966 or even 1976, the absence of comparable data for other years makes this percentage difficult to interpret. Even according to official statistics, however, the private sector's share of economic activity did

TABLE 2.2
Sectoral Distribution of National Income Produced, 1980–1989 (Percentages)

	State sector	*Cooperative sector*	*Private sector*
1980	72.4	9.6	17.5
1981	61.2	8.0	30.4
1982	70.6	9.2	20.0
1983	71.1	8.9	19.6
1984	71.8	9.1	18.8
1985	71.5	9.9	18.2
1986	71.7	9.7	18.2
1987	72.5	9.8	17.2
1988	71.5	8.9	18.8
1989	69.9	9.1	19.2

Sources: Rocznik Statystyczny 1990, 118; *Rocznik Statystyczny* 1989, 84; *Rocznik Statystyczny* 1988, 80; *Rocznik Statystyczny* 1985, 79.

Note: Data are based on current prices.

expand significantly from 1980 to 1989 in industrial production, retail trade, and services to the population, and in the growth rate of the non-agricultural labor force. Official data also indicate that an explosion of private-sector activity took place during 1989. According to a government report, 294,000 private firms were officially established in 1989, increasing

TABLE 2.3
Private Sector Employment, 1980–1989

	Private share of total employment (percentage)	*Percentage of Labor Force Devoted to Private Non-Agricultural Activities*
1980	28.0	3.5
1981	29.1	3.8
1982	30.8	4.1
1983	30.7	4.6
1984	30.5	5.1
1985	30.5	5.3
1986	30.1	5.6
1987	30.1	6.2
1988	30.4	7.0
1989	33.3	10.1

Sources: Rocznik Statystyczny 1990, 93; *Rocznik Statystyczny* 1985, 55.

the number of private firms in Poland by over 50 percent in a single year. In addition, it was estimated that at least another 500,000 private individuals were engaged in various forms of unregistered but legal trade, especially of the informal, street variety (Biuro Pełnomocnika Rządu d/s 1990, 1).

Although policy toward the second economy was generally more liberal during the 1980s than in preceding decades, there was also a good deal of vacillation. The dramatic liberalization of 1981–1982 was followed by more restrictive policies from 1983 to 1986. The principles of the second stage, enunciated in 1986, called for a return to the liberal environment of 1981–1982; this resulted in the passage of the December 1988 legislation promoting the development of the private sector.

The economic collapse of 1979–1982 and the acute political crisis that followed it increased the PZPR's tolerance for sectoral diversity. Although the creation of a more favorable regulatory environment for the legal private sector began in the late 1970s, the real watershed came in 1981 and 1982, during the preparation and initial implementation of the first stage of economic reform. Steps taken at this time included (1) Council of Ministers Resolution 112, in 1981, which significantly liberalized policy towards small-scale enterprises in the private, state, and cooperative sectors; (2) the introduction, on July 1, 1981, of the reform in agriculture, which guaranteed the "inviolability" of private land ownership to peasant farmers, officially confirmed the permanence of Poland's pluralistic ownership relations, and made a commitment (largely honored during the 1980s) to maintaining "income parity" between urban and rural households; and (3) the 1982 liberalization of the regulatory environment for the small-scale foreign-owned *polonia* firms.

The period between 1983 and 1986 period saw continued liberalization of policies toward some components of the second economy mixed with retrenchment in other areas. On the liberalization side, we can point to such developments as the introduction of *zespoły gospodarcze*, economic working groups similar to the Hungarian VGMK, in 1984 (Gąsiorowska 1986; Żmuda 1986),[22] and the legislation of June 1986 authorizing large-scale joint ventures with Western corporations.

Elements of retrenchment first appeared in 1983, when some of the provisions of Resolution 112 were tightened and the first of a series of amendments to the 1982 *polonia* law were introduced. Restrictions were added in July 1983 (the tax rate on gross sales increased by more than 50 percent and the firms were required to sell half of their hard-currency export earnings to the government at the official exchange rate) and in January 1985 (the hard-currency down payment to the government was increased from $50,000 to $100,000). These restrictions, combined with the lapsing of the *polonia* firms' three-year tax holiday after 1984 and the increased emphasis on large-scale joint ventures after 1986 caused the *polonia* sector to lose its dynamism. The number of *polonia* firms decreased between mid-1985 and early 1986, and their share of total exports had begun to decline in 1984 (Loch 1986).

Removing administrative barriers to the expansion of private-sector activity was one of the second stage's central themes. After more than a year of controversy, the Sejm, in December 1988, approved legislation designed to put the private sector on firmer legal footing (Smulska 1989). These laws guaranteed equal legal treatment for all sectors; their purpose was to reduce administrative barriers to creating new private firms and to base the state regulation of economic activity (in all sectors, not just the private sector) on the principle that "everything not explicitly prohibited is permitted." In particular, the new legislation abolished both formal limitations on employment in private firms and the requirement that at least 51 percent of the capital invested in joint ventures with Western firms be held by the Polish government.

In addition to the "traditional" small-scale private firms (mostly artisans), foreign-owned firms, and economic working groups, by the late 1980s the private sector had acquired two other important legal and organizational forms: the leasing of state-owned facilities, and joint-stock companies (*spółki*). Under the leasing plan, private individuals pay a rental fee to manage state establishments for private gain. Originally restricted to shops, restaurants, and kiosks in the 1970s (Aaslund 1985, 103–113) leasing came to be practiced on a much larger scale during the late 1980s. In early 1989, for example, the state-owned electronics firm Omig, in Warsaw, was leased in its entirety to its manager (Federowicz 1990).

Spółki are joint-stock associations of firms and/or other legal entities, including individuals; the association can be intra- or inter-sectoral. *Spółki* are largely a product of the Economic Activity Act of December 1988, which permitted all economic organizations, regardless of their form of ownership, to engage in any legal business activity and to enter into partnerships with firms from other sectors.[23] Along with the liberalization of Poland's 1986 joint venture law, also in December 1988, the Economic Activity Act created a legal framework for privatizing state enterprises via domestic and foreign private investment and subsequently became the basis for the spontaneous privatization that emerged in 1989 and 1990. Because of this, the *spółki* in 1989 seemed more likely to enrich the PZPR *nomenklatura* than to create capitalism. Since the central authorities often controlled the composition and price of stock issued when state enterprises were transformed into *spółki*, party and state officials used their position to become wealthy owners of what used to be state enterprises. In the well-publicized case of the Elpol electronics *spółka*, for example, members of the board of directors (who happened to include representatives of the ministries of Interior and Defense, a former vice premier, and managers of other large state enterprises) received generous financial compensation on the completion of the conversion from state-enterprise status (Rostowski 1989, 203–204).

Of course, not all spontaneous conversions of state enterprises into *spółki* were synonymous with the "propertization of the PZPR" ("*uwłaszczenie nomenklatury*") (Levitas and Strzałkowski 1989). Some conversions were acquisitions of state firms by genuinely entrepreneurial managers; others occurred through the issuing of shares to employees and/or enterprise workers' councils; others resulted from direct foreign investment. Nonetheless, the development of *spółki* in the last months of PZPR rule served to tar the private sector with further instances of *nomenklatura* privilege and corruption.

In sum, the trend toward privatization within the framework of Soviet-type economic structures during the 1980s was a mixed bag. To be sure, a wealth of anecdotal evidence indicates that the importance of informal and illegal private activities increased during the 1980s, and the official statistics almost certainly underestimated the extent of private activity. On the other hand, official statistics show that the private sector's share of national income produced remained essentially constant during this time. They also show that the growth in the private share of economic activity occurred in the late 1980s, accompanied by a symbiotic penetration and further corruption of the private sector by the PZPR *nomenklatura*. The absence of clearly discernible increases in the private sector's share of the Polish economy during the 1980s, combined with the onus of "*nomenklatura* privatization," did not bode well for the private sector's postcommunist regeneration.

Economic Performance in the 1980s

The introduction of the first stage of economic reform essentially coincided with the start of Poland's recovery from its 1979–1982 economic collapse. As Table 2.4 shows, national income produced increased in real terms by almost 16 percent between 1982 and 1985; open inflation during that time

TABLE 2.4
Macroeconomic and External Trends, 1983–1989

	1983	*1984*	*1985*	*1986*	*1987*	*1988*	*1989*
National income produced (% change)	6.0	5.6	3.4	4.9	2.0	4.9	−0.2
Gross industrial production[a] (% change)	6.6	5.6	4.1	4.4	3.4	5.3	−0.5
Gross agricultural production (% change)	3.3	5.7	0.7	5.0	−2.3	1.2	1.5
Retail price inflation	21.4	14.8	15.0	17.5	25.3	61.3	243.8
Labor productivity (% change)	6.9	5.7	3.0	4.8	2.6	5.8	0.7
Hard currency merchandise trade balance ($ billions)	1.44	1.53	1.06	1.07	1.23	1.01	0.77
Net hard currency debt ($ billions)	25.2	25.5	28.1	32.1	37.6	37.5	39.3
Net ruble debt (TR billions)	3.5	4.5	5.3	6.3	6.4	6.3	5.3

Sources: Rocznik Statystyczny 1990, xxxiii, xxxv, xxxix, 122, 170; *Rocznik Statystyczny* 1989, xxxiii, xxxv, xxxix, 132; *Rocznik Statystyczny* 1986, 85; *Rocznik Statystyczny* 1985, 77; *Rocznik Statystyczny: Handel Zagraniczny* 1990, 7, 129; *Rocznik Statystyczny: Handel Zagraniczny* 1989, 90; *Rocznik Statystyczny: Handel Zagraniczny* 1988, 85; *Rocznik Statystyczny: Handel Zagraniczny* 1987, 81; *Rocznik Statystyczny: Handel Zagraniczny* 1986, 81.

Note: Data in rows 1–3 are in constant prices.

a—Gross industrial sales (*produkcja sprzedana przemysłu*).

was reduced from triple-digit to near single-digit levels; and after years of hard-currency merchandise trade deficits, Poland posted surpluses from 1982 to 1989. These improvements were accompanied by apparent improvement in various measures of microeconomic efficiency, such as reductions in the material and energy intensity of national income from 1983 to

1988, as well as by substantial increases in labor productivity between 1983 and 1985. The second stage of economic reform also saw reductions in the number of consumer goods and producer inputs covered by central rationing programs. Among consumer goods, by 1989 only housing, automobiles, and some consumer durables remained subject to large-scale rationing programs.[24]

Closer inspection, however, reveals that the connection between these improvements in economic performance and economic reform was tenuous at best. The militarization of the coal and extractive sectors in 1982 helped provide Poland's energy- and material-intensive industrial base and export offering with fresh infusions of raw materials lacking since 1979. Substantial trade deficits with the Soviet Union eased the shock of drastic restrictions in hard-currency imports, allowing Polish planners to substitute ruble indebtedness for hard-currency debt. Fortuitous weather conditions were instrumental in producing a five-year string of good harvests beginning in 1982, which increased agricultural production and permitted reductions in grain and fodder imports. Decreases in the shares of hard-currency industrial and agricultural imports, combined with increased coal and subsequently agricultural exports, allowed Polish planners to increase hard-currency imports of the raw materials and spare parts necessary to restore growth in industrial production, while at the same time partially servicing Poland's hard-currency debt.

These developments had little to do with economic reform. Rather, they show that the link between changes in economic institutions and economic performance is seldom direct. In this case, changes in economic policy (the militarization of the coal fields, the lengthening the forty-hour work week, etc.) and in the economic environment (favorable weather conditions, Soviet willingness to run trade surpluses with Poland) seem to be more important. Other indicators point to a deterioration in Polish foreign-trade performance during the 1980s. Poland's share of world imports and exports (in value terms) declined between 1978 and 1985 from 1.2 to 0.5 percent and from 1.1 to 0.6 percent, respectively; the export share fell further, to 0.5 percent, between 1985 and 1987. Poland's per-capita trade turnover (the sum of per-capita exports and imports divided by two) fell from $508 in 1980 to $307 in 1986, the lowest among the seven European CMEA countries, although it did register a slight improvement afterward. Poland's net foreign indebtedness increased between 1981 and 1989 increased from $25.2 billion to $39.3 billion, and from 3.5 billion to 5.3 billion transferable rubles (*Polish Economy in the External Environment* 1988, 45–46).

Statistical questions plague measures of Poland's post-1982 economic recovery. The increases in real national income produced (and, given slow or negative labor force growth, improvements in labor productivity) are exaggerated by the well-known practices by enterprises of underreporting inflationary price increases and overreporting production increases.[25] Improvement in labor productivity and in the material and energy intensity of national income must be viewed with skepticism because of their partially cyclical character.[26] Absolute levels of labor and capital productivity in 1986 were still below their 1978 levels (Fallenbuchl 1989, 122). The effects of inflation and disequilibrium prices for energy and raw materials during the 1980s also distorted statistics on materials and energy intensity. Still, the possibility that the reforms' economic pressures on enterprises might have played some role in these improvements cannot be ruled out.

Defenders of the PZPR's economic policies and reforms often blamed the absence of better economic performance on external factors beyond the government's control, such as terms-of-trade reversals and Western economic sanctions. Under close inspection, however, such arguments appear rather weak. While Poland's terms of trade (the ratio of export prices to import prices) declined from 1980 to 1984, they improved between 1984 and 1988. Poland's hard-currency terms of trade were in fact more favorable in 1988 than they had been in 1980. And if the economic sanctions against Poland maintained by the United States and Western Europe during much of decade were beyond the control of the Polish government, the same cannot be said of the act that precipitated the sanctions: the declaration of martial law on December 13, 1981.[27] Instead, the causes of the failure of reform during the period 1980–1988 seemed to lie closer to home.

Because Poland's population increased by some 7 percent during the 1980s, much of the post-1982 increase in economic activity melts away at the per-capita level. As Table 2.5 shows, many per-capita measures of economic activity in 1989 had failed to regain the levels of ten years earlier. Per-capita production of such socially sensitive products as meat, milk, and new housing in 1989 remained significantly below their 1979 levels. Housing construction virtually stagnated after 1983, and at the end of the decade young people were facing the prospect of thirty-year waits for apartments supplied by state and "official" cooperative producers. Since the share of food products devoted to net exports increased during the 1980s, the per-capita production figures in Table 2.5 actually understate the decline in food and milk consumption during that time. Also, repressed and hidden inflation imply that the actual declines in production were almost certainly greater than those captured by the official statistics.

TABLE 2.5
Per Capita Economic Indicators, 1981–1989 (Selected Years, Percentages)

	1981	*1983*	*1985*	*1987*	*1989*
National income used (1970 = 100)	78.6	73.0	78.2	82.7	85.0
Consumption (1980 = 100)	94.6	87.0	91.8	97.8	98.1
Gross investment (1978 = 100)	61.2	57.5	67.0	72.5	74.3
Housing construction[a] (1979 = 100)	66.7	74.1	74.1	74.1	63.0
Meat production (1979 = 100)	77.6	74.2	81.6	89.6	89.8
Milk production (1978 = 100)	87.6	90.1	90.5	84.4	89.8

Sources: Rocznik Statystyczny 1990, XLVII, XLIX, XLVII, XLVII, LI; *Rocznik Statystyczny* 1989, XLVI, XLVII, XLVIII, XLVIX, L, 147.

[a]CUBIC METERAGE OF NEWLY CONSTRUCTED LIVING SPACE PUT TO USE (PER CAPITA).

Data on per-capita economic performance illustrate only one aspect of the stagnation or decline in the quality of life experienced by many Poles during the 1980s. To provide a more complete picture, these data must be supplemented by information about the country's growing ecological problems, increases in work-related diseases and accidents, and the growth of alcoholism and other forms of social pathology.

Industrialization in Poland, both before and after the Second World War, assigned a low priority to environmental protection. In addition to promoting the development of Poland's highly polluting energy and fuels complex, economic policy generally neglected investment in basic ecological infrastructure such as municipal sewage-treatment plants. In 1980, for example, untreated industrial sewage in the majority of Polish municipalities was simply dumped into nearby bodies of water; untreated industrial wastes were disposed of in a similar fashion by almost 62 percent of Polish enterprises. While these figures had fallen by 1988 to 46 and 47 percent, respectively (*Ochrona Środowiska* 1989, XXIV, XXV), this decline did little to reduce the threat such pollution posed to public health. It is noteworthy that even in 1988 some 88.3 percent of industrial and municipal sewage in Warsaw requiring treatment was still being returned, untreated, to the natural environment (ibid., 27). Air-pollution data tell a similarly depressing story. In 1988, 1,554 Polish firms (approximately 20 percent of the total) were officially regarded as "especially damaging" to the environment in terms of airborne emissions. Of these firms, 215 had no pollution-control equipment at all (ibid., XXV). A 49.5 percent increase in the number of motor vehicles (burning leaded fuels) in Poland between 1980 and 1988 also contributed to the air-pollution problem (ibid., 65).

The consequences of decades of ecological abuse range from serious to devastating. In 1988, 11.2 percent of Poland's territory and 35.3 percent of its population were located in one of twenty-seven "ecological danger zones," which had become environmentalatastrophes (ibid., 190). Between 1964 and 1967, for example, the water in 33 percent of Polish rivers was classified as "highest quality" and 22.8 percent of the rivers were classified as "excessively polluted." By 1987 the "highest quality" share had dropped to 4.7 percent, while the "excessively polluted" share had climbed to 40.4 percent.[28] Tap water had to be boiled for drinking purposes in most parts of the country, and dangerously high levels of toxic chemicals, carcinogens, heavy metals, and other industrial, municipal, and agricultural wastes regularly appeared in drinking water and various foodstuffs. While virtually all regions of Poland were facing serious ecological problems by the late 1980s, environmental devastation is especially serious in such major mining and industrial areas as Upper and Lower Silesia, Warsaw, the Cracow/Nowa Huta basin, and the tri-cities region around Gdańsk. In addition to further devaluing Poland's post-1982 economic growth record, ecological problems have forced policymakers into difficult tradeoffs between increased production and environmental protection.

Combined with growing pressures on the food-processing industry and the health-care system,[29] Poland's ecological problems had by the 1980s produced deterioration in numerous public-health measures. Between 1980 and 1988 reported cases (per 100,000 individuals) of dysentery and food poisoning quadrupled, and incidents of salmonella increased by a factor of 2.5. The number of malignant cancers reported (per 100,000 individuals) increased by 16.2 percent from 1980 to 1986. Workdays lost to illness and accidents increased by 14.1 percent between 1980 and 1987, despite declines in the labor force (*Rocznik Statystyczny* 1989, 485, 487, 489). These factors undoubtedly played a key role in the decline in life expectancy in Poland recorded between 1974 and 1985.[30] Together with these maladies, growing problems of alcoholism, nicotine abuse, and other forms of social pathology create a picture of a society under severe, and worsening, strain.[31] The inadequacies of the PZPR's reforms and the perceived hopelessness of Poland's geopolitical situation may have further added to the strain (Nowak 1988).

Despite declines in many aspects of the quality of life, the 1980s did see some improvements in certain indices of personal and collective consumption. The number of automobiles increased by 120 percent between 1980 and 1990; the capacity of natural-gas and water-pipeline networks increased by 104.6 and 75.2 percent, respectively; and the number of telephone subscribers increased by 58.5 percent (Dzierżawski 1991). Even when divided by Poland's 7.0 percent population growth during this decade, these figures imply that, at least in terms of some basic measures of collective consumption, things were getting better for many Poles in the 1980s. Nonetheless, it was painfully apparent that these improvements, whatever their magnitude, did little to satisfy Polish society's frustrated material aspirations.

The Legacies of the Reforms of the 1980s

The reforms of the 1980s left a number of difficult problems for the PZPR's successors. They had created a reform-weary public and a traumatized, suspicious economic administration. The economic growth that had resumed in 1982 came to an end in 1989,[32] inflation had returned to triple-digit levels, inflationary expectations were rampant, and the hard-currency merchandise trade surpluses of 1982 to 1988 were deteriorating. Despite the steps taken during the second stage of economic reform, 1987–1988, and the Rakowski government's subsequent reform policies, much of Polish society had become so skeptical of the reform slogan that the concept had lost much of its credibility as an answer to Poland's problems.

On the other hand, the 1980s left a number of important positive legacies. First, not only did the PZPR's failure to solve Poland's economic problems through reforms discredit attempts at improving Soviet-style socialism, but the reductions in economic security that came with the reforms (e.g., inflation) helped prepare Polish society for the traumas of the transition to capitalism. Second, the events of the 1980s paved the way for Solidarity's rise to power in 1989 and endowed it with a strong initial measure of popular support. Third, while the reforms introduced during the 1980s were unable to solve Poland's economic problems by themselves, they did begin the construction of the institutional basis for market mechanisms. Many enterprises experienced a decade of increased autonomy and responsibility; direct contacts between domestic firms and foreign suppliers and customers were established; and production for export became more important. This is especially true of the economic policies pursued by the Rakowski government in 1988 and 1989, when legislation promoting the development of the private sector and partial zloty convertibility was introduced.

In the end, however, Poland's experience in the 1980s demonstrated the infeasibility and unattractiveness of market socialism and socialist democracy as answers to Poland's problems. The feasibility of a transition to market capitalism and pluralist democracy remained to be determined.

CHAPTER III

Crisis and Economic Transformation, 1990–1992

WHEN the Solidarity government of Prime Minister Tadeusz Mazowiecki assumed power in September 1989, it acquired an inheritance fraught with economic and political obstacles. Opposition leaders realized that Solidarity's electoral victory and the subsequent palace coup d'état had more to do with the electorate's desire to vent its anticommunist frustrations than with grass-roots support for Solidarity per se (Wedel 1989). Solidarity itself was not a coherent political entity, but rather a heterogeneous coterie of opposition forces united primarily by disdain for the PZPR (Zubek 1991b). As a labor union it remained dwarfed in size by the official OPZZ trade union conference. Moreover, Mazowiecki's government was itself a coalition of leaders from Solidarity, the PZPR, and its erstwhile allies, the Peasant and Democratic parties. Internationally, as the head of the only noncommunist government in the Soviet bloc, the Solidarity government faced grudging acceptance at best, and outright hostility at worst, from Poland's neighbors. Hopes for quick, large injections of Western aid and credits failed to materialize. During his visit to Poland in August 1989 the American President, George Bush, offered the Mazowiecki government an aid package of $119 million—roughly 1 percent of the sum that Poland required, according to Solidarity leader Lech Wałęsa.

Most intractable, though, were the country's internal economic problems (Eysymontt 1990b). Because of Solidarity's demands at the Roundtable discussions and the PZPR's own attempts to improve its electoral prospects through easy-money policies, the Rakowski government had effectively lost control of the state budget deficit and the money supply in 1989. The central government's budget deficit increased from 269 billion to 4.7 trillion zloty in 1989, a staggering sixteenfold increase in a single year (*Rocznik Statystyczny* 1990, 139). In September 1989 the government budget deficit stood at 10 percent of GDP (Milanovic 1992, 522). Retail price inflation, which had already begun to accelerate in 1988 (61.3 percent), climbed to 243.8 percent in 1989 (*Rocznik Statystyczny* 1990, 163), largely as a result of the Rakowski government's decision to liberalize food prices following the previous relaxation of controls over wages and nominal incomes. In fact, the population's money income nearly quadrupled in 1989 (ibid., 186). The PZPR's parting shots had brought the Polish economy to the brink of hyperinflation. Meanwhile, the country's more fundamental economic problems continued: the inefficient, highly-monopolized state and cooperative sectors accounted for some 80 percent of Polish national income, and prices and incomes for the most politically-sensitive products were still determined by the central authorities (and the political lobbies standing behind them). Pervasive shortage pressures continued and the servicing of Poland's $40 billion foreign debt was as burdensome as ever. Finally, the 0.2 percent decline in national income produced (in real terms) in 1989 showed that the disappointing recovery from the economic collapse of 1979–1982 was coming to an end (ibid., 121).

On the other hand, the transfer of power to the new government made possible the introduction of radical economic reforms that the PZPR had previously been unable or unwilling to implement. In particular, politicians of virtually all ideological persuasions now joined the public at large in accepting the proposition that Soviet-style socialism had to be replaced by some form of market capitalism and multiparty pluralism. The Polish program for economic recovery and transition to capitalism had to focus simultaneously on six interrelated but not necessarily complementary tasks:[1]

Macroeconomic stabilization. The gathering hyperinflationary firestorm had to be extinguished, in order to allow relative prices to provide accurate information to decision makers and to significantly reduce the extent of macroeconomic, microeconomic, and external disequilibria.

Liberalization and deregulation. The price system, as well as traditional regulations on firms in all sectors, had to be liberalized, to afford enterprises the freedom to respond autonomously to market signals emanating both from the domestic economy and from abroad.

Privatization. A credible program for encouraging the rapid growth of private enterprise had to be designed, aimed at privatizing the bulk of some 7,000 state enterprises as well as encouraging the formation and development of new private firms.

Increasing convertibility. Significantly increasing the degree of zloty convertibility was a necessary precondition for better integrating Poland into the international economy. Increased integration would mean import competition for hidebound domestic firms, increased foreign investment, and better access to technology and know-how, as well as increased export incentives.

Constructing new legal, regulatory, and financial mechanisms. Private firms are unlikely to function in a socially desirable manner in the absence of appropriate legal and institutional constraints on rapacious practices. This meant in particular (1) creating markets for capital and corporate control, (2) reforming the banking system, (3) establishing regulatory agencies to oversee these new or reformed financial institutions, (4) reforming the legal system in order to more clearly define and uphold property rights, and (5) establishing antitrust policies consistent with the development of market competition.

Providing a social safety net. The transition to market capitalism was expected to exact high social costs in the form of unemployment, high (initial) rates of inflation, and reductions in state subsidies. This required redirecting the welfare state away from programs that provided benefits to all, irrespective of socioeconomic position, and toward programs that would furnish aid to those groups most at risk during the transition.

While revamping industrial structures by closing inefficient, energy- and material-guzzling white-elephant enterprises—indeed, entire branches of industry—was widely recognized as an important aspect of the economic transformation, there has been little agreement since 1989 about the proper role of the state in the restructuring process. During most of 1990–1991, however, the view that held sway in policy circles was that reliance on the market forces unleashed by the six restructuring components listed above was preferable to a *dirigiste* industrial policy.

Two additional points about the beginnings of the Polish economic transformation are in order. First, although questions about strategies and tactics for effecting the transition from socialism to capitalism now concern virtually all the countries of Eastern Europe and the former Soviet Union, the first collapse of Soviet-style socialism and the first policy discussions about such a transition occurred in Poland. Since 1989 Poland has been a pioneer in economic transformation, and the results of this most recent Polish "experiment" have been eagerly watched around the world. Second, the economic transition has taken place in tandem with an equally ambitious transformation of the political system. This has meant that the economic transformation has occurred in the context of political flux, in which economic actors face uncertainty over the shape of future political institutions, not to mention the policy decisions produced within those institutions. However, the world views of the democratic opposition that assumed power in 1989 ensured that the economic transition would occur within a political framework in which constituencies whose interests might be threatened by these changes would presumably be better able to publicly articulate their opposition than had been the case under the old regime.

The Origins of the Balcerowicz Plan

The economic program introduced in 1990–1991 was highly controversial and reflected divisions within the Solidarity (and then post-Solidarity) political camp. In general terms, discussions about the program for Poland's economic transformation revolved around the following issues:

Alternatives. Are American and Western European varieties of capitalism the only viable alternatives to Soviet socialism? How relevant are the experiences of the newly industrializing countries, particularly in Asia, to the postcommunist economic transition? Does some sort of viable "third road" between modern capitalism and Soviet socialism exist? If so, what is it?

Sequencing. What is the appropriate sequence of the six elements of the transformation described above? To what extent must stabilization and liberalization precede privatization and other structural changes? To what extent is the simultaneous introduction of all six elements feasible and desirable?

Gradualism versus shock therapy. Is an attempt at rapid transformation—"shock therapy"—preferable to the more gradual introduction of market capitalism? Is shock therapy feasible from a social point of view?

Industrial policy. Is it feasible to rely on market forces to bring about industrial and agricultural restructuring? If so, is that preferable to a more *dirigiste* industrial policy?

Two different ideologies, representing "liberal" (or "neo-liberal") and "social democratic" world views, initially competed for the favor of Solidarity's political leaders during the period 1989 to 1990. While these views continued to play key roles in ideological and policy debates since 1990, the splintering of the Solidarity movement that began in 1990 meant that they were subsequently supplemented by other strains not directly linked to Solidarity's working-class base.

The liberal view assumes the absence of any credible alternatives to Western capitalism and presses the advantages of a rapid break with state socialist institutions and policies (Slay 1993a). Implicit in the liberal view is faith in the market as a socioeconomic institution, both as the *end goal* of the transition (market capitalism) and as the *mechanism* for effecting the transition. A relatively small role for state intervention during the transition, as well as restrictive monetary and credit policies to create foundations for capital, currency, and other asset markets, are also implied by the liberal vision. While liberals realized that reliance on market discipline would mean the liquidation of many firms and industrial branches, such Schumpeterian "creative destruction" was seen as a price that in any case would eventually have to be paid for the institutional and structural transformation of the Polish economy. Many of the reform economists who staffed the Mazowiecki (and subsequently Bielecki) government subscribed to this view, as did most international organizations, at least from 1989 to 1991.

Social democrats, and other groups since 1990, have rejected liberalism as excessively libertarian and inappropriate for Poland, both because of the country's interwar experience with capitalism and especially in terms of the economic situation since 1989. Emphasizing Poland's historical lack of free-market traditions, Solidarity's working-class political base, and the dire straits in which much of Polish society found itself at the end of the 1980s, social democrats have advocated a more gradual and "humane" transition to capitalism. In this they have been joined by representatives of what might be called the "Christian-nationalist-populist" ideological strain that played a strong role in Polish politics during 1991–1993. While not necessarily opposed to markets and private ownership, social democrats, Christian nationalists, and other opponents of liberalism envisioned stronger roles for trade unions, worker self-management, participatory producer and consumer cooperatives, and the welfare state, both during and after the transition. Implicit in this vision is the desire to moderate the austerity associated with the liberals' tight money and credit policies, as well as opposition to shock therapy and the belief that the "visible hand" of state intervention must play a strong industrial-policy role, especially during the transition.

Proponents of the social democratic view include representatives of Poland's labor and self-management movements, as well as left-of-center economists and non-PZPR socialists. The Christian nationalist view is associated first and foremost with the interests of peasant agriculture, with interest groups who claim to be victims of "unfair" foreign and domestic competition, and with various groups close to the Catholic Church.

Mazowiecki's selection of Leszek Balcerowicz, in August 1989, to head the new government's economic team in August 1989 signalled the ascendancy of the liberal view. An economics professor at the Central School of Planning and Statistics in Warsaw, Balcerowicz had for years been working with a group of colleagues on aspects of the transition to market capitalism. Articulate, well versed in Western economic theory and fluent in English and German, Balcerowicz brought to the government a team of dedicated professionals and a degree of credibility in the eyes of Western financial institutions and experts. Balcerowicz's dual role as deputy prime minister and minister of finance demonstrated his authority in economic policy, as well as the government's commitment to a rapid transformation to capitalism along liberal lines. Since the Mazowiecki government's room to maneuver was initially limited by decisions already taken by the outgoing Rakowski government, Balcerowicz and his associates spent the last quarter of 1989 developing a program for executing the transition from socialism to capitalism and securing the approval of the International Monetary Fund (IMF). This program, which became known as the Balcerowicz Plan or Government Economic Program (GPE), was formally introduced on January 1, 1990 (Balcerowicz 1992; Dąbrowski 1992a; Gomulka 1992; Slay 1992d).[2]

Resistance from the PZPR representatives in the Solidarity-led coalition and from Poland's Soviet-bloc neighbors might have initially been expected to hinder the implementation of the Balcerowicz Plan. However, the systemic transformation begun by reform communists in Hungary in 1988–1989, the fall of communist governments in East Germany, Czechoslovakia, and Romania in late 1989, and the subsequent collapse of the German Democratic Republic in 1990 had effectively destroyed the Soviet bloc's cohesion before the introductioni of the Balcerowicz Plan in January 1990. The PZPR's implosion and attempted metamorphosis into a party of "social democrats" at its party congress in January effectively removed the traditional PZPR as a force in Poland's political arena. The local elections in May 1990 removed many (although hardly all) PZPR officials from local government positions, and Mazowiecki's reshuffling of his cabinet in July 1990 (Vinton 1990c), gave the Solidarity government more room to maneuver in the economy. However, the Social Democracy of the Polish Republic (SDRP), the party that inherited a dubious legacy as the PZPR's successor, rose from the PZPR's ashes during 1990–1991 and demonstrated unexpected staying power in the years that followed. In collaboration with the OPZZ, the official trade union federation established during the 1980s, the SDRP formed the Democratic Left Alliance (SLD), which scored impressive gains in parliamentary elections in 1991 and 1993. In fact, to the surprise and consternation of many observers, the SLD gained almost 40 percent of the parliamentary seats in the elections of September 1993.

The Balcerowicz Plan in 1990

As introduced in 1990, the Balcerowicz Plan proposed a relatively clear set of answers to the four questions listed above. According to the Mazowiecki (and later the Bielecki) government, as well as the IMF and most other Western advisers, extinguishing the gathering hyperinflationary storm required shock therapy; gradualism had to be eschewed. "Third roads" were dismissed as "experiments": the destination was to be Western-style capitalism, and it was to be achieved as quickly as possible through the introduction of an economic program based on liberalism.

The perceived need for a rapid transition and clean break with the past was accompanied by the rejection of industrial policy. In terms of sequencing, stabilization, liberalization, and convertibility received the most emphasis.[3]

The new government moved most quickly to douse the inflationary fires. The consolidated government budget, which had been in deficit equal to some 3 percent of gross national product during 1989 (*Rocznik Statystyczny* 1990, 111, 139), was brought into surplus in 1990. Monetary growth slowed in real terms and the share of subsidies in GDP fell from 15 percent in 1989 to 6 percent in 1990 (Gomulka 1992, 366). Real interest rates increased dramatically (although higher-than-anticipated rates of inflation sometimes left them below zero) for both new bank lending and some old loans that had been extended at subsidized interest rates. In addition to the anti-inflationary anchors of interest and exchange rate policies, the stabilization program also relied heavily on a tax-based incomes policy. After convincing the government and parliament to abolish the inflationary wage indexation introduced in July 1989, the Finance Ministry imposed prohibitive taxes on "excessive" wage increases paid by state firms (the so-called *popiwek* tax). The coefficients for nontaxable wage growth in the state sector were set at 0.3 during January 1990, 0.2 for February to April 1990, and 0.6 for the remainder of the year, with the exception of a 1.0 coefficient in July (G. W. Kołodko 1993, 135).[4]

Important progress was also made on convertibility and liberalization. The zloty was significantly devalued in January 1990,[5] providing a dramatic boost to the expansion of zloty convertibility begun with the legalization of black-market currency trading in early 1989. Some 90 percent of prices had been completely liberalized by early 1990 and the deregulation of enterprise activities in all sectors, begun by the Economic Activity Act of 1988, was continued.

The liberalization of Poland's foreign trade regime occurred gradually between January 1989 and October 1990. It featured the virtual abolition of quantitative import restrictions in manufacturing, reductions in average tariff levels from 13.3 to 8 percent (Dziewulski 1992),[6] and the creation of a more favorable environment for direct foreign investment (principally through legislation passed in December 1988 and June 1991). Although average tariff levels in Poland still remained somewhat above European Community (EC) levels (where average tariff levels on imports from other GATT signatories are 6.1 percent), dramatic reductions on effective protection meant that Polish firms were increasingly subjected to the bracing winds of international competition, while reductions in internal demand, central subsidies, and tutelage encouraged firms to export and to find joint venture partners. The guaranteed prices private farmers had received under the old regime were abolished in order to allow market forces to produce a "rational concentration" of agricultural assets and production.

Following a spectacular burst of "corrective" inflation during the last quarter of 1989 and (especially) the first quarter of 1990, the lines and shortages so typical of Polish socialism disappeared and inflation fell dramatically. After registering a 78.6 percent increase during January 1990 (the month of price liberalization), monthly growth in the consumer price index fell to 1.8 percent in August 1990 and remained in single digits for the rest of the year. By the middle of 1990 the Balcerowicz Plan had stopped the hyperinflationary storm dead in its tracks. At the same time, the steep devaluation and the reductions in domestic demand produced by the stabilization program resulted in a record $3.8 billion hard-currency merchandise trade surplus; as Polish exports to the EC increased by 52 percent in 1990 alone. Poland also registered a 2.5 billion ruble trade surplus with the Soviet Union and a $1.4 billion trade surplus with the other "socialist" countries in 1990 (Crane 1991).

These surpluses were all the more remarkable in light of the fact that the nominal zloty-dollar exchange rate was pegged at 9,500 from January 1990 until May 1991. The rates of inflation recorded during 1990 and 1991 indicate that in real terms the zloty appreciated dramatically against the dollar. The apparent contradiction between the expanding trade surplus and zloty appreciation can be explained by the extent of the initial devaluation and by reductions in real wages and the costs of production for export generated by the stabilization program in 1990 (Żukowska 1990).

Critics have pointed to numerous shortcomings of the plan and its implementation. Many have charged that the plan was too dogmatic and inflexible, inappropriate for Polish conditions (Kowalik 1991), or that it was introduced prematurely, before "a more developed groundwork for marketization was in place" (Kamiński 1991b, 187).[7] The implication of these criticisms is that the benefits of improved internal and external balance were more than offset by the costs incurred in the form of declines in production and employment that occurred during 1990 and again in 1991. Less frequently, the Balcerowicz Plan and its implementation were criticized from the opposite side. According to some observers (Dąbrowski 1992a, 1992b), Balcerowicz was too willing to abandon monetary and fiscal rigor in mid-1990 in order to deliver on the promise of an "improvement" after six months of shock therapy. Similarly, Balcerowicz was accused of engaging in excessively discretionary (and ultimately destabilizing) swings from macroeconomic contraction to expansion and vice versa, which in turn damaged the plan's credibility (Winiecki 1992).

While all of these criticisms contained at least some truth, they cannot all be correct simultaneously. It is clear that ex post disparities between projected and actual macroeconomic performance (which, as Table 3.1 shows, were substantial in 1990) provided ammunition for all sides. It is also clear that government promises of a recovery during the second half of the year (which led to loosenings in monetary, credit, and fiscal policies[8]), combined with unexpected (and incompletely sterilized) increases in enterprise liquidity produced by the trade surpluses recorded in ruble and dollar trade, produced an expansionary "correction" in mid-1990. Partly in response to this stimulation, real wages increased by 36 percent between June and December 1990 (Milanovic 1992, 526) and industrial production registered a 20.4 percent increase (in comparable time) from August to December (Winiecki 1992, 193). These more expansionary macroeconomic policies, together with higher oil prices following the Iraqi invasion of Kuwait, led to an uptick in inflation in the second half of 1990, however, and convinced the government and the National Bank of Poland to resort to

TABLE 3.1
Projected and Actual Macroeconomic Indicators in 1990

	Projected	*Actual*
Consumer price inflation (percent)	267.6	352.2
Gross domestic product (% change)	−3.1	−11.6
Industrial output[a] (% change)	−5.0	−24.2
Unemployment rate (percent)	2.0	6.1
Merchandise trade balance		
In Dollars (billions)	−0.8	3.8
In Transferable Rubles (billions)	0.5	4.4
Consumption (% change)	−1.0	−11.7
Real Wages (% change)	−20.0	−22.3

Sources: Rocznik Statystyczny 1991, 107, 117, 196, 275, 380; G. W. Kołodko 1993, 136–137, 141.

[a]Gross industrial sales (*produkcja sprzedana przemysłu*).

tighter monetary controls.[9] The growth in industrial production stalled in early 1991 and, despite a slight upturn in late 1991, did not resume again until March 1992.

These developments can be seen as a confirmation of all three of the above criticisms. According to the "too tight" view, the contraction introduced in late 1990 choked off a nascent recovery. According to the "too loose" position, the premature loosening during the summer of 1990 produced an unsustainable expansion that subsequently had to be smothered. And according to the "excessive discretion" view, oscillation in 1990 between tightening (in the first half), loosening (in the third quarter), and tightening (in the last quarter) undermined credibility in the entire program and compounded the economic problems that appeared in 1991.

A more charitable interpretation would emphasize the following two points. First, given the immense and unprecedented difficulties faced in negotiating the simultaneous retreat from hyperinflation and transition to capitalism, the correct mixture of flexibility and stability must inevitably be determined through trial and error. Second, since none of the other economies in the former Soviet bloc had, prior to 1993, experienced a sustained economic recovery, prospects for maintaining the upturn in Polish industrial production that began in the second half of 1990 must in hindsight be viewed as dim. Still, judging by official statistics, the threat of hyperinflation in 1990 was averted at the cost of greater declines in production and higher "corrective" inflation rates than anticipated, while the recovery promised for the second half of 1990 was not sustained.

Numerous problems with both the quality and interpretation of Poland's official statistics introduce further confusion into the picture (Winiecki 1991). As in the other postcommunist economies, the official statistics in Poland almost certainly overstated declines in production, for two reasons. First, the official data-collection system was established to measure the activities of a relatively small number of state enterprises, and is therefore ill equipped to monitor the activities of the thousands of private firms (and individual entrepreneurs) that appeared after 1989. Second, because incentives under the old system encouraged state firms to maximize output (or at least produce greater-than-profit-maximizing levels of output), enterprises had incentives to exaggerate reported production to the statistical authorities. By contrast, incentives since 1989 generally encourage underreporting in order to reduce tax liabilities. This is especially the case with private firms, which have spent decades perfecting the art of tax evasion. Underreporting of enterprise production and sales means that official statistics overstate the decline in economic activity.[10]

Important problems appear in interpreting these data as well. A (probably significant) share of the output that "disappeared" after 1989 represents goods or activities that could not be profitably produced under market conditions. To the extent that production of these goods reduced the social welfare, declines in their production constitute improvements in resource allocation. Also, since production declines have been concentrated in the state sector, they can be defended by advocates of privatization as desirable structural changes. While inflation certainly reduced the real value of the population's zloty holdings, prior to 1990 many of these zloty were "hot money" that their holders were either unable to exchange for shortage goods, or had to pay considerable waiting and search costs to do so. These costs largely disappeared once macro- and microeconomic equilibria were established, increasing the incentive to hold wealth in zloty form. Still, there can be little doubt that aggregate economic activity in Poland, and the incomes generated thereby, shrank in 1990–1991.

Similar problems are apparent in statistics concerning the growth of unemployment. Since open unemployment was not permitted under the old system, the wages received by "unproductive" workers (i.e., workers whose labor incomes exceeded their marginal revenue products) were a disguised form of unemployment compensation. The financial pressures introduced by the stabilization program encouraged firms to shed these workers first, thus translating hidden into open unemployment. Moreover, the unemployment compensation system, as initially introduced in 1990, allowed individuals who had not previously been in the official labor force to register as unemployed and qualify for benefits. For these reasons, official statistics exaggerate the post-1989 growth of unemployment.

In any case, except for inflation, Poland in 1990 met and often surpassed the stabilization targets agreed on with the IMF. The $668 million current-account surplus recorded in 1990—the first since the 1960s—(Crane 1991, 2) was particularly impressive and boded well for the reestablishment of Poland's creditworthiness. This occurred in spite of the fact that Poland's energy imports increased by some $1 billion in 1990 as a result of higher oil prices (and shrinking deliveries from the Soviet Union) and despite the economy's loss of another $2.9 billion as a result of the country's participation in the international embargo against Iraq (Żukowska 1991). Although the government suspended debt servicing in February 1990, Poland became the darling of the international financial community and the IMF and the World Bank agreed to aid programs totalling some $2.5 billion.[11] This paved the way for a landmark agreement concluded in April 1991 with the Paris Club of creditor governments. According to this agreement, 50 percent of Poland's publicly-held foreign debt would be forgiven, provided that economic development in Poland continued along the path begun in 1990, debt servicing was renewed, and the targets in the IMF agreements were met (Crane 1991).

The stabilization program's accomplishments were accompanied by progress in a number of other areas of the transformation, including the use of competition policy to break up monopolies in the extractive and cooperative sectors, external liberalization, the passage of landmark privatization legislation, and the introduction of unemployment programs (Dąbrowski 1991, 128). As seen from the West, a more promising start for Poland's economic transformation could hardly have been imagined, especially considering Poland's previous track record of unsuccessful reforms (Milanovic 1992).

Not surprisingly, the Balcerowicz Plan and Balcerowicz himself were major issues in the presidential campaign in the autumn of 1990. The demagogic populist Stanisław Tymiński, who eliminated Prime Minister Tadeusz Mazowiecki during the first round of voting, made attacks on Balcerowicz a central campaign theme, describing the Balcerowicz Plan as part of a Western conspiracy to bankrupt Poland. However, Lech Wałęsa's crushing defeat of Tymiński during the elections' second round, and Wałęsa's ambiguous campaign rhetoric about the economy, muddied the electoral verdict on the Balcerowicz Plan. In any case, the continuation of the plan was endorsed in 1991 by President Wałęsa and his new prime minister, Jan Krzysztof Bielecki. By maintaining his position as deputy prime minister, Balcerowicz—and his economic program—provided a crucial element of continuity between the Mazowiecki and Bielecki governments.

In many ways, the economic victories of 1990 came too easily. The high rates of inflation increased the nominal value of income tax and turnover tax revenues and depressed real wages paid by state firms. These developments both increased enterprise profitability and reinforced the state budget. Firms were therefore able to raise prices to compensate for lost subsidies and higher import costs (resulting from the devaluation of January 1990) while simultaneously avoiding unpleasant decisions about layoffs and restructuring. Sales of foreign exchange and inputs acquired prior to the large devaluation and price liberalization in January, as well as the large trade surplus, also provided unanticipated increases in enterprise liquidity.[12] Therefore, the stabilization program in 1990 did not immediately have the liberals' desired microeconomic effect on the state enterprises, that of "holding their feet to the fire" to force them to restructure and become more efficient.[13]

Moreover, while the "small privatization" of shops, stores, and small factories was begun in 1990, virtually no progress was made in privatizing or restructuring the thousands of large industrial firms comprising the bulk of the state sector. Much of the dirty work in stabilization, and especially privatization, remained to be done in 1991.

THE BALCEROWICZ PLAN IN 1991

Although the Bielecki government continued the stabilization program in 1991 under Balcerowicz's guidance, the program was not up to the challenge (see Table 3.2). Although inflation continued to moderate in 1991, the 70.3 percent rate of consumer price inflation was approximately double the anticipated level. Gross domestic product fell by another 7.4 percent in 1991, despite official forecasts of 3 to 5 percent growth.[14] Unemployment stood at 11.8 percent at the end of 1991. Despite a projected increase of 20 percent in real terms (Winiecki 1992, 195), investment spending declined by another 4.4 percent in 1991 (following a 10.1 percent decline in 1990), leaving more than half of Poland's capital stock completely depreciated (*Mały Rocznik Statystyczny* 1992, 104, 157, 171, 343; Telma 1991, 1; Misiak and Żukowska 1992).[15]

These declines in production and employment occurred relative to levels attained in 1990, when prices had already been liberalized and many distortions removed from the official statistics. The declines therefore implied relatively greater reductions in socioeconomic welfare than had been the case in 1990, since 1990 data were compared to 1989 statistics that still contained the "quirks" of the old system. Similarly, while the higher-than-expected inflation rates in 1990 could be partly written off as "corrective" inflation necessary to absorb the zloty overhang left over from the PZPR's economic mismanagement, above-forecast inflation rates in 1991 were a sign of more fundamental economic problems, including the rapid growth in the budget deficit and nominal wages.

The macropolicy loosenings in mid-1990, and then again in the second half of 1991 during the run-up to the parliamentary elections on October 27, contributed to a partial reflation that undid some of the restrictions on real incomes and consumption introduced in 1990. Although real wages grew by some 2 percent in 1991, this growth masked significant variation of income changes around this trend. Real income for pensioners increased by some 15 percent and real wages for workers in the so-called productive sphere increased by 4 percent, while peasant family incomes fell (in real

TABLE 3.2
Macroeconomic and External Trends, 1990–1991

	1990	*1991*
Gross domestic product (% change)	−11.6	−7.4
Industrial production (% change)	−24.2	−11.9
Consumer price inflation (percent)	352.2	70.3
Unemployment (percent)	6.1	11.8
Consumption (% change)	−11.7	0.5
Merchandise trade balance (convertible currencies)	$2.2 billion	$51 million
Current account balance (convertible currencies)	$716 million	−$1.36 billion
Gross investment (% change)	−10.1	−4.4
Real wages (% change)	−20.0	2.0

Sources: Rocznik Statystyczny 1991, 107, 117, 196, 244, 275, 380; *Mały* Rocznik Statystyczny 1992, 104, 157, 171, 177, 343; *Rocznik Statystyczny: Handel Zagraniczny* 1992, 67; "Uwiąd sektora państwowego" 1992.

terms) by seven percent and real wages paid by organizations funded from the state budget fell by 11 percent ("Uwiąd sektora państwowego" 1992). In real terms, consumption also registered a slight increase in 1991.

Most disquieting was the appearance and rapid growth of the government budget deficit, which by the end of November 1991 had reached some 30 trillion zloty (approximately $2.7 billion), a sum comprising approximately 15 percent of budgetary expenditures and 4 percent of gross domestic product (ibid., 12). The deficit and the above-forecast inflation rates violated Poland's agreement with the IMF, which suspended disbursement of the $2.5 billion aid package in September 1991. Combined with shrinkage in the surplus on merchandise trade (to $51 million) and the reappearance of a current account deficit of $1.36 billion (*Rocznik Statystyczny: Handel Zagraniczny* 1992, 67),[16] Poland's inability to comply with the IMF's terms imperiled the debt-forgiveness agreement concluded with Western governments in April 1991.

Part of the problem lay in the policy of fiscal discrimination against state firms, employed in 1990–1991 to promote the development of the private sector. While levying the *popiwek* wage tax and the *dywidenda* asset charge on state but not private firms can be justified on microeconomic grounds,[17] fiscal discrimination against the state sector had the effect of closely linking budgetary revenues to state enterprise liquidity—too closely, as it turned out. The recession that decimated state enterprise finances left the budget without viable alternative revenue sources. As much as 23 trillion of the 30 trillion zloty budget deficit that had developed by November 1991 could be accounted for by outstanding tax payments owed by state firms ("CUP o 1991 r.: Recesja" 1992). Rising enterprise illiquidity also contributed to growing insolvency problems in Poland's banking and financial systems (Slay 1992b).

Exchange-rate policy also contributed to the recession and to budgetary tension. Although the zloty was devalued on May 17, 1991 (to approximately 11,000 zloty per dollar) and again on February 25, 1992 (to approximately 13,400 zloty per dollar), and despite the adoption of a crawling peg in October 1991, the zloty became significantly overvalued in 1991. The zloty's nominal value (vis-à-vis the dollar) fell by some 37 percent between January 1990 and February 1992, while retail prices rose by over 400 percent.[18] The unwillingness to adopt a more active exchange-rate policy reflected the anti-inflationary "nominal anchor" role the fixed exchange rate played in the stabilization program. Although inflation declined in 1991, its continued high level (70 percent) and the weakening of other anti-inflationary tools (such as the *popiwek*) meant that the zloty's overvaluation produced rapid import growth, especially of consumption goods. This also meant that exporters (chiefly West Europeans), rather than Polish producers, reaped the benefits of the 2 percent increase in real wages during 1991. Imports increased by 37.8 percent in real terms, while export volume fell by some 2.4 percent (*Rocznik Statystyczny: Handel Zagraniczny* 1992, 5). Increased import competition and stagnant exports put the squeeze on domestic producers already hit by rising real wages. According to the Central Planning Office, 39 percent of state enterprises were running in the red at the end of 1991, and about one state firm in three had lost its creditworthiness ("CUP o 1991 r.: Recesja" 1992). Rising unemployment and enterprise insolvency in turn meant falling tax revenues, greater spending pressures, and rapid growth in the state budget deficit.

The trade shock emanating from the collapse of the CMEA also contributed to the budget deficit. The transition in 1991 to the use of convertible currencies (rather than the transferable ruble) and world-market prices in intra-CMEA trade led to significant declines in trade affecting state enterprises in the former CMEA countries. Official and unofficial Polish statistics paint a chilling picture of this shock. According to preliminary official estimates, the volume of Polish exports to the former CMEA countries declined by 42 percent in 1991 (*Polski Handel Zagraniczny* 1992, 12); other sources place the decline at as much as 60 percent (Bińczak 1992). Import prices from the former CMEA countries rose by an estimated 126 percent in 1991 (ibid.);[19] the application of world-market prices to energy products (which constituted some 70 percent of Poland's CMEA import bill in 1991 [ibid.]) were a major factor in this increase. According to press reports, this trade shock brought 150 Polish firms traditionally oriented toward exports to the USSR to the verge of bankruptcy (A. Rutkowski 1991). Whereas many firms in 1990 had been able to shift production away from CMEA toward Western markets, the zloty's appreciation made such attempts at reorientation less profitable by 1991.

The CMEA trade shock was not an exchange-rate problem, of course, since the insensitivity of Polish exports to the former USSR with respect to price and exchange rate changes implies that a different zloty-ruble exchange rate in 1991 would not have moderated the decline in Polish exports. Moreover, many Polish firms used to servicing the Soviet market had neither the capabilities nor the desire to reorient their production to meet Western standards. This produced a large trade deficit with the USSR in 1991 and major output declines in those industrial branches devoted to servicing the Soviet market. According to preliminary official statistics, Poland recorded a deficit of 6.65 trillion zloty (approximately $600 million) in merchandise trade with the former Soviet Union in 1991 (*Biuletyn Statystyczny* 1992, 93). In 1991 production of electrical machinery and metallurgical products in 1991 fell by 26 and 22 percent, respectively, from 1990 levels. This trade shock was particularly hard on CMEA-dependent sectors like textiles, electrical machinery, and metallurgy and was an important factor in the rising unemployment figures. The trade shock also had a particularly strong effect on Łódź, the center of the textile industry, as well as on many smaller towns (e.g., Starachowice) whose largest employers produced almost exclusively for the Soviet market.

On the other hand, estimates of declines in intra-CMEA trade in 1991 are fraught with methodological and statistical questions. The transitions to hard-currency accounting and the use of world prices within the CMEA, the differing (and generally accelerating) inflation rates in the region, and the absence of corresponding exchange-rate revaluations for intra- and inter-regional trade—all this played havoc with attempts at separating the effects of prices and exchange-rates from changes in intra-CMEA trade volumes in 1991. Also, official statistics probably underestimate the extent of private trading activities, which, considering their rapid growth in 1991, would exaggerate the officially recorded declines in CMEA trade.[20]

Finally, reductions in CMEA trade accelerated Poland's reorientation away from the former USSR: according to one estimate, by the end of 1991 the share of Poland's imports and exports to the former Soviet Union (measured in constant prices) had fallen to 8.0 and 5.5 percent, respectively (Bińczak 1992).[21] In any case, tensions on the trade front did not prevent further expansion of zloty convertibility. By the summer of 1991, foreign firms were authorized to repatriate their zloty profits, thus making the zloty almost completely convertible on current-account transactions.

For all these reasons, definitive judgments on the stabilization program in 1990–1991 are difficult to make. Recession had afflicted all the postcommunist economies, and the declines in volumes and terms of CMEA trade certainly were factors beyond Poland's control. The experience of many countries indicates that high rates of inflation are virtually never reduced without significant declines in employment, incomes, and output. Questions about sins of omission and commission in macropolicy during 1990 and 1991—whether these mistakes were avoidable and whether an alternative program (or the same program "better implemented") would have been more effective—are so fraught with technical and normative issues as to defy simple answers. In this author's view, however, given the desperate economic situation in which Poland found itself in late 1989, the results of the stabilization program during 1990 and 1991 were generally favorable, and certainly more so than most specialists had expected.

Privatization in Poland, 1990–1992

The expansion of private economic activity in Poland was one of the success stories during 1990–1992 (see Table 3.3).[22] According to official data, the private sector created almost a million new jobs between January 1990 and July 1991 ("Prywatnych przybywa" 1991); during 1992 job losses in the state sector during 1992 were counterbalanced by job growth in the private sector. By 1993 the private sector officially accounted for over 50 percent of total employment and, unofficially, close to 50 percent of GDP. 1,631,000 private entities had come into existence by the end of 1992 (Balicka 1993), including 59,000 wholly private domestically owned joint-stock companies and 10,800 joint ventures (including *polonia* firms) (*Statystyka Polski* 1993a, III).[23]

A dual approach to privatization was taken by the Mazowiecki government in 1990 and was continued by its successors. This approach involved (1) supporting the development of the indigenous private sector by creating a more favorable financial environment for private (as opposed to state) firms, and (2) developing programs for state enterprise privatization that

TABLE 3.3
Shares of Private Activities in Selected Sectors, 1991 and 1992 (Percentage)

	1991	*1992*
Industry	24.6	31.0
Construction	62.2	77.7
Transport	25.2	39.3
Trade	88.3	90.5

SOURCE: Statystyka Polski 1993b, i.
Note: End-of-year data.

would transfer large numbers of these firms to private owners while simultaneously guaranteeing the integrity of the privatization process. While efforts to promote the development of the indigenous private sector were quite successful, the goal of effecting a rapid, scandal-free transfer of state property into private hands was much less so.

The Ministry of Ownership Transformation was created, in July 1990, in order to subject privatization to closer supervision by the new Solidarity government.[24] This concern was driven by the popular backlash against the "spontaneous privatization" of the late 1980s, when state-owned assets became the property of enterprise managers and other members of the old *nomenklatura* in an unsupervised and morally questionable manner. The July 1990 legislation also created the legal foundation for a stock market and afforded workers special privileges in obtaining stock in their firms. Provision was made for the universal public distribution—free of charge, if necessary—of privatization vouchers, which could be exchanged for enterprise stock. The legislation also authorized the creation of investment funds and other types of institutional investors. In sum, virtually all forms of privatization were authorized in 1990; the specifics would be determined by practice.

The first step in the privatization of large and medium-sized firms is their "commercialization" into joint-stock companies. Although stock in the companies is held by the state, commercialized firms are managed by independent boards of directors rather than by central ministries or local authorities, as is the case with other state enterprises. This is supposed to reduce central interference in managerial decisions to a minimum. The firm's value is "established" at this stage, by estimating the discounted stream of future profits or the firm's book value, or some combination of the two. Once the firm is fully commercialized, its stock is sold, via auction, public offer, or agreements between the government and larger buyers. From 1990 to 1992, 51 such firms were sold (*Prywatyzacja przedsiębiorstw państwowych* 1993, 21).

Privatized firms do not have to pay wage taxes (the notorious *popiwek*) or dividends (*dywidendy*, a form of capital taxation) to the state budget. This provision provides strong incentives for firms to choose to privatize themselves. The sale of shares to other state-owned institutions is generally forbidden, in order to prevent the appearance of Hungarian-type cross-ownership patterns among state institutions (Grzegorzewski 1991).

The physical assets of state enterprises can be privatized through "liquidation" or "asset privatization," either in their entirety or through the piecemeal sale of plant and equipment. This usually takes the form of a manager or worker buyout (or lease with an option to buy) of the assets in question, and contrasts with the approach to privatizing large and medium-sized firms (so-called large privatization), in which ownership shares (stock) in privatized enterprises are sold (or given away).

Privatization efforts under the Mazowiecki government focused on selling large industrial firms via public offers. This "British model" approach reflected in part the liberal ascendancy over social democratic advocates of worker-ownership strategies. In practice, however, the British model proved incapable of quickly privatizing many large firms. This reflected a number of factors, including the technical difficulties of determining enterprise value in the absence of a well-functioning stock market (Wellisz 1991a) and the lack of domestic capital.

By November 1990, some 15 months after the Solidarity government had come to power, only 20 of the 157 state enterprises selected for large-scale privatization had been commercialized (Kowalska 1990), and by January 1991 only five large state firms had actually been sold (Kowalska 1991). Though touted by the government as a great success, the sale of the first five firms was not without its problems. Although months were required to estimate these firms' value (which was determined to be some 500 billion zloty) and prepare them for privatization, when finally sold the five firms yielded only some 300 billion zloty in revenues, 67 billion of which went for the costs incurred in administering the privatization of these firms (Doliniak 1991). The slow pace of this process increased uncertainty among managers and workers about the ultimate fate of their firms. Criticism of the slow pace of privatization under the Mazowiecki government was an important element of Lech Wałęsa's "acceleration" theme during the November 1990 presidential campaign. During the campaign Wałęsa supported the universal distribution of state property, promising voters that they would each receive 100 million zloty (approximately $10,500) in privatization vouchers as their "share" of the state's wealth.

The Bielecki government therefore announced a "privatization offensive" in February 1991. Janusz Lewandowski, head of the Ministry of Ownership Transformation, promised a more ambitious program featuring a wide variety of privatization techniques. As the coauthor, in 1988, of one of Eastern Europe's first voucher-based privatization plans (Lewandowski and Szomburg 1989), Lewandowski advocated universal distribution as a way to turn Poland into a "society of capitalists."

Lewandowski's "mass privatization" program, announced in June 1991, envisioned the commercialization of 400 of the largest state-owned industrial firms (producing about 25 percent of industrial output and employing 12 percent of the industrial labor force) and the creation of five to twenty investment funds as joint-stock companies initially owned by the state. Shares in the funds would be distributed free of charge to the public, with each of Poland's 28 million adults receiving stock in the funds. The funds would in turn receive 60 percent of the stock in the 400 firms; the funds would become the firms' owners, while the funds themselves would be owned by Polish citizens. Directors of the funds were to be appointed by the president. Incentive systems and personnel matters in the management of the 400 enterprises would be handled by Western consulting and financial-management firms hired by the funds. These "experts" were to help the funds restructure the enterprises in their portfolio. Of the remaining 40 percent of the firms' stock, 10 percent would be given to the firms' workers gratis, and 30 percent would remain state property.

This grandiose scheme was meant to privatize the "mass" of the large firms that dominate state industry, while simultaneously turning the "masses" into property owners. However, mass privatization fell victim to a number of problems in 1991 (Slay 1991a). Pressures on the state budget made the giveaway of 400 of Poland's large firms a fiscal nonstarter; fears that the investment funds would become superministries unaccountable to their 27 million owners made for further opposition. The possible inflationary consequences of creating trillions of zloty worth of new paper assets, which could be exchanged for cash to help increase consumption, was an issue, as were charges that the funds would be manipulated by the Western firms hired to manage them. The recession, which brought previously profitable firms to the edge of bankruptcy, also reduced the program's viability. While mass privatization remained a cornerstone of the successive Bielecki,

Olszewski, and Suchocka governments' privatization programs, it did not receive parliamentary approval until April 1993 (and then in slightly modified form), some two years after the program was developed.

The rise and fall of mass privatization in 1991 was accompanied by the development of the "sectoral privatization" program, which attempted to integrate privatization with industrial policy. The core of this program was to be the synthesis of analyses of current and future prospects for firms in a given sector with policies for privatization and foreign investment for that sector. According to this approach, the feasibility of restructuring and privatizing entire branches was to be evaluated by Western consulting firms, with one consulting firm assigned to "handle" an entire branch. The consultants would then attempt to sell large chunks of stock in the firms belonging to that branch. In theory, a number of enterprises could be sold at once through this program. While both domestic and foreign buyers would be welcome, the program was oriented toward foreign investors. In July 1991, 173 Polish enterprises of various sizes, in 34 (mostly industrial) branches, were selected for this program; a total of 250 firms, employing some 304,000 workers, had been included by December 1991.

The appeal of sectoral privatization lay in its emphasis on providing state enterprise managers and workers with a comprehensive picture of their future, which was intended to reduce uncertainty about and opposition to privatization. On the other hand, placing responsibility for industrial policy in the hands of the Ministry of Ownership Transformation raised some doubts—especially in other central bureaucracies. Questions were also raised about whether the use of Western consulting firms could be justified on budgetary and national security grounds. In any case, sectoral privatization was scaled back by Tomasz Gruszecki, the Olszewski government's privatization minister, and was essentially marginalized after 1991.

The "privatization offensive" was not limited to the mass privatization and structural privatization programs. The concept of "restructuring" privatization based on business and managerial contracts was also developed during Lewandowski's tenure ("Prywatyzacja restrukturyzacyjna" 1991; "Prywatyzacja połączona z restrukturyzacją" 1991). Like sectoral privatization, the restructuring privatization program linked privatization directly to enterprise restructuring and industrial policy. Under the "business contract" scheme, groups of Polish and/or foreign managers "bid" for the right to manage commercialized state enterprises by submitting competing business plans for the firms' restructuring and future development. The "winning" group—the one whose program for restructuring the firm was deemed most promising by the Ministry of Ownership Transformation—

would make a down payment equal to 5 percent of the firm's book value; this collateral would be lost if the program is unsuccessful. The group would then be given a free hand in managing and restructuring the firm; the prerogatives of the workers' council would be dramatically reduced. Once restructured, the firm's stock would be sold, with the managerial group obtaining a significant share of the revenues accruing from the capital gain. The attraction for managers lay in the possibility of a large payoff for relatively little risk; the central authorities, for their part, would be relieved of some of the burden of enterprise restructuring.[25]

Privatization through liquidation was one of the success stories of the Polish privatization effort from 1990 to 1992. In addition to providing a mechanism for bankrupting insolvent firms and reallocating their assets, liquidation was an effective avenue for privatizing relatively healthy small and medium-sized firms as well. Some 90 percent of the state enterprises actually privatized during the 1990–1992 period were privatized via liquidation (*Prywatyzacja przedsiębiorstw państwowych* 1993, 21).[26] On the other hand, the fact that leasing schemes far outnumbered outright sales of state enterprise assets under "liquidation" raised questions about the permanence and completeness of this approach.

The so-called small privatization process—the sale or lease of state-owned housing, stores, shops, and small firms to single individuals or small groups of private investors—was also regarded as a success. Approximately 35,000 state-owned and cooperative stores were transferred to private hands in 1990 (Fallenbuchl 1991, 14), some through leases, others through outright sales. However, progress with small privatization was rather uneven. Local officials in some areas resisted small privatization and local governments often seemed to prefer to lease state-owned shops and stores rather than sell them. As with liquidation privatization, the end result was that small privatization often left "privatized" property in state ownership. And whereas leasing arrangements made under liquidation privatization often broke up state firms' assets, thus reducing the state's direct control over the property in question, small privatization via leasing was more likely to leave the physical structures (and thus official control) intact.

Reprivatization of properties expropriated by the government during and after the Second World War has perhaps been the greatest weakness of Poland's privatization efforts (Wellisz 1991b). All of Poland's first four post-1989 governments resisted calls for a general restitution of confiscated property to former owners. Financial motives played a large role in this position, since "giving away" properties that could otherwise be sold would have reduced the budgetary revenues privatization was expected to produce, and offering financial compensation to former owners would have been a further budgetary strain. From 1990 to 1992 official policy sanctioned the return of only those properties whose expropriation was clearly illegal at the time of seizure and whose restitution was not clouded by issues of property alteration or modernization.

Perhaps these governments' most important concern was that the reprivatization issue would forestall all other forms of privatization, since sorting through conflicting claims for restitution could quickly become a bureaucratic morass: How can title to a piece of property that has undergone significant changes during 45 years be documented? What should be done, for example, about state-financed modernization and expansion of facilities taken from private owners 45 years ago? Should Germans and other non-Polish nationals evicted from Poland or disenfranchised during the 1945–1948 period be eligible for compensation or restitution? The sheer number of claims for restitution could be an even bigger problem. Although only 3,709 claims were actually filed during 1991 ("Bilans prywatyzacji" 1991), Jerzy Grohman, the presidential privatization plenipotentiary in the Bielecki government, estimated that the number of claims could reach 500,000 (Wellisz 1991b). Since the state might be unable to sell disputed properties until this mess had been cleared up—which could take more than a decade—acknowledging the legitimacy of restitution claims could bring the privatization process to a halt. In the worst-case scenario, the costs of adjudicating claims and compensating former owners could be as high as 250 trillion zloty (approximately $18 billion—roughly half the size of Poland's foreign debt) ("Oddzielić reprywatyzację od budżetu" 1992).

Privatization in other areas has generally proceeded slowly. The privatization of state farms received legislative approval only in October 1991, some two years after the Mazowiecki government took power; the Agricultural Property Agency, charged with implementing agricultural privatization, was created only in 1992; and while housing subsidies have declined and the importance of market forces in housing policy has increased since 1989, the privatization of state-owned housing stock remained unresolved during the period 1990 to 1992, in part because of the lack of resolution of the reprivatization question.

So while important progress was made in terms of small privatization and asset privatization, uncertainty over the fates of reprivatization and mass privatization left Poland's privatization program in a state of confusion as late as mid-1993. Because the general legal framework created by the legislation of July 1990 failed to impose a well-defined structure on the various privatization processes that developed in 1990 and 1991, the large number of state agencies that became involved in the process added to the confusion. According to one former privatization minister, as many as 60 different central and local organs could block or impede the privatization process (Brzeg-Wieluński and Urbaniak 1992). In addition, powerful officials of trade unions and workers' councils within firms often acted as a brake on entrepreneurial managers seeking to privatize their firms (Bieńkowski 1992). This slow pace had a negative impact on the stabilization program, which counted on privatization to improve enterprise supply response to the eventual relaxation of macroeconomic austerity. The slow pace of privatization also helped reduce privatization revenues to a trickle. Only about 4.5 trillion zloty in privatization proceeds accrued to the state budget in 1991, for example, instead of the anticipated 15 trillion ("Bilans Prywatyzacji" 1991; "10 bilionów z prywatyzacji" 1992).

The difficulties encountered in the privatization of state properties make the development of new private firms look even more impressive by comparison. The indigenous private sector was not without its problems, however. Its small-scale, atomistic nature was essentially preserved: at the end of 1992 the 1.6 million private firms employed only some 8 million people. While the private sector's rapid growth reflected an explosion of grass-roots entrepreneurship, the "visible hand" of the Ministry of Finance also played an important role. While state enterprises were burdened with the *popiwek* tax on "excessive" wage increases and *dywidendy* (the levy on state firm assets), private enterprises were not, after mid-1990, subject to these taxes. Moreover, on May 18, 1990, the Finance Ministry granted one- to three-year sales and turnover tax holidays for private proprietorships (Nasierowska 1991). The private sector's rapid development was thus accompanied by concerns about whether it was paying its fair share of taxes, especially after the sharpening of the budgetary crisis in 1991.

The harshest criticisms of the private sector focused on corruption. In addition to routinely underreporting sales and turnover figures in order to reduce tax liabilities, the private sector was known to create dummy enterprises for the purpose of conducting a single transaction. Once the transaction was completed, the firm vanished without a trace, thus avoiding taxes and customs duties. Private corporations took advantage of the abovementioned sales and turnover tax holidays for proprietorships by establishing dummy proprietorships through which large shares of their business could be funnelled. Losses to the state treasury in 1992 resulting from tax evasion and underground economic activity are estimated to have been in the range of 40–60 trillion zloty (approximately $3–4.5 billion)—a sum of greater magnitude than the budget deficit in 1991 (Doliniak 1992).

The basic problem was that the Economic Activity Act of 1988 liberalized the financial and legal environment for the private sector without putting in place regulatory and enforcement mechanisms appropriate to the new setting. Entrepreneurs straddling the public and private sectors were able to take advantage of loopholes and lax enforcement of fiscal and financial regulations to bilk the state treasury out of trillions of zloty. While the resulting "scandals" were many and varied, the "Art-B" and "FOZZ" affairs are the best known and most instructive.

The Art-B firm allegedly exploited the primitive technical state of Polish banks to earn millions of dollars in interest via a kiting scam made possible by the underdeveloped financial regulatory system. Before 1992, interbank check clearing had to be done by mail. Art-B developed a computer program, called the "oscillator," to simulate the interbank check clearing mechanism. By moving funds back and forth between banks, Art-B could earn interest on the same money in various accounts. The Polish press reported that as much as 500 billion zloty (approximately $53 million) may have been bilked out of the banking system by running this scam in over 100 bank accounts. Although arrest warrants were issued for Art-B's owners in mid-1991, such practices may have been legal under the banking regulations then in force. Art-B's activities led to the arrest, in August 1991, of Wojciech Prokop, first deputy director of the National Bank of Poland (NBP), the central bank, allegedly for providing Art-B with unwarranted credit guarantees prior to his tenure at NBP. Prokop's arrest was followed by the dismissal and subsequent arrest of Grzegorz Wójtowicz, the NBP president, for failure to exercise effective supervision over the banking system (McQuaid 1991b; Andrzejczak, Ćwikliński, and Ziarno 1991).

The FOZZ scandal revolved around the state-owned Fund for Servicing the Foreign Debt (*Fundusz Obsługiwania Zadłużenia Zagranicznego*), established in 1985 allegedly for the purpose of repurchasing (and thus annulling) Poland's foreign debt (McQuaid 1991b). Although not illegal in themselves, such repurchases by debtor nations are not looked on favorably by international creditor agencies, and Poland in 1988 explicitly agreed to refrain from such activities. As a debt-repurchasing institution FOZZ was a questionable success, since the costs it allegedly incurred in covertly repurchasing Polish debt through Western intermediaries exceeded the market price of Poland's debt by a factor of two to three. These losses may have been small potatoes compared to the internal chicanery engineered by the fund's own officials, however. Between February 1989 and FOZZ's abolition in December 1990, FOZZ management allegedly lost, embezzled, or misappropriated up to 9.5 trillion zloty (approximately $864 million). This malfeasance led to the arrest, in August 1991, of the fund's general director, Grzegorz Żemek, and its vice director, Janina Chim. Although Żemek and Chim had been removed from their posts in 1990, it appears that the private firm TRAST, whose owners included Żemek, Chim, and other members of FOZZ's supervisory board, continued to spend money in FOZZ's name in an essentially unsupervised manner, up until the time of Żemek and Chim's arrest. While the FOZZ affair was primarily a matter of government incompetence, the role played by TRAST and its co-owners Żemek and Chim, acting in the name of the Polish government, provided another example of rapacious private firms vandalizing the state treasury to line the pockets of a few privileged individuals.

Combined with the outcry against spontaneous privatization, these scandals deepened public cynicism about private enterprise. They also gave ammunition to populists like Prime Minister Jan Olszewski (in power from December 1991 to June 1992), who declared that "the invisible hand of the market has often turned out to be the hand of the swindler, garnering public funds from the state treasury" ("Wystąpienie Premiera Olszewskiego" 1991). On the other hand, the media's ability to scrutinize the sordid details contrasts sharply with the public's ignorance of the details of official corruption that existed in communist Poland. How many FOZZ-like cases of hard-currency malfeasance by the PZPR *nomenklatura* went unreported under the old regime? Seen in this light, the reaction against postcommunist corruption in the private sector is somewhat ironic, to say the least.

Between "Breakthrough" and "Continuity" in 1992

The parties that formed the parliamentary coalition for the government of Prime Minister Jan Olszewski in December 1991 had campaigned on populist economic platforms. While the groups that had supported the Bielecki government called for continuity (*kontynuacja*) with the essence of the Balcerowicz Plan, the center-right parties that supported Olszewski called for a "breakthrough" (*przełom*), a break with the policies of 1990–1991. In economic terms, this attitude was linked to (1) the shortcomings of the liberal approach to systemic transformation that had become apparent during 1990 and 1991 and (2) the growing atmosphere of scandals and corruption surrounding the liberal Bielecki government and the private sector during the second half of 1991.

The recession, tight money, and fiscal discrimination against state firms had, by mid-1991, laid bare the economic and political weaknesses of liberalism in the Polish context. Continuing declines in output and incomes had put the Mazowiecki and Bielecki governments on the defensive, especially after forecasts of "recovery" in mid-1990 and early 1991 went unfulfilled. Opponents could persuasively argue that the shortcomings of industrial policymakers paled in comparison to the folly of leaving strategic decisions about Poland's future to the "invisible hand" of a private enterprise economy that had not yet come into existence. According to this view, the liberal emphasis on "creative destruction" turned out in practice to be long on the latter and short on the former. Polish farmers could plausibly claim to be victims of EC agricultural subsidies. State firms laboring under the *dywidenda* could persuasively argue that their capital stock resulted from investment decisions made under the old regime and over which they had no control, and that its continued employment was a barrier to investment. The *popiwek* was increasingly criticized for the obstacles it placed in the path of labor market liberalization.

According to the parliamentary groups supporting the Olszewski government, the Balcerowicz Plan had led to the decimation of Polish industry and agriculture by exacerbating the recession and refusing to intervene to help stricken firms and farms.[27] The stabilization program's anti-inflationary emphasis should therefore be replaced by anti-recessionary policies; a more interventionist, protectionist industrial policy was needed to repair the damage done by the liberals. This would mean relaxing the (relatively) tight money policies of 1990–1991, as well as the partial cancellation of enterprise indebtedness. The previous two governments' privatization policies came in for criticism: privatization was to be subordinated to industrial policy in order to provide a comprehensive "road map" for Poland's industrial development. Since these macroeconomic principles were inconsistent with Poland's agreement with the IMF, the terms would have to be renegotiated. The liberal response—that many state firms and small farms are doomed anyway, that intervention by the central authorities was unlikely to be effective, that profitable activities will eventually be taken over by private producers (Polish or foreign), that systemic transformation is easier with IMF support than without it, and that the pace of privatization needs to be accelerated, not delayed—may have been satisfying intellectually but was less so politically.

The favorable climate for private enterprise began to deteriorate in late 1991, as the liberals' enthusiastic support for the private sector was rejected by their opponents. Tax holidays for private firms were increasingly blamed for decoupling private-sector growth from its revenue-generating abilities. Private firms were providing only 8.4 percent of budgetary revenue through taxes and tariff duties in October 1991, despite the fact that the private sector had accounted for 46.1 percent of all imports at year's end (Kostrz-Kostecka 1992; "Podatki bez mitów" 1991). The relatively small share of the tax burden borne by the private sector was increasingly irritating to many Poles, who found it difficult to reconcile the closure of schools and libraries with the conspicuous consumption of the *nouveau riche*. Approximately half of the respondents in a poll conducted in January 1992 believed that the budget crisis "results from the fact that the state is unable to extract tax revenues from private entrepreneurs," while only 13 percent believed that "the state coffers are empty because of the absence of privatization" ("Koniec Pogody dla reformy?" 1992).

Social policy in 1990 and 1991, in terms of programs funded by the state budget, was more complicated than these sentiments suggested. On the one hand, expenditures on social services (education, health care, etc.) declined by 22.8 percent in real terms during this time. Reductions in support for education (26.3 percent), culture (50.3 percent), and sports and tourism (58.1 percent) were particularly large. On the other hand, transfer payments increased by 17 percent in real terms during this time, with particularly large increases in illness payments (42.3 percent) and retirement pensions (30.9 percent). These trends indicate a drastic budgetary reallocation away from product, enterprise, and sectoral subsidies towards cash transfer payments (Golinowska 1992).

In any case, when it took office in late December 1991 the Olszewski government was faced with the task of reconciling its populist rhetoric with the financial and economic constraints facing the country. These included the imperative of maintaining macroeconomic stability as a condition for the restoration of IMF aid, as well as the lack of budgetary resources with which to finance ambitious anti-recessionary and industrial restructuring programs. As a consequence, the "breakthrough" campaign slogan was quietly abandoned and economic policy assumed a greater degree of continuity with the Balcerowicz era than might have been expected.

Continuity also resulted from the fact that the Bielecki government had been forced to adopt a more interventionist industrial policy during the second half of 1991. In the summer it had pledged support for guaranteed minimum agricultural prices. A new tariff regime, which tripled average tariff levels to 18.1 percent, was introduced in August (Dziewulski 1992). Bailouts for the giant tractor firm Ursus and for the armaments and aircraft industries were promised during the parliamentary electoral campaign. While partly motivated by political considerations, these deviations from liberalism also reflected a certain tempering of the liberals' free-market ideological zeal and its replacement by a more pragmatic, problem-solving approach to economic problems.

This reconciliation was not an easy task. The genie of economic populism that Olszewski's coalition had uncorked during the parliamentary election campaign provided a most unfriendly welcome for the new government. When Olszewski and his economic tsar, Jerzy Eysymontt, decided to go ahead with 20–100 percent price increases for electricity, hot water, and energy products—introduced on January 1, 1992, as part of the draconian provisional budget for the first quarter of 1992 prepared by the Bielecki government—they immediately faced strikes by Solidarity and other trade unions. The government was able to defuse the situation, in part by blaming its predecessor, in part by threatening to resign if its program were overturned by the Sejm, and in part by claiming that it would soon offer a program for recovery.

The government attempted to articulate its economic program in the white paper "Principles of Socioeconomic Development," submitted to the Sejm in mid-February 1992 ("Założenia polityki społeczno-gospodarczej" 1992), and in the auxiliary planning document "Principles of Socio-Economic Policy for 1992–1994," released in March. Although the latter document included optimistic and pessimistic projections for the Polish economy through 1994, even the optimistic version forecast levels of GDP and consumption (15 percent and 8.7 percent, respectively) considerably below 1989 levels, and an unemployment rate of 14 percent (Aleksandrowicz 1992b). The main difference between the two versions was that in the optimistic version the recession would be stopped in 1992, while the pessimistic version forecast a continuation of the recession until 1994.

Although these documents emphasized the need to replace the anti-inflationary macropolicy regime with an anti-recessionary one, in most other respects they exhibited much greater continuity with the Balcerowicz era than would have been expected during the electoral campaign. The budget deficit was to be held to 5 percent of GNP in 1992 and gradually eliminated by 1994. The Olszewski government introduced changes in the tax system that had been prepared by Balcerowicz's Finance Ministry. The average level of indirect consumption taxes was increased from 5.4 to 7.5 percent in 1992 (Bobinski 1992), in effect diverting resources away from private consumption to reduce the budget deficit. Withholding for a universal personal income tax (collectable in 1993) was introduced in January 1992, and a value-added tax was slated for introduction in 1993. These tax changes were intended to reverse the increase in consumption recorded in 1991 and implicitly to finance the reallocation of resources toward investment and export, both of which were intended to grow significantly between 1992 and 1994.

Despite some slippage, during Olszewski's tenure no large-scale retreat from the liberalization of prices and business activity engineered in 1990–1991 occurred,[28] the tax burden on the private sector was not significantly increased, and the government's rhetoric on privatization warmed considerably. In essence, the policies framed by the "Principles" documents were an attempt to find a programmatic compromise between sociopolitical demands for reflation and the need to maintain a dialogue with the IMF, without undermining either fiscal stability or the achievements of 1990–1991.

Politically, this attempt at programmatic compromise was a thankless task. The lack of a clear-cut emphasis on reflation dampened enthusiasm for the government from the populist forces in parliament, while those deviations from the Balcerowicz Plan sanctioned by the new government received withering criticism from the liberal parliamentary opposition, financial circles, and much of the Western press. Most controversial were the small increases in the real money supply envisioned in the Principles of Socio-Economic Development submitted for the year 1992, intended to provide the liquidity necessary to finance increases in production for investment and export. This liquidity was to be allocated to exporting and investing branches and enterprises through discretionary reductions in the ***popiwek*** and ***dywidenda***. To tight-money advocates, this combination seemed to be both inflationary and an excessive weakening of Balcerowicz's hard line toward state enterprises. These concerns precipitated the resignation of Olszewski's first finance minister, Karol Lutkowski, shortly after the Principles were submitted to the Sejm in early 1992. The Principles for 1992 were in any case defeated in the Sejm on March 5 by an "unholy alliance" of left-wing, liberal, and right-wing votes.

However, the absence of a clear-cut alternative to the Olszewski government allowed Eysymontt and the new finance minister, Andrzej Olechowski, to continue with the economic program. The program, and especially the 1992 budget, with the deficit limit set at 5 percent of GNP, received the IMF's conditional imprimatur in March 1992. The budget was not passed until shortly after the Olszewski government was voted out of office during a heated confrontation over the decision in early June to release secret police dossiers on members of parliament. Although the acceptance of the 5 percent budget deficit was a major concession on the IMF's part, it also recognized that the Olszewski government had done all that could reasonably have been expected, given the political realities in Poland.

For this reason, it is doubtful whether Balcerowicz would have been able to effect a different scenario had he still been holding the reins of macroeconomic policy.

On the other hand, privatization slowed noticeably during Olszewski's tenure. This slowdown can in part be traced to the hysterical atmosphere created around privatization during the parliamentary election campaign in 1991. This atmosphere was carried over into the Olszewski government, where a partial reassessment of Poland's privatization experience took place. Tomasz Gruszecki, in his first press conference as head of the Ministry of Ownership Transformation, in January 1992, criticized his predecessors' policies and said that certain elements of the privatization program must be reviewed. Gruszecki's statements—that privatization should be subordinated to industrial policy, that "in order to move forward, sometimes you have to step back," and that "just because you privatize 10 percent a year doesn't mean that the other 90 percent should not be looked after"—were widely seen as a renunciation of Poland's commitment to rapid privatization (Lindemann 1992). This made Polish enterprises less willing to privatize themselves and introduced new uncertainties for potential Polish and foreign investors.

Despite rhetoric during the campaign and in parliament about the need for a more interventionist industrial policy, significant departures from the Bielecki era were not undertaken. A number of factors seemed to be at work here. First, the Bielecki government had itself adopted more interventionist policies during the second half of 1991—higher tariffs, promises of help for Ursus, the defense industry, and guaranteed minimum prices on some farm products. Second, the financial collapse of many state enterprises and the resulting shock waves for large state-owned commercial banks (the firms' creditors) made a more hands-on approach to enterprise and bank restructuring imperative, as even the liberals recognized. Third, budgetary tensions and the need for the IMF's imprimatur prevented the introduction of sweeping restructuring measures.

In comparison with its populist rhetoric during the electoral campaign and its first weeks in office, the Olszewski government's effect on the economy proved to be much more benign than its critics had feared. Although the pace of privatization was slowed somewhat, harebrained industrial restructuring schemes were avoided, the overall framework of the macroeconomic stabilization remained largely in place, and fences were mended with the IMF. Moreover, blame for some damaging economic policy decisions made during the winter and spring of 1992, such as the Constitutional Tribunal's invalidation of the 1991 freeze on public sector salaries and pensions and the Sejm's failure to overturn the ruling,was appropriately laid on other branches of government.

The fall of the Olszewski government, in June 1992, led to the formation of a new government in July under Prime Minister Hanna Suchocka. The Suchocka government continued the programs of its predecessors and made no bones about the imperative of doing so.[29] This facilitated the passage of a budget resolution, in February 1993, maintaining the limit on the fiscal deficit at 5 percent of GDP; this was followed by the finalization of the on-again, off-again agreement with the IMF, which paved the way for a resumption of the $2.5 billion aid program suspended in 1991. The Suchocka government's most important policy contributions came in the microeconomic arena, however. These included the passage of Poland's long-delayed mass-privatization legislation, the approval of a landmark bill on enterprise debt restructuring and the recapitalization of the banking system, and particularly the introduction of a new approach to labor relations in the state sector.

When the most serious strike wave since 1989 shook Poland in July and August 1992, the Suchocka government's response was to propose a "social pact" on state enterprises (Sabbat-Swidlicka 1992). The social pact was a far-reaching social contract between trade unions, enterprise management, and the central authorities. In exchange for labor peace, Solidarity and its larger rival, the postcommunist OPZZ trade union confederation, were offered an expanded role in the management and privatization of state enterprises (Vinton 1992a). Had it been adopted, this arrangement would have had profound implications for enterprise governance, privatization, and restructuring, as well as for wage determination.

State enterprises not previously slated for privatization were to establish special committees to decide on one of four privatization paths: (1) worker or manager buyout, (2) public offering, (3) sale to a single buyer (domestic or foreign), or (4) sale of a controlling packet of shares to an institutional investor (e.g., a mutual fund). Firms with outstanding tax or loan liabilities would have to secure their creditors' approval for their selection; other firms could select the path on their own. Firms that did not make a selection within three months' time would be forcibly commercialized and placed under the supervision of the Ministry of Ownership Transformation. Trade union representatives would be guaranteed seats on the privatization committees and on boards of directors in the privatized firms. Individual workers would receive 10 percent of their firms' stock for free and firms' after-tax profits would fund "privatization accounts" to subsidize further employee stock purchases. Both state and private enterprises would contribute to a "guarantee" fund to improve the safety net for workers who lost their jobs as a result of privatization and restructuring.

The social pact, as a program for state enterprise privatization and restructuring, was widely criticized. The creation of enterprise privatization committees, the new privatization paths, and the lack of clear responsibility for enterprise restructuring would have introduced new elements of bureaucracy, uncertainty, and delay into privatization. Many of the firms plagued by outstanding fiscal liabilities and labor turmoil—the "lemons" that were already poor candidates for privatization or restructuring—would also be less likely to agree on a restructuring/privatization program with their creditors. These firms would therefore end up on the doorstep of the Ministry of Ownership Transformation. Pressures on the Ministry of Ownership Transformation and the Finance Ministry (the agency charged with supervising the financial system in general and these firms' creditors in particular) to micromanage these problem firms could have been difficult to resist. The social pact would thus have provided an additional task for two of Poland's most overburdened central ministries. There were also doubts about whether Poland's dispirited workers would accept increases in ownership rights and participation in enterprise governance in lieu of higher real wages. In any case, the Suchocka government lost a vote of confidence in the Sejm in June 1993, before the pact could obtain legislative approval.

Despite the political instability of this period, an economic recovery began in Poland during early 1992 and continued into 1993. As Table 3.4 shows, industrial production increased significantly during 1992, and GDP was estimated to have increased slightly. Labor productivity in industry increased by 10 percent in 1992 (*Statystyka Polski* 1993b, v). Inflation continued to fall, the budget deficit remained within the 5 percent limit agreed on with the IMF, and the increases in unemployment moderated relative to 1990–1991. Although the status of the current account and the merchandise trade balance was enveloped in a controversy over a new statistical system, it seemed clear that improvement in the balance of merchandise trade and the current account was achieved, relative to 1991. And although the private sector was the locomotive for this expansion (Rostowski 1992),[30] there was also evidence indicating that at least some state enterprises were beginning to restructure themselves and adapt to the new environment (Hume and Pinto 1993).

On the other hand, these data and claims of recovery are somewhat difficult to interpret (Slay 1992a; Rosati 1993). The stabilization of the unemployment rate was linked in part to tightened eligibility requirements

TABLE 3.4
Macroeconomic and External Trends, 1991–1992

	1991	*1992*
Gross domestic product (% change)	−7.4	1.0
Industrial production[a] (% change)	−11.9	4.2
Consumer price inflation (percent)	70.3	43.0
Unemployment rate (percent)	11.8	13.6
Gross investment (% change)	−4.4	0.0
Merchandise trade balance (convertible currencies)	$51 million	$734 million[b]
Current account balance (convertible currencies)	−$1.36 billion	−$36 million[b]
Real wages (% change)	2.0%	−7.6[c]

Sources: Mały Rocznik Statystyczny 1992, 104, 157, 171, 177, 343; "Uwiąd sektora państwowego" 1992; *Statystyka Polski* 1993(b), I, III, IV, VI (PRELIMINARY); *Rocznik Statystyczny: Handel Zagraniczny* 1992, 67

Note: Data in rows 1–2, 5, and 8 are in constant prices.

[a]Gross industrial sales (*produkcja sprzedana przemysłu*).

[b]NBP financial data for 11 months. Not consistent with customs data.

[c]Includes transfer payments.

introduced in October 1991 and February 1992. The profitability, liquidity, and creditworthiness of state enterprises and banks did not improve significantly during 1992, which indicates that much of the increased production was incurred at a loss. In addition, drought conditions helped produce an 11.9 percent decline in gross agricultural production in 1992 (*Statystyka Polski* 1993b, v). Investment remained flat at best in 1992, which did not facilitate enterprise restructuring. Perhaps most important, the decline in real incomes that made possible the simultaneous declines in import growth and inflation also paved the way for the industrial unrest of August 1992, the most serious in three years. The decline in real wages continued into 1993[31] and helped produce a strike by workers in budget-funded institutions that ultimately led to the Suchocka government's demise (Vinton 1993a). While a recovery had taken hold, it was too weak to quickly redress many of the Polish economy's structural problems.

The economic recovery of 1992 was an extremely important development, and not only for Poland, since it demonstrated that a restoration of economic growth after the postcommunist recession was possible. However, the fact that the recovery proceeded well into 1993 without significant improvement in unemployment, corporate profits, financial stability, or the budget deficit indicated the distance that remained to be travelled in the postcommunist economic transformation.

In sum, sweeping judgments about the success of Poland's 1990–1992 transition from socialism to capitalism are difficult to make. On the plus side, hyperinflation was brought under control, the private sector grew rapidly, shortages were eliminated, the construction of many new market and regulatory institutions was begun, zloty convertibility was restored, and important strides were made in regaining external creditworthiness. On the minus side—statistical and methodological issues aside—significant declines in output, incomes, employment, and trade with former CMEA countries were recorded in 1990 and 1991 and many firms, farms, and banks fell on increasingly hard times. Budgetary pressures had forced painful cuts in social services and prevented the development of rescue programs for sectors at risk. More complete answers to questions about the extent and success of the economic transformation require two other types of analysis: (1) examinations of the imperfections with which market mechanisms function in individual sectors of the Polish economy and (2) a comparison of the transformation in Poland with that of other postcommunist countries. These analyses are undertaken in chapters 4 and 5, respectively.

It is clear that the economic transition placed severe strains on Poland's postcommunist political system. In addition to the dangers these strains posed for the development of a democratic political system per se, they had important implications for the economic transition as well. Indeed, many of the most serious threats to Poland's economic transformation after 1989 came not from the economy but from the political sphere. This was most apparent in the results of the September 1993 parliamentary elections, in which the Democratic Left Alliance (SLD), the PZPR's successor party, and the Polish Peasant Party (PSL), the PZPR's former ally, won an outright majority of seats in the Sejm and the Senate.

The Politics of the Economic Transition, 1989–1993

As with the economic transformation, the post-1989 political transition from the PZPR's increasingly pluralistic but ineffectual rule to a more open system based on parliamentary democracy, multiple political parties, and the rule of law, has both pluses and minuses. On the one hand, free elections were held at the local (May 1990) (Vinton 1990d), presidential (November-December 1990), and parliamentary (October 1991 and September 1993) levels of government; civil, economic, and political freedoms increased and were safeguarded; a free and quite vibrant press emerged; and official barriers to Poles' ability to travel abroad were abandoned (limitations still existed, however, in the form of economic constraints and the unwillingness of other—especially Western—governments to grant work and tourist visas). To a much greater extent than previously, Polish society since 1989 gained the ability to hold its political leaders accountable for their economic policies and programs. This resulted not only from the collapse of PZPR rule within Poland in 1989, but also from the dissolution of the Soviet bloc in 1990–1991. At the same time, Poland took important strides toward "finding its place in Europe" by becoming increasingly integrated into Western European political and (to a much smaller degree) security structures (de Weydenthal 1990a).

On the minus side, a growing trend of dysfunctionality was apparent in Polish politics in the years after the collapse of communism, and many of the hopes that were raised by the events of 1989 were dashed by the behavior of Poland's postcommunist political elite (Curry 1992). The Polish electorate became increasingly apathetic; voters were increasingly unwilling to take advantage of the controls over the political leadership afforded by electoral institutions. This was most apparent in the parliamentary elections of October 1991, the first democratic elections to the Sejm since the 1920s, in which only 40 percent of the eligible voters participated. Although participation in the parliamentary elections of September 1993 increased to 52 percent under the majority electoral system employed (in which parties had to receive at least 5 percent of the total popular vote in order to seat any of their victorious candidates in parliament) more than one-third of the popular vote went to center-right parties that did not gain representation in the Sejm.

Part of the problem may have been that before these elections Poland had labored for more than two years with the communist-dominated parliament elected under the April 1989 Roundtable Agreements between the PZPR and Solidarity. Although it initially gave the Mazowiecki government wide latitude in most policy areas, by 1991 the "Roundtable Sejm" had become increasingly obstructive. This prompted President Wałęsa and Prime Minister Bielecki during 1991 to request "special powers" to allow the government to introduce legislation accelerating the political and economic transition. (Their attempts were unsuccessful.) The Olszewski and Suchocka governments also requested "special powers" in 1992 and 1993, even after the Roundtable Sejm had been replaced in the democratic elections. Despite the democratic ethos of the Solidarity movement, governments wearing the

Solidarity mantle have had to seek extraparliamentary means of governing postcommunist Poland.

In contrast to the 1980s, the 1990–1992 period was not really marked by struggle between the PZPR and Solidarity. Instead, the dominant trend was that of Solidarity's disintegration. Solidarity was dramatically weakened as a coherent political force during the presidential elections in the second half of 1990 and decomposed further in the next three years. This was most evident in the fall of the Solidarity-based Suchocka government in June 1993, when it lost a vote of no confidence submitted by Solidarity deputies in parliament. In effect, the "thousand-headed monster" of the underground movement in the 1980s collapsed into a plethora of political groups and programs once the threat of the PZPR had ceased to be a unifying force (Zubek 1991b). This process of disintegration ultimately returned the political initiative to the postcommunist SLD, which had emerged after the parliamentary elections in October 1991 as a key force in Polish politics.

The decomposition of the Solidarity political camp produced a confusing spectrum of political parties and groupings, whose ability to govern effectively declined after 1990. This is most clearly seen in the October 1991 parliamentary elections, which created a fractious parliament unable to produce a government capable of exercising firm direction over Poland's economic and political transitions. Perhaps the most serious problem was the institutional failure of the cabinet, parliament, and presidency to develop well-defined, mutually compatible functions. While the approval of the so-called "little constitution" in late 1992 helped resolve some of this confusion, it is instructive to note that some four years after the PZPR fell from power Poland's constitution had not been rewritten to reflect the fundamental political changes that had occurred.

Lech Wałęsa, the former union leader who oversaw the parliamentary coup d'etat that brought the first Solidarity government, under Prime Minister Tadeusz Mazowiecki, to power in September 1989, has been the key figure in Poland's postcommunist politics. Wałęsa declined to serve in the Mazowiecki government, taking on the supragovernmental role of reform advocate, roving ambassador, trouble shooter, and president-in-waiting. Wałęsa's initial support for the Mazowiecki government was crucial, since it lent legitimacy to the Balcerowicz Plan and facilitated the social contract between the Solidarity trade union and the Solidarity government. In the summer of 1989 this strategy was a sensible one for Wałęsa and Solidarity; Wałęsa could keep the mantle of Solidarity from being tarnished if the Mazowiecki government should fall or become compromised. Given the apparently precarious nature of Eastern Europe's first noncommunist government in 45 years, holding the democratic opposition's largest trump card in reserve seemed quite appropriate.

By mid-1990, however, this strategy was no longer consistent either with Wałęsa's political self-interest or, in his view, with Poland's needs (Sabbat-Swidlicka 1990b, 1990d). Not only had the Soviet bloc collapsed and noncommunist governments been established throughout Eastern Europe, but Wałęsa's star was being eclipsed by Mazowiecki, parliamentary leader Bronisław Geremek, labor minister Jacek Kuroń, and other intellectuals in the Solidarity government. Wałęsa, a worker by background and more populist in orientation, also chafed at what he regarded as the slow pace of Mazowiecki's reforms and especially at Mazowiecki's willingness to abide by the terms of the Roundtable Agreements and accept General Jaruzelski's continued role as president.

Wałęsa's provocative but ill-defined call in May 1990 for a "war at the top" of the political system was a populist summons to those who believed that the tribulations facing postcommunist Poland were not the inescapable consequences of the economic and political transitions but were attributable to, or at least aggravated by, mistakes made by the Mazowiecki government. The governing "intellectuals in Warsaw," in turn, read Wałęsa's impatience as excessive personal ambition and a lack of commitment to democracy.[32] For both personal and programmatic reasons, a political split in the leadership of Solidarity was inevitable. By the late summer of 1990 Wałęsa's parliamentary allies had succeeded in rescheduling the presidential elections, which had been slated for 1993 under the Roundtable Agreements, to November and December of 1990 (Vinton 1990a). Wałęsa, Mazowiecki, and a host of other, lesser-known figures subsequently announced their candidacies. General Jaruzelski, the incumbent president, did not seek to continue in office.

The presidential election was initially regarded as a contest between Wałęsa and Mazowiecki. Given their long history of common cause against the PZPR and their lack of stark ideological differences, the campaign, not surprisingly, focused largely on differences in personality, images, and sloganeering between the two men and their entourages (Vinton 1990b). Wałęsa's campaign slogan, calling for an "acceleration" (*przyspieszenie*) of the transformation, was a simultaneous appeal to economic liberals' mistrust of the state bureaucracy and to workers' frustration with the lack of wholesale change in state enterprises and the central administration. Wałęsa coupled his demands for rapid change with promises that no one would be hurt by his policies and even promised to distribute 100 million zloty to every citizen as "compensation for their years of sacrifice" under the communist regime (Weschler 1990, 130).

In effect, Wałęsa's campaign combined strains of liberal and populist rhetoric in a way that promised something for everyone without hurting anyone except the remnants of the PZPR *nomenklatura*, which had become everybody's favorite whipping boy. Wałęsa's campaign insinuated that retrograde communists were being protected by the Mazowiecki government and that if Wałęsa were elected the communists would get what they had coming to them. When directed at the Mazowiecki government, these charges often bordered on red-baiting and at times acquired an anti-Semitic flavor as well. To the charge that he was sacrificing Solidarity's unity, ethos, and political stability for his own presidential ambitions, Wałęsa replied that his candidacy was introducing genuine pluralism into Poland's postcommunist political system.

Mazowiecki, for his part, emphasized the absence of rapid and painless solutions to Poland's problems and called for staying the course of gradual change and not upsetting the country's political stability or the initial progress made in constructing the institutions of market democracy. The Citizens' Movement for Democratic Alternatives (ROAD) was created by Warsaw intellectuals, many of whom had previously been affiliated with KOR, to promote Mazowiecki's candidacy; his campaign appealed to the intelligentsia and those most concerned with stability, continuity, and gradualism. Mazowiecki partisans responded to the attacks of Wałęsa's campaign by portraying Wałęsa as "an authoritarian, populist demagogue on his way to erecting a Peronist-style, perhaps even fascistic movement by exploiting mob politics and even plotting a coup d'état" (Zubek 1991b, 593). As a campaigner, though, Mazowiecki could not compete with Wałęsa's dynamism and charisma.

Given the focus on sloganeering and personalities, the lack of clear-cut ideological differences between the two camps, and the confusing political configurations that crystallized around the two men, it was difficult to read much policy significance into the presidential campaign. Its real importance lay in the rupture it caused in Solidarity and the precedent it set in demagogic and simplistic pandering to the Polish electorate's basest political instincts. Wałęsa assumed such a commanding lead in the polls that the only question seemed to be whether he would receive the absolute majority of votes cast during the first round of the elections on November 25, 1990, and obviate a runoff election with the second-place finisher two weeks later.

The results of the first round voting surprised everyone: not only did Wałęsa fail to obtain an absolute majority of popular votes, but Mazowiecki was eliminated from the second round by Stanisław Tymiński, an emigré businessman and political novice. By mixing appeals to Polish nationalism and traditional values with allegations that the Mazowiecki government was conspiring to sell the country's wealth to foreigners for a song, Tymiński portrayed himself as a sort of redneck populist, the quintessential anticandidate. In contrast to Wałęsa and Mazowiecki, Tymiński unambiguously criticized the Balcerowicz Plan and, implicitly, the transition to capitalism. Tymiński's fresh face, Western business experience, and promises of imminent prosperity upon his election conveyed an air of difference, success, and perhaps hope, which many Polish voters were desperately seeking.

Stunned by his defeat and by the electorate's rejection of his gradualist approach, Mazowiecki announced the resignation of his government. Mazowiecki endorsed Wałęsa's candidacy, and the remnants of Solidarity closed ranks around its former leader as best they could. The result was an overwhelming (if somewhat pyrrhic) victory for Wałęsa who, on December 9, 1990, received 77 percent of the votes cast in the runoff election.

The results of the presidential election had important implications for the economic transformation. Perhaps most important, Lech Wałęsa, Poland's leading political figure, had undermined a government committed to implementing this transformation. To the extent that the government's economic program was well defined, had important achievements to its credit, and was widely supported by the international community, the conduct of Wałęsa and his political entourage convinced many observers that Poland's postcommunist political elite was not necessarily any more responsible or mature than the PZPR had been. The resignation of the Mazowiecki government also raised questions about Poland's political stability. Although Wałęsa attempted to restore external and domestic confidence in Poland's commitment to economic and political transformation after the election, the damage had been done.

Wałęsa's succession of Jaruzelski as president signified more than the definitive end of the communist era in Poland. It also marked a certain return to Poland's precommunist political culture and traditions. The unwillingness of Wałęsa and other Solidarity leaders to subordinate their own political self-interest to the imperative of stability during a national crisis recalls the behavior of the Polish magnates in the eighteenth century who chose to sacrifice their country to the partitions rather than subordinate themselves to the king. One observer also ascribed the split among Solidarity's leaders in part to the "resurfacing of the intelligentsia's traditional anti-working class prejudices" (Zubek 1992a, 589). Tymiński's outlandish allegations that Mazowiecki had committed high treason were a contemporary example of the *liberum defaecatio*, the "right to vilify one's opponents" practiced in Polish politics for centuries. In a sense, Tymiński attempted to cast himself as a modern-day insurrectionist, the only candidate not tainted by collaboration with communism, the true patriot who had emigrated rather than risk moral compromise. Wałęsa and Mazowiecki, by implication, were contaminated by the Roundtable Agreements and their willingness to seek accommodation with the communists. In this sense, the presidential election can be seen as a throwback to Poland's past as well as a gateway to its political future.

Wałęsa moved quickly to consolidate his position and prevent the "Tymiński factor" from further destabilizing political life (Vinton 1991b). Wałęsa's appointment of the liberal economist Jan Krzysztof Bielecki as the new prime minister, as well as his retention of Balcerowicz as deputy prime minister and finance minister, demonstrated continuity in economic policy. In continuing the Mazowiecki government's emphasis on stabilization and privatization, Wałęsa both downplayed the populist rhetoric of his campaign and informed Poland's Western creditors that the transition to capitalism would be continued.

The Bielecki government attempted during 1991 to continue the work begun in 1990. In theory, the popular election of Wałęsa as president should have made this task easier, since Solidarity's largest trump card was now on the table. However, the game had changed, in large measure through the events of 1990 surrounding Wałęsa's decision to seek the presidency. These changes had two important dimensions: the breakdown in the social contract between the government and society (Vinton 1991a) and the accelerated disintegration of the Solidarity movement.

The relative social peace that accompanied the introduction of the Balcerowicz Plan in early 1990 had by midyear given way to increased labor conflicts. In the first six months of 1990 there were only 87 strikes, involving 24,500 employees. But a three-month rail strike, settled in June, marked the end of the honeymoon between labor and the Solidarity government. The second half of the year saw 163 strikes, involving 134,500 workers. Many of these were wildcat strikes, not authorized by union leaderships (Brown 1992, 54; Stefanowski 1990). Metallurgy, local public services, and other sectors were affected. In addition, sharpening tensions throughout 1990 between Warsaw and the peasant movement contributed to farmers' estrangement from the Mazowiecki government (Sabbat-Swidlicka 1991, 29).

The net effect of these changes was that, despite Wałęsa's overwhelming electoral victory and his desire to act as a "political shield" for the Bielecki government (Vinton 1992c, 92), Bielecki was quickly faced with a storm of opposition in the parliament and in the countryside. Privatization increasingly came to be a lightning rod for criticisms of the government and the hardships of the economic transformation. According to Janusz Lewandowski, head of the Ministry of Ownership Transformation in the Bielecki and Suchocka governments, "Our privatization program was immediately confronted with all sorts of strikes, protests, and resistance. I don't recall a single transaction that went unprotested" (Zaryczny 1992). The intensity of the opposition to the economic transformation was a reflection of the passions unleashed during the presidential campaign.

The disintegration within the Solidarity movement accelerated during the presidential campaign and continued into 1991. In addition to the Center Alliance (PC) party, which had been created to support Wałęsa during the presidential campaign, and ROAD's successor, the Democratic Union, other post-Solidarity parties sprang up in anticipation of the parliamentary elections to be held in 1991 (McQuaid 1991a). These included left-wing parties such as Labor Solidarity, liberal groups like Bielecki's Liberal Democratic Congress (KLD), Catholic parties such as the Christian National Union (ZChN), and the Peasant Alliance (PL). Two "postcommunist" parties emerged from the wreckage of the old system: the Democratic Left Alliance (SLD) and the Polish Peasant Party (PSL), both of which had previously been subordinated to the PZPR.[33] The post-Solidarity and postcommunist parties were joined by the Confederation for an Independent Poland (KPN), a right-wing, nationalist, anti-Soviet group that had functioned conspiratorially throughout the 1980s. These groupings, which formed the heart of the party system that emerged in 1991, were accompanied by dozens of smaller fringe organizations, ranging from Tymiński's "Party X" to the pro-business "Beer Drinkers" party (which subsequently split into "Big Beer" and "Little Beer" factions).

The unseemly "war" over Poland's 1991 parliamentary elections, and the electoral law passed in July after months of bitter infighting within the Solidarity camp, also facilitated Solidarity's decomposition into numerous smaller political parties (McQuaid 1991a, 1991c). In March 1991 an alliance of postcommunist deputies and Mazowiecki supporters in the Democratic Union rejected Wałęsa's proposed parliamentary elections in May, pushing them back to late October. This alliance reflected the postcommunist parties' fears of the electoral extinction that might result from a majority-based voting system. The SLD, the PSL, and the Democratic party thus favored a "hyperproportional" system under which parties receiving as little as 0.2 percent of the popular vote could be represented in parliament. In contrast, Wałęsa and his supporters, seeking to ensure a stable parliamentary regime, advocated a majority system in which smaller parties that failed to receive a certain minimum of popular votes would be excluded from parliament. Although the Democratic Union, as one of the largest parties, would have benefited from Wałęsa's proposal, its leaders were so incensed by the "dictatorial" tactics Wałęsa and his allies in the Center Alliance used during the skirmishing over the legislative framework for the elections that they chose to side with the postcommunist forces and block Wałęsa's initiatives.

In addition to furthering Solidarity's decomposition, infighting over the election law had two other important political consequences. First, the postponement of the parliamentary elections until late October 1991 prolonged the political interregnum and the uncertainty associated with the Roundtable Sejm at a time when both Wałęsa and the Bielecki government wanted to accelerate the political transformation and when virtually all the other East European countries had undergone democratic parliamentary elections. In political terms, Poland was beginning to lag behind some of its postcommunist neighbors. Second, the electoral law that finally, in July 1991, received the approval of both parliament and (after two vetoes, the second of which was overridden) the president had a strong proportional emphasis, in that it discriminated against the larger parties in favor of smaller political groupings. This predictably facilitated the proliferation of political parties—more than 100 fielded candidates in the October parliamentary elections (McQuaid 1991a)—and further balkanized Polish politics. So although a degree of pluralism within the Solidarity camp was arguably necessary and unavoidable, it occurred in a manner that had damaging implications for Poland's political transition.

This trend toward fragmentation had two important economic consequences. First, it encouraged the numerous individual political groupings to attempt to differentiate themselves in the public mind, and to distance themselves from the Bielecki government's economic program, by adopting distinctive (frequently populist or demagogic) economic platforms, programs, and slogans. The Center Alliance, for example, which had essentially supported the liberal economic program during the presidential election in 1990, a year later had become one of the "liberal" Bielecki government's strongest critics—despite the fact that Jerzy Eysymontt, the director of the Central Planning Office, and Adam Glapinski, the housing minister, were both members of the Center Alliance. Second, the prospect that the elections would produce a fractured parliament incapable of creating a strong, stable coalition government increased uncertainty about Poland's economic future.

The results of the October 27 elections, therefore, did not come as a shock, but they did contain some surprises. Predictions of a fractured Sejm were correct: no single party received more than 13 percent of the popular vote and thus held no more than 13 percent of the seats in the Sejm. Most unexpected was the relatively strong showing of the PZPR's successor party, the Democratic Left Alliance (SLD), which garnered 60 seats in the Sejm, almost as many as the leading vote-getter, Mazowiecki's Democratic Union, which gained 62. Parties associated with the Solidarity movement received only 44 percent of the seats combined, and the divisions between them resulting from the fallout of the Balcerowicz plan, the presidential campaign, and the election law prevented them from forming an effective coalition. Nationalist and Christian democratic parties received about 23 percent of the seats, as did the postcommunist SLD and PSL.[34] The remainder went to smaller parties and independents.

The ensuing interregnum lasted until late December, when, against Wałęsa's wishes, a five-party center-right coalition succeeded in electing Jan Olszewski (from the Center Alliance) as prime minister and confirming his cabinet. The coalition was initially composed of four of the parties with roots in Solidarity (the Center Alliance, the Liberal Democratic Congress, the Peasant Alliance, and the Christian National Union and the Confederation for an Independent Poland (KPN). The Liberal Democratic Congress and the KPN subsequently deserted the coalition, however, and subsequent attempts at broadening it proved unsuccessful. Its weak parliamentary base and Wałęsa's opposition meant that the Olszewski government was under constant threat of political isolation and impotency.

This did not bode well for the government's ability to carry out a consistent economic program. Although the appointment of Andrzej Olechowski as finance minister in late February 1992 increased the government's cohesion and credibility in budgetary and economic matters, in May Olszewski was unable to muster the two-thirds vote necessary to override the Constitutional Tribunal's invalidation of the freeze on public-sector wages and pensions declared in 1991. The government's failure to hold the line in parliament precipitated Olechowski's resignation and deepened the impression that "Poland was becoming increasingly ungovernable" ("Poland: Country Report" 1992, 9). Although dire predictions of the collapse of the reform program and the demise of fiscal discipline proved incorrect, the privatization program effectively stalled and some foreign investment deals that had been concluded by the Bielecki government were put on hold or cancelled.

The Olszewski government's weakness did not prevent its adoption of combative rhetoric and programs. The parties in the coalition wanted a break with the liberal policies of the Mazowiecki and Bielecki governments and rallied around the twin slogans of an anti-recessionary "breakthrough" (*przełom*) in economic policy and the "decommunization" (*dekomunizacja*) of political life. Although budgetary pressures forced the Olszewski government to essentially abandon the "breakthrough" goal in the economy, the "decommunization" objective was pursued by attempting to purge officials who were not members of the ruling coalition parties from important positions in the state administration. Relations with Wałęsa, which were strained throughout Olszewski's tenure, dropped to a new low in April, when Defense Minister Jan Parys accused Wałęsa of plotting a coup d'état.

The end came in June 1992. Prompted by the Sejm's decision in late May to authorize the release of the communist secret police files, Interior Minister Antoni Macierewicz provided parliamentary leaders with lists of public officials suspected of collaborating with the PZPR's security organs. Coming as it did on the eve of a scheduled vote of no confidence against the Olszewski government in the Sejm, the interior minister's actions had strong overtones of blackmail, and the secretive, almost conspiratorial manner in which the information was released antagonized even those MPs who had favored opening the files. Moreover, as the contents of the lists began to leak to the press, it became clear that they included some of Poland's most ardent anticommunists—men like KPN leader Leszek Moczulski, who had served many years in prison for his underground activities. According to some sources, Wałęsa himself was even listed as a collaborator (Vinton 1992b, 1). This further discredited the entire operation and reduced the Olszewski government's parliamentary base to minuscule proportions.

The Sejm was only too happy to accept Wałęsa's motion on June 5 to dismiss the government and to accept PSL leader Waldemar Pawlak, Wałęsa's nominee, as prime minister. Wałęsa and Pawlak moved quickly to secure control over the ministries of Interior and Defense, in order, they said, to prevent further tampering with the secret police files and to forestall a possible coup attempt by Olszewski loyalists. Olszewski responded, in a nationally televised address, that his government had itself been the victim of a coup engineered by neocommunist forces acting through Wałęsa and the parliamentary opposition. This was apparent, Olszewski's partisans maintained, in the choice of Pawlak, leader of one of the postcommunist parties, to be the new prime minister.

Wałęsa's choice of Pawlak was initially seen by many commentators as the end of the Solidarity camp's ability to set Poland's political agenda. After five weeks of trying, however, Pawlak was unable to form a government capable of obtaining parliamentary confirmation. Then, in early July, a post-Solidarity coalition converged around the Democratic Union's Hanna Suchocka, who, apparently over Wałęsa's objections, was confirmed by the Sejm as prime minister on July 9, 1992. The formation of the Suchocka government—and the end to the political turmoil it seemed to imply—was initially greeted with a strong sense of relief, both within Poland and abroad. The parliamentary coalition that supported Suchocka, her desire to seek an accord with Wałęsa, and the fact that many of her ministers had previously served in the Mazowiecki and Bielecki governments all seemed to indicate a return to the policies and (relative) stability of 1990–1991 (Vinton 1992a).

The Suchocka government's year in power (July 1992 to June 1993) helped restore a measure of stability and order to Polish politics. The focus was clearly on facilitating the economic transition; legislation on a number of important economic issues, including mass privatization and debt restructuring, was passed and the renewal of IMF assistance was successfully negotiated during Suchocka's tenure. Indeed, Suchocka's success in getting Poland's political and economic house in order and the novelty of having a woman prime minister, combined with the dissolution of the Czech and Slovak Federal Republic and increasing signs of instability in Hungary (Pataki 1993), elevated Poland's star during 1993.

In the end, though, Suchocka was as much a captive of Poland's postcommunist political foibles as her predecessors had been. When her government lost a vote of confidence in the Sejm on May 28, 1993, Wałęsa responded by dissolving parliament and calling new elections for September. The failure of Poland's fourth postcommunist government in as many years sentenced the country to another lengthy political interregnum full of economic uncertainties. On the other hand, because a sustained economic recovery had occurred in the face of such political turmoil, these uncertainties may not have been as threatening for the Polish economy in 1993 as they would have been a few years earlier.

The surprisingly strong showing of the SLD, the PZPR's successor, and of the PSL, which had been subordinated to the PZPR until 1989, in the September 1993 parliamentary elections heightened this uncertainty. Even if these postcommunist parties were to attempt to continue the economic policies of the previous years, friction between the parties could generate economic discord. Despite their past alliances and their majorities in both the Sejm and Senate, SLD and PSL leaders experienced difficulties in the fall of 1993 in forging a government under PSL leader Waldemar Pawlak, and sharp differences over economic policy between the two parties were apparent.

The variety of political interpretations placed on the results of the parliamentary elections also gave rise to uncertainty about the future of the Polish economic transition. To be sure, voter dissatisfaction with the slow pace of the economic recovery and growing fears of unemployment certainly worked to the left's political advantage, and indicated gathering resistance to the economic transformation. This did not bode well for the transformation's prospects. On the other hand, the failure of right-of-center political forces to form the coalitions needed to surmount the 5 percent popular-vote threshold required to seat victorious candidates in the Sejm obviously contributed to the right's debacle. The vote may also have been a reaction against the right's shrill "decommunization" rhetoric (which seemed to invite political witchhunts), as well as an anticlerical protest against the growing power of the Catholic Church, which had forced a restrictive antiabortion bill through parliament in early 1993. To the extent that the left's victory in these elections reflected noneconomic factors, the prospects for continuing the economic transition would be improved.

Is the Polish Crisis Over?

In an important sense, the crisis that plagued People's Poland disappeared with the collapse of communism in 1989. To the extent that the Polish crisis before 1989 resulted from a fundamental incompatibility between Poland's political culture and national traditions, on the one hand, and the institutions of Soviet-style socialism, on the other, that dimension had essentially disappeared by 1991. In contrast to the PZPR, the postcommunist political elite has been able not only to live with autonomous social movements but also to implement unpopular macroeconomic policies. In economic terms, the crisis of the 1980s derived largely from the steep decline in incomes and production between 1979 and 1982 and from the PZPR's unwillingness or inability to remove the obstacles created by the Soviet system to establishing a "normal" Western consumer economy. Long queues, the gray drabness of a frustrated consumer society, and bureaucratic suffocation were endemic features of daily life for most Poles. The reforms introduced since 1989 obviously changed this.

However, the crisis motif has been a constant theme of Polish historiography, predating the establishment of the People's Republic. Poland's borders, socioeconomic institutions, sovereignty, and statehood have come and gone, but the crisis element has remained. Before 1918 the "Polish question" concerned prospects for the reattainment of statehood and its implications for the European order. The Second Republic (1918–1939) was marked by a crisis of underdevelopment and the incomplete construction of a nation-state. History would suggest that the end of the People's Republic should not be taken to mean that the crisis is over. Instead, as postcommunist Poland is changing, the crisis may simply be undergoing change, reflecting the new realities and conditions in which Poland finds itself.

Many of the socioeconomic problems inherited from the communist era will continue into the 1990s and beyond. The average life span for Polish men declined during 1990 to 66.5 years, falling to the level of 1961–1965 (*Rocznik Statystyczny* 1991, 53). Infant mortality, which had declined from 21.3 deaths per 1,000 live births in 1980 to 15.9 per 1,000 live births in 1989, stabilized at that level during 1990, and seemed to have increased during 1991–1992 (ibid., 49; Semprich 1993).[35] Problems of environmental devastation and public health (aggravated by the abuse of alcohol and especially of cigarettes)[36] continued largely unabated. Deaths from malignant cancers increased from 18 per 10,000 inhabitants in 1985 to 18.8 in 1989 and 19.1 in 1990 (*Ochrona Środowiska* 1991, 14). Moreover, while declines in industrial production in 1990 and 1991 may have reduced yearly increments of new pollution,[37] the number of factories (*zakłady*) classified as "extremely damaging" to the environment increased in 1990 and stood about 47 percent above the level recorded in 1985 (ibid., 16). Even a rapid and successful transformation of Poland's economic and political institutions would do little to reverse these statistics. In this sense, the unhappy consequences of Soviet-style socialism are likely to haunt Poland for decades to come.

In other ways, the crisis motif inherited from People's Poland has changed beyond all recognition. The collapse of Soviet-style socialism effectively took with it the sense of all-encompassing crisis, and the concept had taken on different shapes for different regions and social groups in the postcommunist transition. The key trend has been that policies of public-sector austerity and privatization has both reduced the quality and quantity of public services and increased the inequality in the distribution of wealth and income in Poland. While this combination has lifted certain social groups—entrepreneurs, managers, bankers, some professionals, and enterprising people in general—out of the postsocialist morass, it has also pushed other groups—low-skilled workers, small-scale farmers, public-sector employees—deeply into poverty. Likewise, while Warsaw, Cracow, and other urban areas with diversified economies and stronger ties to foreign capital have enjoyed booms in construction and tourism that have kept unemployment rates well below the national average, smaller rural communities based around a single state factory or farm have been decimated by the post-1989 declines in economic activity. While the concept of "crisis" has lost its meaning for some parts of the "new Poland," it has become even more relevant for others. On the other hand, the rapid increase in the (reported) incidence of crime, and the resulting fear of crime, affected even the nouveau riche (Siemaszko 1993).

The post-1990 trend toward growing political dysfunctionality would seem to be the strongest crisis element in the postcommunist political system. The widespread distrust of politics, politicians, and public organizations in general that Poles inherited from the pre-1989 system has obviously continued. It is most visible in the low rates of electoral participation, as well as in the press and in numerous public opinion surveys.[38] Poland's first "free" parliament was characterized by absenteeism,[39] public grandstanding, corruption, and flagrant abuse of the congressional immunity from prosecution.[40] This did little to endear the Sejm to the public, which generally supported President Wałęsa's dissolution of parliament in May 1993. The surprisingly strong performance of the SLD in the September 1993 parliamentary elections, therefore, may have reflected strong anti-incumbent sentiments among voters. After the political antics of Solidarity politicians during 1990-1993, the electorate may well have concluded that a "kinder, gentler" form of neo-PZPR rule might be an improvement over the instability delivered by the PZPR's anticommunist successors. If so, a more damning indictment of Solidarity's political legacy could scarcely be imagined.

The ultimate danger was that the inability of the new elites and institutions to consolidate their positions and function in a democratic manner could ultimately lead to the failure of political democracy in Poland, replicating in a sense the failure of democracy during the interwar period. Warning signs of this trend were seen in the "Tymiński phenomenon" of 1990, in the "nostalgia" for certain elements of the PZPR era that was already becoming apparent in 1991 (Henzler 1991), and in the strikes that plagued the Suchocka government. The obvious contempt with which the strikers viewed the government and the politicians, and their willingness to pander to the basest instincts of the body politic, showed how far the Solidarity movement had fallen since the summer of 1989. It also showed that the divisiveness and personal ambition that have characterized Polish politics since 1989 had yielded bitter fruit indeed. The right combination of these factors could derail the program for systemic transformation—an outcome that, should it come to pass, would certainly add a new dimension to the crisis, both for Poland and for the region.

Indeed, by mid-1992, some three years after the elections that led to the PZPR's demise, public opinion polls commonly disclosed strong negative attitudes toward the general direction of post-1989 change. According to one specialist, by early 1992 only 20–25 percent of Polish society was declaring itself in favor of privatization and private enterprise. This contrasted with figures of 70 percent recorded during the autumn of 1989 (Lamentowicz 1992a, Kruszewski 1992).[41] If Poland was experiencing a postcommunist political crisis, one of its elements was the feeling that, despite the political and economic transformations, the more things change, the more they stay the same. Wałęsa seemingly captured the popular mood when he remarked, in May 1992, when he remarked, "Regardless of the political changes, the average citizen has the impression of still living in the same world, the world of permanent crisis which has become kind of a curse on Poland" (Mapes and Mitraszewska 1992).

Various explanations for this extensive distrust of politicians may be offered. The gradual manner in which the political transition began in 1988–1989, within the framework of the Roundtable accords, may account for some of this disillusionment, since it may confirm the view that the postcommunist political leadership "let the communists off too easily." The contrast between the high hopes raised by the Mazowiecki government in 1989–1990 and the economic hardships associated with its policies may also account for some of the disaffection. The infighting between Wałęsa and Mazowiecki (and their supporters) during 1990 and 1991 probably alienated many of Solidarity's supporters and contributed to the belief that Poland's postcommunist political elite was no less cynical and incompetent than the PZPR had been (Lamentowicz 1992b; Staniszkis 1992).

In any case, this cumulative disaffection resulted in a "general crisis of trust," according to one commentator:

> During the presidential campaign, Mazowiecki's supporters had painted Wałęsa as a power-hungry demagogue with authoritarian tendencies, damaging his domestic reputation and undermining his international standing. Wałęsa's behavior in 1991 belied this image; the president respected the limits of the existing legal system, however loudly he railed against them. The stereotype persisted nonetheless, buttressed by the accounts of Western jour-

> nalists, who preferred to portray Wałęsa as a dictatorial bumpkin rather than as a complex statesman. Wałęsa's domestic opponents were misled as well and spent much of the year on guard against anticipated threats to democracy from the president and his men. With hindsight, it seems clear that the real threat lay elsewhere—in the steady erosion of all state authority. While Wałęsa's erstwhile foes would blame him for having begun this process by moving prematurely to split the Solidarity movement in 1990, their own refusal to admit that the president's motives could be anything other than self-serving in 1991 merely exacerbated the general crisis of trust. (Vinton 1992c, 93)

Political developments during the period of the 1991–1992 coalition government must have been especially disheartening for many Poles. Voters who cast their ballots for the parties that created the Olszewski coalition believed they were supporting a government committed to an antirecessionary breakthrough in the economy and the cleansing of communism's legacy in the polity. Instead, the constraints of the IMF conditions and Poland's budget crisis made continuity in economic policy largely inevitable, and "decommunization" boiled down to parliamentary and interparty bickering and the ludicrous (even dangerous) incompetence displayed in the handling of the secret police files that precipitated the Olszewski government's collapse. This cannot have improved the esteem in which Polish voters held the country's major parties.

This general disillusionment with the postcommunist political system and politicians, culminating in the "general crisis of trust" in state institutions, implies that many Poles continue to view the state as something foreign and illegitimate, something less than their own. In economic terms, these attitudes manifest themselves in corruption, scandals, and tax evasion, as seen in the Art-B, FOZZ, and numerous other affairs since 1989. Despite the farthest-reaching liberalization of private enterprise in the former Soviet bloc, the underground economy continued to be substantial, accounting for the equivalent of an estimated 10–30 percent of GDP (Doliniak 1992). It would seem that the rapacious attitude toward state institutions impressed upon many Poles by 40 years of communism and 123 years of the partitions is being only slowly unlearned.

Just as the 1990 presidential election can be read as a return of sorts to prewar Polish political traditions, certain characteristics of Poland's prewar economic development can be seen in the shape of the economy that emerged from 1990 to 1992. There are some interesting parallels between the tasks of economic reconstruction faced by Leszek Balcerowicz and those faced by the leaders of the nascent Second Republic. Like Balcerowicz, Władysław Grabski was an economic liberal who stopped the hyperinflation of the early 1920s and strengthened (actually created) the zloty through macroeconomic austerity policies. Grabski also established the commercial and financial institutions necessary for Poland to participate in the international economy, as Balcerowicz intended to do. The emphasis placed on a strong currency throughout the interwar period (when a stable zloty was regarded by Józef Piłsudski as a symbol of the Polish nation-state), even at the cost of slow economic growth (or recession) at home, finds its equivalent in the zloty's dramatic overvaluation from 1990 to 1992. The interwar economy's inability to break out of the traps of underdevelopment; the underutilization of its labor and capital resources; the depressed agricultural conditions; the desperate need for, and dependence on, foreign capital—all these characteristics were also apparent in 1990–1993. While there are, of course, many differences between these two periods in Polish economic history, these parallels imply that the future of Polish capitalism may have as much in common with the interwar period as with its post–World War II experience up to 1990. Historians are divided on whether Poland would have broken out of problems it faced during the interwar period if the Second World War had not intervened. If nothing else, Poland's postcommunist development will provide an interesting new perspective on this question.

CHAPTER IV

Transformations in Key Markets and Sectors

AS THE PRECEDING chapter's description of developments from 1990 to 1993 shows, sweeping judgments about the first years of Poland's transition from socialism to capitalism are not easily made. On the plus side, hyperinflation was brought under control, shortages were eliminated, the private sector grew rapidly, the construction of many new market and regulatory institutions was begun, zloty convertibility was restored, trade with Western Europe expanded significantly, and important progress was made in restoring Poland's external creditworthiness. On the minus side, significant declines in output, incomes, employment, and regional trade were recorded, and many firms, farms, and banks fell on hard times, with few prospects for recovery. Budgetary pressures forced painful cuts in social services, prevented the development of rescue programs for sectors at risk, and made the long-term outlook for inflation anything but hopeful.

Given these conflicting developments, judgments about the success or failure of Poland's economic transformation depend on how these pluses and minuses are weighed by the observer. Alternatively, the progress of the Polish economic transformation can also be examined in terms of the degree to which market mechanisms began to function effectively in individual sectors of the Polish economy. This chapter focuses on the extent to which key sectors underwent transformation during the 1990–1992 period. Special attention is devoted to industry, agriculture, the banking and financial systems, the labor market, and external economic relations.

INDUSTRY

Numerous difficulties impede any attempt to gauge the changes in Polish industry since 1989. On the one hand, the official statistics depict steep production declines in virtually all industrial branches during 1990–1991 (see Table 4.1)—so deep that the moderate increases recorded in 1992 still left production well below 1989 levels. These drops in industrial production were accompanied by declines in profitability and investment spending, which resulted in the further depreciation of industrial plant and equip-

TABLE 4.1
Percentage Changes in Industrial Production, 1990–1992 by Branch

	1990	*1991*	*1992*[a]
Industry (overall)	−24.2	−11.9	4.2
Fuels and power	−22.1	−8.2	0.1
Metallurgy	−19.7	−22.8	−4.3
Engineering	−22.0	−19.8	7.7
Chemicals	−24.6	−12.7	6.8
Minerals	−21.5	−3.2	0.0
Wood and paper products	−24.9	−1.6	13.9
Light industry	−33.8	−11.9	4.0
Food processing	−23.7	−1.8	4.2
Other branches	−33.6	−6.4	—

Sources: Rocznik Statystyczny 1991, 275–276; *Rocznik Statystyczny: Przemysł* 1992, 23, *Statystyka Polski* 1993(b), v.

Note: Gross industrial sales (*produkcja sprzedana przemysłu*), constant prices.

[a]Preliminary official data.

ment. The welfare loss associated with declines in overall levels of industrial production would have been moderated, however, if they had been accompanied by a reorientation away from value-subtracting branches toward the production of more highly valued goods and services. Given the traditional policy emphasis on heavy industry and the energy and fuels complex, the introduction of market forces was expected to lead to decreases in the share of industrial production represented by these branches and increases in the share of such branches as light industry and foodstuffs.

However, according to the official statistics, the branch restructuring of Polish industry between 1990 and 1992 did not proceed in accordance with this hypothesis. As Table 4.2 shows, the share of light industrial output in total industrial output fell by 47 percent during this time, while the share of fuels and power nearly doubled. Although the share of food processing increased by 11 percent, the share of engineering products, a sector that includes many technology-intensive and consumer products, declined by about 21 percent. The implication is that, beyond contributing to the aggregate decline in industrial production, the impact of market forces in restructuring from 1990 to 1992 was rather weak.

However, in important respects the figures in tables 4.1 and 4.2 paint an excessively bleak picture of the changes that have occurred in Polish industry since 1989. The bias described in Chapter 3 toward underreporting in the official statistics implies that the actual extent of the decline was almost

TABLE 4.2
Percentage Changes in the Composition of Industrial Output, 1989–1992 by Branch

	1989	*1990*	*1991*	*1992*[a]
Industry (overall)	100.0	100.0	100.0	100.0
Fuels and power	11.2	15.9	20.5	21.5
Metallurgy	10.1	12.7	8.9	7.3
Engineering	25.3	24.2	20.9	19.9
Chemicals	9.1	9.5	9.3	9.2
Minerals	3.9	4.2	4.4	3.9
Wood and paper products	5.0	4.8	5.3	4.9
Light industry	12.2	8.1	7.4	7.0
Food processing	20.9	18.6	21.2	23.2
Other branches	2.3	2.0	2.1	3.1

Sources: Rocznik Statystyczny 1991, 276; *Rocznik Statystyczny: Przemysł* 1992, 25–26; *Statystyka Polski* 1993b, v.

Note: Gross industrial sales (*produkcja sprzedana przemysłu*), current prices.

[a]Preliminary official data.

certainly less than that depicted in Table 4.1. The data on industrial restructuring in Table 4.2 are also misleading. Since the private sector is represented much more strongly in light industry, food processing, and engineering than in fuels and power,[1] more accurate reporting of private-sector activities would have shown an increase in the share of the former branches at the expense of the latter. Declines in industrial production also helped reduce the scale of Poland's pollution problem. Moreover, even if the picture of industrial restructuring presented in Table 4.2 is more or less accurate, it does not necessarily follow that market forces failed to take hold between 1990 and 1992. The declines in light industry and engineering reflected in part the collapse of CMEA markets during this time, as well as stiff competition from Western imports; the increase in the share of fuels and power can be explained in part by the relative price- and income-inelasticity of demand for these products, with the result that sales and production in these branches held up better in the face of higher prices and lower real incomes than in other branches.

The demonopolizing tendencies that began to take hold in Polish industry during the late 1980s (Slay 1990) accelerated in 1990–1991. As Table 4.3 shows, within the state sector alone the number of industrial firms increased by about 42 percent between 1987 and 1991 and concentration ratios for industrial branches generally fell as well. This occurred despite the completed privatization of 554 state enterprises in 1990 and 1991 (*Prywatyzacja przedsiębiorstw państwowych* 1993, 21). Moreover, the number of private industrial firms increased by almost 60 percent (from 210,150[2] to 335,663[3]) during 1988–1991; by the end of 1992 the private sector officially accounted for almost one-third of industrial output.[4] Finally, the import competition that followed the dramatic increase of zloty convert-

TABLE 4.3
Changes in Structural Concentration (State Industry), 1987–1991 by Branch

	Total Number of Firms		*Number of firms whose share of gross branch sales jointly exceeds:* 50 percent		80 percent	
	1987	*1991*	*1987*	*1991*	*1987*	*1991*
Non-ferrous metallurgy	9	19	1	4	2	4
Energy	11	84	1	12	3	33
Fuels	20	25	1	1	6	7
Coal	18	85	2	21	5	45
Ferrous metallurgy	37	44	3	3	11	12
Animal feeds	14	33	4	5	7	12
Ceramics	30	38	5	4	14	14
Paper products	54	89	6	4	16	18
Transportation equipment	232	310	8	10	32	42
Precision tools	116	155	9	15	30	49
Glass products	79	91	11	10	27	26
Leather	198	298	12	28	44	86
Machine tools	429	656	19	50	110	176
Printing	118	134	20	17	51	50
Electronics	252	325	21	23	65	81
Metals	412	496	24	31	88	105
Chemicals	356	445	27	23	83	81
Food processing	732	1130	27	86	159	347
Building materials	240	463	33	45	95	166
All other branches	167	153	36	18	85	57
Wood products	384	535	44	41	110	126
Clothing	343	677	52	67	182	240
Textiles	370	417	55	50	130	131
TOTALS	4712	6702	141	232	853	1129

Sources: Rocznik Statystyczny: Przemysł 1988, 36; *Rocznik Statystyczny: Przemysł* 1992, 14.
Note: Figures based on gross industrial sales data, current prices. Data for private firms, and state firms employing less than 50 workers, not included.

ibility in 1990 introduced much stronger competitive pressures into Polish industrial markets. In addition to effectively deconcentrating industrial structures, market entry by private producers and importers effectively demolished the shortages and product-level monopoly that had been so pervasive under socialism (Kharas 1991; Slay 1990).

On the other hand, the degree of marketization in Polish industry in 1990–1991 declined as one moved upstream in the production process. Although virtually all industrial prices had reached equilibrium levels by the end of 1990, price increases were generally greatest for energy products. The price of coal, Poland's key fuel source, rose 600 percent in January 1990 alone, and increased further after controls were removed in July (Eysymontt 1990a). These price increases allowed energy and mineral suppliers to remain profitable in 1990, despite reductions in central subsidies. Indeed, with the exception of the breakup of the coal *wspólnota* during the second quarter of 1990, few if any structural changes occurred in this sector. Still, equilibrating these markets was certainly important in helping to rationalize energy and material usage.

As inflation began to subside after mid-1990, the impact of tougher subsidy and credit policies began to cause other problems for many firms, especially in heavy industry and the energy and fuels complex. The recession, the zloty's appreciation, the loss of CMEA markets, the stiffer application of environmental regulations and fines, and the growth in real wages—these combined pressures pushed many firms into insolvency. Although joint-venture partners were found for some of these firms (e.g., in steel and automobiles), for most, privatization was not an option. The authorities during 1989–1992 were generally unwilling to include chronically insolvent firms in the mass privatization program, and the size of many of these firms made them poor candidates for liquidation privatization. With fresh subsidies from the state budget ruled out by rising fiscal tensions (not to mention programmatic concerns), many of these firms simply stopped paying their bills. This informal interenterprise debt mechanism created fresh problems for the state budget and the banking system; these problems are taken up below.

The problems were most severe in the inefficient, heavily polluting extractive sector, which had been largely unaffected by the first and second stages of economic reform during the 1980s. They came to a head in the strike wave of July and August 1992 that followed the formation of the Suchocka government. Some steps were taken between 1990 and 1992 to marketize the extractive sector: the coal mines were formally made independent of administrative organs in 1990, monopolistic coal distribution chains were broken up, and the *Polska Miedź* copper monopoly was commercialized into a state-owned joint-stock company. The price liberalization introduced in January 1990 allowed firms in the extractive sector to raise prices tenfold and to record profit rates above the industrial average, despite a decline in sales volume of over 25 percent.[5]

However, these branches responded extremely unfavorably to other aspects of marketization, especially in 1991–1992. Price increases slowed noticeably in 1991, while costs rose dramatically, owing to higher real wages,[6] the liquidation of remaining subsidies, and steep increases in pollution charges—on the order of 75–300 percent for the coal industry ("Górnictwo" 1992). Although output in the energy and fuels sector fell by another 8.3 percent in 1991 (*Biuletyn Statystyczny* 1992, 5, 94), domestic and export demand fell more rapidly, producing rising inventories[7] and falling profits. The coal industry recorded losses of 3.6 trillion zloty (approximately $360 million) in 1991 and some 14 trillion zloty (approximately $1 billion) in 1992; 60 of Poland's 66 coal mines were running in the red at the end of the year ("Górnictwo" 1992; Polish Television, February 2, 1993). Predictably, few of the now "independent" mines and foundries tried to restructure themselves, nor did many make headway in improving the polarized labor-management relations inherited from the PZPR era. In light of these developments, the strikes affecting Poland's coal and copper mines in mid-1992 came as no surprise.

A program to restructure the coal industry was developed by the Olszewski government and approved by the Council of Ministers in May 1992. If implemented, this program would close 11 "permanently unprofitable" mines in 1993 and lay off some 40,000 workers (Wielopolska 1993). These moves would accelerate the development and modernization of profitable mines. Profitable mines would in turn be commercialized and then integrated into seven concerns that would be strong enough to handle market competition. These concerns would thus supervise the intra- and inter-mine restructuring process and coordinate inter-firm cooperation in matters of production and sales, as well as oversee the liquidation of mines unable to survive.

This program raised a series of questions. Although liquidation proceedings had already begun at six mines by mid-1992, both political and budgetary tensions seemed likely to prevent their rapid closure. According to one source, liquidating a single coal mine costs 1–1.5 trillion zloty (approximately $75–100 million). No funds were allocated for this purpose in the 1992 budget and, given the likely pressures on public spending in the next years, the state budget would be unlikely to be able to fund the closure of many mines in the near future—assuming that such closures would be politically feasible. Moreover, the creation of such concerns to "supervise" the restructuring process by coordinating production and sales policies among the mines could lead to the recreation of the intermediate-layer administrative organs that proved to be the bane of economic reform during the 1980s. The regeneration of this layer, combined with traditional managerial practices in the extractive sector and the practical infeasibility of rapidly closing unprofitable mines, implies that the concerns' real functions would probably be (1) using revenues generated by profitable mines to "temporarily" keep unprofitable mines afloat, (2) promoting cartel-like behavior among coal sellers, and (3) bargaining with the central authorities for increased subsidies and protection from market forces—to keep labor peace, if nothing else. If so, this would represent a major defeat for the attempts to marketize the extractive sector and, indirectly, much of heavy industry.[8]

Agriculture

Unlike industry, the bulk of Polish agriculture in 1990 was already in private hands, as a result of the spontaneous decollectivization that followed the events of 1956.[9] Improvement in Polish agricultural performance is thus not primarily a matter of privatization, but is instead viewed by many observers as a question of encouraging the "rational concentration" of landholdings and capital. This belief reflects the fact that while 76 percent of Polish land was in private hands in mid-1989, the average farm was undercapitalized and contained only 7.2 hectares (17.8 acres) of land (*Rocznik Statystyczny* 1990, 322, 329). As Table 4.4 shows, compared to the Western European economies, Polish agriculture was dominated by peasant farms that were too small and poor to capture economies of scale and effectively utilize modern technology. The resulting low levels of agricultural productivity trapped a comparatively large share of the Polish labor force in agriculture (see Table 4.5), and these farmers received correspondingly low personal incomes. According to the ascendant liberal view, the transformation of Polish agriculture was to be based on the "farmerization" of peasant farming. Market forces should be allowed to force smaller, less efficient farms to merge into (or sell out to) larger, more profitable units.

Both market and policy forces therefore squeezed Polish agriculture during 1990 and the first part of 1991. According to official statistics, while agricultural incomes had increased in real terms in 1988 and 1989 by 21.9

TABLE 4.4
Polish Land Ownership Structure Compared to EC Countries, 1990

	Percentage of Farms Larger Than Ten Hectares[a]	*Percentage of Arable Land Cultivated by Farms Larger Than Ten Hectares*[a]
Poland	19	56
West Germany[b]	52	87
Belgium	54	95
Holland	57	98
France	64	87
Great Britain	75	88
Denmark	81	96

Source: A. Kołodko 1992a.
[a]Ten hectares is approximately 22 acres.
[b]Pre-unification.

and 13.6 percent, respectively, they fell by a staggering 51.4 percent in 1990 and by another 7 percent in 1991 (*Rocznik Statystyczny* 1991, 342; "Uwiąd sektora państwowego" 1992). These income trends resulted, in part, from dramatic fluctuations in the prices of agricultural inputs and outputs. The so-called marketization of the agricultural and food-processing sectors introduced by the Rakowski government on August 1, 1989, had allowed farmers to raise output prices toward market clearing levels (although, given the inflation occurring in the last quarter of 1989, whether they ever

TABLE 4.5
Comparative Agricultural Employment Shares, 1990

	Percentage of Agricultural Employment in Total Employment
Poland	28.0
Hungary	20.0
Bulgaria	16.5
Czechoslovakia	13.0
France	6.5
Denmark	5.5
Holland	4.0
Belgium	2.5
Great Britain	2.0

Source: A. Kołodko 1992b.

reached those levels was unclear). At the same time, interest rates and the prices of some farm inputs remained well below market levels. These favorable movements in the terms of trade provided Polish farmers with a one-time windfall; however, coming at the end of a decade in which maintaining parity between rural and urban incomes was a key tenet of agricultural policy, they left Polish farmers quite unprepared for the events of 1990 and 1991.

The large increases of 1988–1989 in agricultural incomes and the commitment to income parity disappeared with the general price liberalization and introduction of market-clearing interest rates, as well as reductions in subsidies, introduced in January 1990. The terms-of-trade shock was substantial: the number of quintals of wheat required to purchase an Ursus tractor increased from 248 in the last quarter of 1989 to 618 in the third quarter of 1991 (*East European Agriculture*, February 1992, 14). The effects of positive, often extraordinarily high, real interest rates were particularly damaging, since many agricultural loans were taken at flexible rather than fixed interest rates.[10] The ensuing collapse in farm incomes was so extensive that, according to Gabriel Janowski, minister of agriculture in the Olszewski and Suchocka governments, farm incomes in mid-1992 had fallen to 40 percent of their 1989 levels (Szot 1992).

In part, this decline in farm income reflected the fact that the harvests from 1990 to 1992 were less bountiful than the 1989 harvest had been. Global agricultural production fell in 1990 and 1991 by 5.8 and 1.2 percent, respectively, and then by a stunning 11.9 percent in the drought year of 1992 (*Rocznik Statystyczny* 1991, 324; *Mały Rocznik Statystyczny* 1992, 198; *Statystyka Polski* 1993b). Part of the explanation for this could be found on the demand side: consumers reacted to higher food prices by reducing their consumption of numerous products, although these declines were generally moderate (in the range of 2–3 percent in 1990 [A. Kołodko 1991]). Instead, the general availability of better-quality food and agricultural products, often driven by the fear of import competition,[11] in addition to the new difficulties in inter-regional wholesale trade that followed the collapse of the monopolistic trade and distribution networks in 1990, made it difficult for farmers to sell all their output, as they had been able to do in the past. Continued uncertainty about reprivatization and regulation of land sales, as well as the fate of cooperative and state farms, also hung over the formulation of agricultural policies.

In light of these problems, Polish farmers' ability to keep agricultural production in 1990 and 1991 close to 1989 levels was a strong testament to their capacity to persevere in the face of adversity. The rapid increases in agricultural exports recorded during this time were just as impressive. Polish exports of food and agricultural products in 1990 increased by 22.4 and 77.4 percent, respectively, in volume terms (*Rocznik Statystyczny: Handel Zagraniczny* 1991, 11). For 1991, agricultural exports were up 25.5 percent, in volume terms, while food exports were up some 3 percent, in value terms (Telma 1992, 19).

In spite of their relative success, the Mazowiecki and Bielecki governments' agricultural policies were extremely unpopular in the countryside, and farmers were some of the most vociferous critics of the Balcerowicz Plan during 1990–1991. In light of this opposition, the government's unwillingness to consider preferential agricultural policies in credit policy, pricing, or foreign trade proved to be politically untenable. The Agricultural Marketing Agency was created in 1990 to help stabilize farm prices through strategic purchases and sales of agricultural products, and the Bielecki government was forced to accept farm price supports during the parliamentary election campaign 1991. This led to the introduction of minimum prices for grain and milk and to the establishment of the Agricultural Restructuring Fund, to provide preferential credits for indebted farmers, in 1992. The drought of 1992, which reduced gross agricultural output by about 12 percent, produced a surge of (ultimately successful) protectionist demands for "temporary" surcharges on agricultural imports.

While the policies pursued during 1990 and early 1991 may have squeezed farmers, their success in promoting the "rational concentration" of agricultural landholdings and production was questionable. Virtually no changes were recorded in 1990 or 1991 in the average private farm size (*Rocznik Statystyczny* 1991, 323) or in the sectoral shares of agricultural land ownership or production (see Table 4.6). The privatization of Poland's 1,500 increasingly hard-pressed state farms had barely begun by 1993. The fate of the agricultural cooperatives also remained in limbo pending revision of Poland's cooperative law. And although some of the monopolistic distribution and supply organizations were broken up between 1989 and 1991, many of the rest of the industries servicing Polish agriculture (the so-called agricultural environment) did not undergo fundamental change during this time.

Prospects for a smooth transformation of Poland's state farms in mid-1993 seemed especially bleak. The Agricultural Property Agency, created by the privatization legislation of October 1991, received the ambitious mandate of restructuring and privatizing all of these farms by the end of 1993. Privatization could take the form of the sale or rental of farm assets; proceeds were to finance the agency's activities. However, as of mid-1992

TABLE 4.6
Sectoral Distribution of Gross Agricultural Production, 1989–1991 (Percentages)

	State Sector	*Cooperative Sector*	*Private Sector*
1989	17.1	3.9	79.0
1990	18.2	4.6	77.2
1991	16.5	4.2	79.1

Sources: Rocznik Statystyczny 1990, 331; *Rocznik Statystyczny* 1991, XVIII; *Mały Rocznik Statystyczny* 1992, 198.

Note: Globalna produkcja rolnicza, current prices.

some 400 farms were virtual bankruptcies and another 800 were teetering on the edge (Mozolski 1992b). Since state farms were often the sole employers in the towns where they were located, their collapse frequently had dramatic socioeconomic implications; a 1992 report warned that 100,000 people could be added to the unemployment rolls by 1995 (ibid.).[12]

According to press reports, in 1992 only 40 percent of state farm land offered for privatization was actually transferred to private hands (mostly via leasing), and only two farms were sold ("Cud się nie nadarzył" 1993). Agricultural privatization had been impeded by the unresolved reprivatization issue, the lack of rural capital, and the need to use proceeds from privatization to subsidize unprofitable farms and offer new employment to former state farm workers. Although the authorities had resisted popular pressures for the breakup and parcelization of state farm land and assets, given the poor fiscal condition of many farms and the tensions in the state budget this may be the only viable privatization option for state farms. This could lead to the further atomization of Polish agriculture rather than its rational concentration.

These problems aside, by 1993 Polish agriculture had clearly emerged as one of Poland's leading and most hopeful sectors. The large role of the private sector in agriculture, the relatively far-reaching liberalization of prices and the regulatory environment, and the rapid increases in exports to the developed capitalist countries, compared favorably with many other sectors of the economy. The resolution of Polish agriculture's problems seemed to hinge on domestic and international political factors rather than economic issues. Domestically, Poland's postcommunist governments had succeeded in alienating a large part of the Polish peasantry, which constitutes about some 25–30 percent of the population, from the program for economic transformation. Of course, small farmers in many societies are often opposed to economic liberalism, and this opposition does not always prevent agricultural modernization. Still, the fact that Polish farmers' political representatives were able during 1991–1992 to impose more interventionist agricultural policies before the "farmerization" trend could really take hold raises questions about the viability of farmerization as an agricultural modernization strategy.[13] Indeed, according to some observers, rising unemployment and poverty in both urban and rural areas will force more Poles into small-scale subsistence farming, which would work against the tendency towards "rational concentration" (*East European Agriculture*, April 1992, 18). These problems are likely to sharpen as Polish agriculture becomes more closely integrated with, and faces stiffer competition from, the much more productive farm sectors of the European Community.

Internationally, agricultural trade relations between Poland and the EC deteriorated during the first years of the transition, culminating in a skirmish over hoof-and-mouth disease in April 1993. The EC decision to ban Polish animal and meat imports—without any proof that this disease was, in fact, present in Poland—produced a retaliatory ban on EC imports of these products into Poland. Although the bans were reciprocally revoked in July, the EC action reduced Poland's revenues from the export of these products by an estimated $30 million, or about one-third of the yearly total. This incident illustrated both the intensely political nature of agricultural trade with the EC and Poland's growing frustration with the Community's unwillingness to live up to its promises of market access. As long the EC's Common Agricultural Policy is in place, it will cast a shadow over the long-term prospects for Polish agricultural exports to the EC, Polish farmers' natural external market.

Banking, Capital, and Financial Markets

Restructuring banking and financial systems and creating workable capital markets are among the largest institutional challenges of the postcommunist economic transition. The nominal privatization of state enterprises is unlikely to induce desired changes in enterprise behavior if it does not take place within a framework of effective financial intermediation and capital allocation and reallocation. In addition to the creation of markets for stocks and bonds, as well as regulatory institutions to supervise them, reform of the banking system is required. This new framework is necessary not only to provide firms with decentralized, commercial sources of investment and working capital, but also to impose a greater measure of financial discipline on enterprises, as well as to provide market estimates of enterprise and property values.

Although the Warsaw securities market was reestablished in April 1991 (Wellisz 1991b), and programs to "marketize" the state insurance funds were developed during 1990–1992, the capital-allocation role of these institutions in this period was insignificant. As of June 1993 only 17 firms were traded on the Warsaw stock exchange, which was open only two days a week. Throughout the 1990–1992 period the stock market generally languished, as share prices declined by large measures in real terms. Foreigners generally stayed away from Polish stocks and bonds because of fears about inflation and political instability: according to one source, foreigners accounted for only 10 percent of the turnover during the Warsaw exchange's first year, in contrast to the 90 percent role played by foreigners in the Budapest stock market (*East European Markets,* June 10, 1992, 8). However, the Warsaw stock exchange did experience a boom during the first half of 1993, as share values increased by some 300 percent (Pomfret 1993). While this bull market was a hopeful sign, the general insignificance of the stock market as a source of capital for (and control over) Polish enterprises made this boom difficult to interpret.

While private insurance companies emerged after 1989, their capital-allocation role in the Polish economy remained minuscule, and the state insurance funds required increasing government subsidies to remain solvent. The private insurance sector was also damaged by the spectacular collapse of the Westa corporation in 1993, which left the state Insurance Protection Fund with the prospect of picking up the tab for potentially as many as 100,000 claimants (Czechowski and Raczko 1993). Other types of private financial institutions (e.g., pension funds and mutual funds) generally stayed away from Poland during 1990–1992 as well. All this placed a premium on banking reform and on more effective financial intermediation between demanders of financial capital (firms) and the suppliers of capital.

Banking reform in Poland had begun in 1982, with the passage of legislation authorizing the partial decentralization of the National Bank of Poland (NBP).[14] "Commercializing" relations between banks and enterprises, in order to impose greater financial discipline on state enterprises, had been a theme of the second stage of economic reform of 1986–1988. This led in 1989 to the spinning off of nine regional divisions from NBP into state-owned commercial banks. Legislation in 1989 also attempted to increase the NBP's independence from the government. The establishment of private banks was authorized by the Economic Activity Act of 1988. The intent was to improve the banking system's ability to perform financial intermediation by separating the commercial banks from the central bank and the central bank from the government, ultimately affording firms a choice among private banking institutions, helping the NBP pursue tighter monetary and credit policies, and allowing administrative controls over money and credit to be replaced by indirect monetary policy instruments. The NBP would then be able to influence commercial-bank liquidity and lending practices by changing interest rates, capital requirements, and other variables. Initially, however, the accounts of state enterprises were simply transferred to the appropriate regional commercial banks, with the result that the banks began their new "commercial" lives as regional monopolies with loan portfolios created by administrative fiat. Private banks were also in an initially disadvantageous position vis-à-vis the behemoth state banks. In 1989, when private banks began to appear, the choice among competing financial institutions was still, for all intents and purposes, quite limited.

The liberalization of prices in 1990, and the willingness of NBP and Balcerowicz's Finance Ministry to push interest rates to market-clearing levels, marked a watershed in the development of the Polish financial system. Higher interest rates helped rationalize the demand for credit and increase incentives to save. They also helped liquidate credit shortages, so that the NBP in early 1990 was able to move away from the administrative allocation of blocs of reserves and credits to individual banks in favor of indirect controls over the money supply. This was meant to encourage commercial banks to tighten lending policies—to take a tougher line with inefficient state enterprises and deny working and investment capital to uncreditworthy firms and investment projects. Enterprises that could not meet the market test were to be pushed into insolvency and then bankruptcy by the banking system.

These changes did not always have the desired impact on banks and firms, however, and instead produced side effects that posed a serious threat to both macroeconomic stability and the economic transformation (Slay 1992b). From 1990 to 1992 most of the largest Polish banks and their enterprise clients were state-owned, and state-owned commercial banks continued to allocate the bulk of Poland's business credit.[15] As of mid-1991, the "big nine" state-owned commercial banks that were carved out of the NBP in 1989 were allocating some 90 percent of Poland's commercial credit pool (Białkowska 1991),[16] and they were funneling some 90 percent of this share to the credit pool to state firms in early 1992 (Lipiński 1992b). Combined with the lack of well-developed bankruptcy procedures and slow progress in privatizing state enterprises, the dominance of the state-owned commercial banks perpetuated many traditional property-rights pathologies among state firms and between state firms and banks.

This situation produced rapid increases in interenterprise debts, as many firms squeezed by the tight money and credit policies of 1990–1992 simply refused to pay their bills, in effect forcing interest-free loans out of their creditors. Andrzej Lipko, minister of industry and trade in the Olszewski government, wrote in April 1992 that interenterprise debt had at that point reached some 200 trillion zloty (approximately $14.8 billion, or 15 percent of Polish GDP) (Lipko 1992). Creditors generally had neither the legal ability nor the economic incentive to push insolvent debtors into bankruptcy in order to obtain a share of their assets. And since the threat of bankrupting banks had, before April 1992, not been at all credible, bankers' incentives to deal firmly with nonperforming loans were weak. If anything, banks were more likely to loan out additional funds in order to help debtor firms get back on their feet. This growth in interenterprise debt was accompanied by increasing amounts in outstanding bank loans and credits, which by mid-1991 had reached 145 trillion zloty (approximately $13 billion), 118 trillion of which was owed by state institutions (Balicka 1991). Outstanding enterprise tax liabilities reached 43 trillion zloty (about $3.2 billion) in March 1992 ("Wzrosło zadłużenie przedsiębiorstw" 1992). The emergence of these problems in 1991–1992, combined with the rapid growth of the government budget deficit, gave the appearance of a fiscal meltdown waiting to happen.

The expansion of interenterprise debt weakened Poland's economic transformation program in three ways. First, it allowed enterprises to informally expand the supply of credit, thus increasing the velocity of money and softening the stabilization program's money and credit policies. Second, because it distorted the financial picture of state enterprises (the banks' main clients), interenterprise debt introduced a new element of uncertainty into the financial system. Third, by permitting firms to borrow, in effect, from suppliers, irrespective of market performance or creditworthiness, the interenterprise debt mechanism weakened the pressures for enterprises to restructure. In fact, whereas large, well-connected state enterprises with the greatest monopsony power vis-à-vis suppliers, banks, and the fiscal authorities could obtain informal credit for free, smaller private firms without such leverage had to borrow at exorbitant market interest rates. Private farmers, for example, received loans from banking cooperatives in 1991 at average nominal interest rates of 85 percent (Dowda 1992), which, given farm price inflation in the 30 percent range, translated into real farm interest rates on the order of 50–55 percent.

As a result of the bureaucratic procedures and high interest rates charged on loans from the commercial banks, creditworthy firms generally chose to finance investment and working capital out of retained earnings, while the lion's share of the de facto credits extended by the banking system went to finance the budget deficit or to sustain uncreditworthy state enterprises that the banks were unwilling to push into bankruptcy.[17] Meanwhile, many private firms had virtually no access to bank credit. These problems were aggravated by the banks' inability to process the foreign loans and credits made available to Poland. According to data released by the Central Planning Office in January 1992, of the $8.1 billion in foreign credits and loans pledged to Poland by Western and other foreign financial institutions—most of which was pledged to the private sector—only $1.7 billion had actually been used. While this situation was the result of many factors (including, for example, the fact that many credits are tied to purchases of specific exports from the loaning countries), the Polish banking system's inability to allocate these funds to private users is widely perceived as an important part of the problem (Małachowski 1992).

Since the root of the interenterprise debt problem is the fact that the state is the owner both of the largest commercial banks and of their industrial clients, the ultimate solution would seem to be to privatize both parties. However, the privatization of the banking system progressed even more slowly between 1990 and 1992 than the privatization of large industrial firms. Although the "big nine" state-owned banks were commercialized during the second half of 1991, only one more (the Wielkopolski Credit Bank) had been privatized by May 1993.[18]

The recession was a second major cause of the banking system's problems. Although high rates of inflation in 1989–1990 and the commercial banks' monopoly position produced (on paper) high profit rates for the banks in 1990, the recession had pushed growing numbers of loans into the "nonperforming" category by 1991. Reclassifying these nonperforming assets as liabilities in turn pushed the banks toward insolvency. Seven of the "big nine" were in serious trouble after mid-1991 as a result of declines in the performance of loans (comprising 80–90 percent of the banks' "assets") made to large state firms (Kowalska 1992). According to a World Bank report, 30–40 percent of the bank credits extended to state enterprises were classified as "doubtful" or "unrecoverable" by February 1992, up from 10 percent in mid-1990 (Lipiński 1992b; "Oczyszczenie finansów i polityka strukturalna" 1992).

By 1992 the growing budget deficit had imposed harsh limits on the central authorities' ability to recapitalize the banks and the firms in their portfolios. However, the failure to recapitalize at least some of the large banks could have led to their collapse, and then to a general financial breakdown. The macroeconomic implications of such a turn of events could have been quite unpleasant. The debt-reduction (*oddłużenie*) program, developed during the Olszewski and Suchocka governments and passed into law in May 1993, was meant to deal with these problems. If introduced as planned, this legislation would deal simultaneously with the interenterprise debt problem, the commercial banks' bad loans, and the lack of effective bankruptcy procedures. It would also accelerate the privatization of the financial system and promote foreign investment in the banking system (Gadomski 1992; Mizsei 1993).

Under the law, the commercial banks would be issued some 21 trillion zloty (approximately $1.5 billion) worth of treasury bonds to finance the recapitalization of their balance sheets (Aleksandrowicz 1992a). In return, the banks would face stronger incentives to take a tougher line with bad debtors. In particular, the Finance Ministry would be authorized to (1) force banks to develop programs for restructuring bad loans held by large debtors, (2) order recalcitrant banks to initiate liquidation or bankruptcy proceedings in uncreditworthy enterprises whose loans appear on the banks' balance sheets as assets, and (3) force banks to sell these "assets" for whatever price the market will bear. These steps could be taken by banks holding as little as 20 percent of the debt in an uncreditworthy firm. Banks not willing to take these steps would not be recapitalized.

Bank loans whose performance was regarded as "below standard," "doubtful," and "losses" would be recapitalized at 20 percent, 50 percent, and 90 percent of their nominal value, respectively. This scale would give the banks an incentive to take a hard line with the most creditworthy debtors, while loans made to truly hopeless firms (often predating the banking system's 1989 commercialization) would be recapitalized almost in full. Commercial banks would thus be freed from the burden of their worst loans, while the least creditworthy large debtors would no longer enjoy reverse leverage over the banks. Moreover, banks—and creditors in general—would be able to exchange bad debt for equity in debtor firms, provided they held at least 30 percent of the firm's debt.[19]

If effective, this program would create strong incentives for commercial banks to get tough with recalcitrant debtors and would simultaneously make the banks better candidates for privatization (and for foreign purchases) by cleaning up their balance sheets. And in laying the foundations for "vulture capitalist" markets, this law would increase the viability and economic significance of bankruptcy in general. Creditors would have more incentive to initiate bankruptcy proceedings against debtors, since the former would be able to recoup at least some of their losses by selling the debtors' assets on vulture capital markets or through debt-equity swaps. The interenterprise debt problem would also be addressed by the creation of special clearing agencies (*izby powiernicze*) to supervise the annulment of mutual debts that cancel each other out. This would reduce the scale of the interenterprise credit phenomenon from a gross to a net problem (Wrąbec 1992). All this would help break some of the Gordian knots of the interenterprise debt mechanism, since creditors could either exchange their claims on other firms for equity or sell them for cash. Finally, debt-equity swaps would create another avenue for privatizing state firms.

Despite the hopes raised by this legislation, it faced a series of possible pitfalls. The first concerned financing. The program would be funded externally by a $400 million World Bank loan and by tapping half of the $1 billion stabilization fund issued in 1990, none of which had been used. The issuance of 20 trillion zloty worth of new bonds would represent an additional financial burden on the Polish financial system, putting upward pressure on interest rates and crowding out productive investment. It was also ironic that Poland was proposing to increase its external debt in order to bribe commercial banks into restructuring their bad loans. It was also possible that the 21 trillion zloty budgeted for the program would be insufficient. According to NBP president Hanna Gronkiewicz-Waltz, the amount of bad loans had reached 40 trillion in mid-1992 (Aleksandrowicz 1992a). Second, it was possible that the incentives included in the legislation could prove to be too weak to influence some creditors. Banks could conceivably refuse the carrot of recapitalization, or even ignore the stick of Finance Ministry directives, to push debtors into bankruptcy. In either case, bad debts would not be sold or swapped for equity, which would short-circuit the program. Perhaps most important, this legislation would make possible the application of strong measures (including bankruptcy proceedings) against large, insolvent state enterprises. For this reason, it was likely to encounter fierce political opposition. It was unclear whether the government, which had previously been unwilling or politically unable to declare these firms bankrupt, would be willing and able to permit banks and other creditors to do the dirty work for them.

Bankers and regulators have moved to clean up the Polish banking and financial system, especially since the appointment of Gronkiewicz-Waltz as NBP president in March 1992. Liquidation proceedings were initiated on March 30, 1992, against the Katowice Commercial Credit Bank, which had lapsed into insolvency, in part as a result of its connection to the Art-B affair.

Legislation approved in April 1992 closed some of the regulatory loopholes that facilitated banking scandals, and a more modern interbank clearing system, based on a computerized check-clearing facility and the creation of a "national interbank accounting chamber" (*krajowa izba rozliczeniowa*), was established in April 1993 to prevent repetitions of Art-B's kiting scheme. Poland's associate membership status with the European Community, the first elements of which went into effect in March 1992, should ultimately impose European financial and accounting standards on the Polish banking system. Despite these measures, allegations of banking malfeasance, especially in regard to money laundering, continued to abound in 1993.

Despite large measures of liberalization and deregulation, Poland's banking and financial systems were unable to effectively meet the challenge of financing Poland's transition to capitalism during 1990–1992, and their foibles helped weaken the stabilization program to boot. Prime Minister Jan Krzysztof Bielecki was certainly correct when he declared in October 1991 that the banking system was "the Polish economy's greatest weakness" ("Bielecki" 1991). Capital market development was facilitated by the success of "small" and asset privatization, as well as the post-1988 legalization of numerous gray-market transactions in convertible currencies and small-scale producer goods. However, capital markets remained shallow and poorly integrated, and the slow pace of large-scale privatization—and especially the mass privatization program, with its emphasis on the state-inspired creation of investment funds—made rapid changes in this sphere unlikely. The effects of the recession and the government budget deficit were also placing immense fiscal burdens on nascent financial markets. The uneven progress in transforming Poland's financial system between 1990 and 1992 makes the rapid development of the private sector look all the more impressive.[20]

Labor Markets and Social Policy

Labor markets in Poland underwent an important degree of liberalization and marketization during 1989–1992.[21] Shortage pressures essentially disappeared and wage-push inflationary forces weakened considerably. On the other hand, the continued presence of numerous distortions prevented the full rationalization of employment patterns and significant increases in labor mobility. These included the *popiwek* tax on excess wage growth, the chaotic nature of collective bargaining arrangements, the effects of the chronic housing shortage, and weaknesses in the social safety net. The waves of strikes in the Polish mining and manufacturing sectors during the summer of 1992 and in the public sector in the spring of 1993 were obvious reflections of these problems, as was the post-1989 appearance of unemployment rates that were high by both regional and European standards.

The Polish labor market before 1990 was characterized by a high degree of excess demand. In 1988 there were 86 registered vacancies for every job seeker (Brown 1992, 51). The 1980s were marked by endemic wage-push inflationary pressures, as well as the inability of the communist governments to apply consistent, effective wage controls (Baczyński 1986). The effects of the 100 percent wage indexation provision that Solidarity forced on the Rakowski government during the Roundtable negotiations in early 1989 added significant new pressures to nominal incomes, which increased by 284 percent in 1989 (*Rocznik Statystyczny* 1991, 194). The last years of the PZPR's increasingly ineffectual rule were marked by growing chaos in industrial relations, as organized and wildcat strike activity by disgruntled workers often undermined the authority of enterprise management, the central authorities, and other political actors. Grass-roots wage-push pressures, which had been a constant feature of economic life during the 1980s, essentially spun out of control in 1988 and 1989 and real incomes increased in those years by 13.8 and 6.5 percent, respectively (ibid.).

These trends made the inclusion of a wage-based incomes policy in the stabilization program introduced in 1990 almost inevitable, and the *popiwek* tax on excess wages was the instrument through which this occurred. While the *popiwek* was relatively effective during 1990 in forcing enterprises to accept reductions in real wages, its effectiveness dramatically lessened after 1990. This was apparent in the higher coefficients for the *popiwek* adopted in mid-1990, in the increasing numbers of firms which were exempted from paying the tax, and in the growing arrears in *popiwek* payments that began in 1991.[22] Not surprisingly, the large declines in real wages (20 percent) that occurred during 1990 were reversed in 1991, when real wages grew by about 2 percent. Although a decline in real wages was again recorded in 1992, continued growth in *popiwek* arrears implies that other factors, such as increases in unemployment, were responsible for this decrease.

Despite its increasing irrelevance, the *popiwek* was widely criticized for hindering the rationalization of employment patterns, preventing wages from better reflecting labor productivity, penalizing those firms with above-average productivity growth, and preventing the depoliticization of the wage-determination process. The Solidarity trade union forced major modifications in the *popiwek* in May 1991 and calls for weakening or abolishing the *popiwek* were frequently heard during the parliamentary election campaign that fall.

With the notable exception of the *popiwek*, however, labor markets had been substantially liberalized by the end of 1990. Legislation derived from the Roundtable Agreements and passed in 1990 attempted to establish a more modern, consensus-oriented collective bargaining system in which workers' right to strike was guaranteed once all other stages of the collective bargaining process had been exhausted. Wage setting was formally decentralized to the level of the enterprise, although it was understood that both the importance of moderating nominal wage growth and the supra-enterprise nature of trade union structures would tend to create industry-wide or regional collective bargaining frameworks.

Despite the early cooperation between the Solidarity government and the Solidarity trade union, the development of Poland's labor relations framework during 1990–1993 has been more chaotic than orderly. The collapse of the PZPR's cells within state enterprises was accompanied by the growth of workers' councils and trade union activities, from the OPZZ (former communist) trade union confederation as well as from Solidarity and its radical, anti-Wałęsa offshoot, "Solidarity '80." The important role played by workers' councils in the operational management of at least some state enterprises led to what became known as the "Bermuda Triangle" syndrome (Bieńkowski 1992b), in which authority was divided three ways, among the enterprise director, workers' councils, and trade union officials. Since privatization of "their" enterprise was not necessarily consistent with any of these actors' self-interest, this "unholy alliance" constituted one of the more important forms of grass-roots opposition to privatization after 1989. Also, enterprise managers were often constrained by the workers' councils and/or trade union officials from taking unpopular but necessary entrepreneurial decisions. Instead, managers were often tempted to seek intrafirm alliances in order to improve the firm's bargaining position vis-à-vis the central authorities.

Combined with the continued state ownership of most large enterprises, this triangle also militated against the emergence of effective collective bargaining and labor-management arrangements. Instead, disputes among different union groups and between workers and management often exacerbated intra-enterprise conflicts and produced wildcat strikes beyond the control of national or even local union officials. This was most apparent in the strike wave of July and August 1992 that greeted the formation of the Suchocka government.

The inability of the Roundtable labor relations system to put a halt to this confusion led the Suchocka government in August 1992 to propose the "social pact" with workers in state enterprises. The pact was never ratified. In addition to the corporatist implications for enterprise management, privatization, and restructuring discussed in Chapter 3, it would also have centralized wage determination. Permissible yearly wage increases for state enterprise workers would have been authorized by the Sejm as part of the approval process for the state budget. This would seemingly have left little room for wage flexibility at the plant level, thus exacerbating unemployment problems in the state sector. On the other hand, given the imperative of defusing Poland's labor relations tensions, sacrificing some degree of labor market efficiency in exchange for fewer strikes and less industrial conflict may well have been desirable.

The rise in open unemployment, from zero at the start of the stabilization program in 1990 to 14.2 percent at the end of March 1993, symbolized the costs of the transition to capitalism and the failure of policies designed to smooth the labor market transition. Rapid increases in the official unemployment statistics between 1990 and 1992 were matched by the authorities' inability to predict this growth. Government forecasts had anticipated some 400,000 unemployed workers at the end of 1990 (Dryll 1990; G. W. Kołodko 1991), but 1,125,000 Poles were classified as unemployed at year's end (Dryll 1991), producing an unemployment rate of 6.1 percent. On the other hand, the 13.6 percent unemployment rate at the end of 1992 was below the 17 percent forecast for that year's end under the Central Planning Office's "optimistic" scenario and well below the 19 percent envisioned in its "pessimistic" scenario (Aleksandrowićz 1992b).

The unanticipated severity of the recession of 1990–1992 largely overwhelmed efforts to develop active labor market policies, and sharpening budget tensions forced reductions in the scope and magnitude of unemployment compensation. The initial employment legislation passed by the Mazowiecki government in December 1989 was in many respects quite generous: benefits were paid out of the newly established Labor Fund to anyone who claimed to be unemployed, even those who had not previously been in the labor force. Those who had been previously employed received, for a three-month period, compensation equal to 70 percent of the wage earned at their previous place of employment. While benefits declined to 50 percent during the next six months and to 40 percent after that, there was no cutoff date for benefits. (On the other hand, given the high rates of inflation prevailing during 1990, the real value of these benefits diminished quickly.) Those receiving unemployment compensation were also eligible for publicly funded health care and other social programs, and the time spent registered as officially unemployed counted toward the retirement pension (Leśnicka 1992).

These provisions subsequently proved too lavish for Poland's meager budgetary resources, and progressive restrictions were introduced on September 1, 1990, December 1, 1991, and February 15, 1992 ("Statystyka mówi" 1992). The amendments of September 1990 made individuals who had never formally been in the labor force, or who had not worked at least 180 days in the previous 12-month period, ineligible for benefits. They also reduced the lowest benefit level. In December 1991 the duration of benefits was limited to 12 months, with the result that the long-term unemployed increasingly lost benefits after 1992; by March 1993, almost half of those officially registered as unemployed were no longer eligible for benefits (*Statystyka Polski* 1993a, II). The amendments of February 1992 lowered all benefit levels to 36 percent of the average wage from the previous quarter.

The rapid growth in the unemployment rate forced the transfer of funds that had been earmarked for active labor market policies to unemployment compensation: some 80 percent of the public funds spent on labor market activities in 1991 went to unemployment benefits.[23] Job retraining programs were among the casualties: from 1990 to 1992 less than 2 percent of the workers classified as unemployed were able to participate in such programs. According to Polish press reports, about 20 percent of the unemployed workers in the OECD countries generally participate in job retraining programs (Dryll 1993; Kraus 1992).

The introduction of unemployment compensation was only one social-policy reform during 1990–1992. A dramatic reallocation in budgetary priorities occurred during this time, transferring funds away from product, enterprise, and sectoral subsidies toward direct-transfer payments to the population (Golinowska 1992). Real expenditures on social services such as education and health care declined by 22.8 percent in 1990–1991; reductions in spending on education (26.3 percent), culture (50.3 percent), and sports and tourism (58.1 percent) were particularly large. Transfer payments, by contrast, increased by about 17 percent in real terms during this time, with particularly large increases in health care payments (42.3 percent) and retirement pensions (30.9 percent). The share of the state budget devoted to pensions alone increased from 3 percent in 1988 to an estimated 29 percent in 1993—this despite cutbacks introduced in 1991, 1992, and 1993 (Vinton 1993b). These trends helped to increase the share of transfer payments in personal incomes (*przychody pieniężne ludności*) from 16 to 22 percent in 1990–1991, while the share of labor income fell from 40 to 31 percent. Cuts in social services contributed to reductions in public consumption by some 15 percent in 1990–1991, while consumption as a whole fell by approximately 8 percent during this time (Sonntag 1992).

This reallocation in budgetary priorities had important implications for income distribution. While real incomes declined in workers', peasants', and pensioners' households in 1990 and 1991, the declines were hardly even. Pensioners' incomes fell by "only" 5 percent over the two-year period (thanks largely to a 15 percent increase in 1991), while real incomes in worker and peasant households declined by 25 and 45 percent respectively (ibid.).[24] Within worker households, employees of the "budgetary sphere" (public services and state administration) were especially hard hit after the indexation of their wages to remuneration in the "productive sphere" was suspended in 1991.

In addition to decimating public services, expanded transfer programs, together with the revenue shortfalls linked to the recession and the growth of the more lightly taxed private sector, did not necessarily help the groups most at risk during the transition. For example, continued subsidies for central heating and water benefited urban apartment dwellers at the expense of rural residents and the homeless, and free university educations subsidized relatively well prepared students from middle- and upper-class backgrounds. A similar trend was apparent in unemployment policy during 1990–1992, where the tightening of eligibility requirements reflected the imperative of ensuring that benefits went to those who were genuinely unemployed. According to various estimates, the number of workers actually employed in the "second economy" during this period ranged from 30 to 80 percent of those registered with the unemployment offices (Wandycz 1990; Walicki and Adamczuk 1992).[25]

Given the budgetary pressures Poland faced in 1991–1992, this miscast social safety net was widely regarded as unsustainable and its reform was the subject of spirited debate. Unfortunately, the growth in transfer payments reflected fundamental demographic and labor market trends and could not be quickly and easily reversed. The rapid growth in pension expenditures was driven primarily by a 25 percent increase in the number of pensioners between 1989 and 1992 (Balicka 1992) rather than by increases in benefit rates. Despite increases in payroll tax rates levied on the declining numbers of gainfully employed workers—the social security tax rate in 1993 stood at 48 percent, one of the highest in the world—the State Insurance Office (ZUS) required growing subsidies from the central budget in order to meet its pension obligations.[26] ZUS was also making workers' compensation payments to some 3.5 million workers.

To be sure, some aspects of Poland's social safety net seemed lavish, even in comparison with Western European welfare states, and provided tempting—if politically explosive—targets for fiscal austerity. These included retirement ages (65 for men, 60 for women) and the number of years of work required to receive a state pension (30) that were well below European norms.[27] (As one observer put it, "Poland is 40 years behind Western Europe in terms of national income per capita, and 20 years ahead of Western Europe in terms of public expenditures" (Kowalska 1993). The point is that although reductions in benefit levels may have been seen as a painful necessity, the sheer number of recipients and the essential immutability of their status (as retirees or invalids) meant that even severe cuts in benefit levels were unlikely to produce significant cost savings in the short term.

How serious was Poland's unemployment problem during 1990–1992? According to one estimate, frictional unemployment (i.e., people between jobs, moving from one part of the country to another, etc.) accounted for up to 600,000 of those registered as unemployed in March 1992 (ibid.). If the official statistics can be taken at face value, some 1.6–1.7 million workers would have been cyclically or structurally unemployed as of June 1992. If 50 percent of this number were employed in the underground economy, some 800,000 workers (about 4.5 percent of the labor force) would have been involuntarily, and genuinely, unemployed. By postwar Central European standards this figure is quite high, though less so in terms of the generally higher unemployment rates of the recessionary years of the early 1990s.

These are figures for the entire country, of course, and as such they provide relatively little insight into the specifics of the unemployment problem. When disaggregated by region, gender, or age group, a rather different picture emerges. The official statistics depict a wide regional variance in unemployment rates. As of March 1993, unemployment ranged from 6 to9 percent in the counties in which Warsaw, Cracow, and Katowice are located, while in the counties containing Koszalin, Elbląg, Słupsk, and Olsztyn, as well as in the Suwałki region, rates exceeded 22 percent (*Statystyka Polski* 1993a, II). Other hard-hit areas included the Wałbrzych coalmining region, Łódź (the center of Poland's textile industry), and some of the southeastern rural counties (former Galicja). Large metropolitan centers with diversified economies and stronger ties to the international economy seemed to be doing rather well, while the areas most devastated by unemployment had none of these advantages. The geographic proximity of Elbląg, Olsztyn, Suwałki to the former Soviet Union may have contributed to the high employment in those areas, in the aftermath of the reductions in Polish-Soviet trade in 1990–1991. This certainly was a factor in the collapse of Łódź's textile industry and the rise in unemployment there.

As was the case across Eastern Europe, unemployment in Poland was highest for women, the unskilled and uneducated, and the young. At the end of March 1992 women accounted for 52.4 percent of the unemployed.[28] Workers with only basic or basic technical education (or less) were hardest hit by unemployment: at the end of 1992, these groups comprised 31.2 and 38.4 percent of the total number of unemployed, respectively. Young workers were also disproportionately afflicted by unemployment: youths in the 18–24 and 25–35 age brackets comprised 34.0 and 29.7 percent of the total unemployed at the end of 1992, respectively (*Statystyka Polski* 1993b, IV). Among all socioeconomic groups, the unemployment problem was most serious for young, poorly educated women from large families living in small towns or villages.

Unemployment seemed to contribute to the growth of poverty which, according to Minister of Labor and Social Affairs Jacek Kuroń, had by early 1993 overtaken 30 percent of the population (Dryll 1993). One study found that income levels in 90 percent of the households "touched" by unemployment were below the social minimum and 52 percent of those families lived in severe poverty, near biological subsistence (Kraus 1992). The trend toward tightened eligibility for unemployment compensation was likely to further exacerbate the poverty problem because those who lost their eligibility for unemployment benefits would likely find their access to other social services, such as public health care, reduced as well.

Perhaps the most serious costs of involuntary unemployment are the lost output represented by the unemployed and the burden unemployment places on for the state budget. According to one source, if all 2.2 million Poles who were officially registered as unemployed in March 1992 had instead been working in the official economy, they could have added as much as 150 trillion zloty (approximately $11 billion, or 15 percent of national income in 1991) worth of goods and services to the Polish economy ("Bezrobocie po polsku" 1992). In budgetary terms some 10 trillion zloty were devoted to unemployment compensation in 1991 and another 10 trillion went to fund early retirement for workers who might otherwise have been laid off (ibid.). These are considerable sums.

Some observers have argued that despite Poland's already high unemployment rate (compared to both Eastern and Western European levels), the trend during the next years may continue upward even if the economic recovery continues. Because GDP and industrial production fell more rapidly than employment in 1990–1991, the extent of hidden unemployment may have increased during that time, on top of increases in the official unemployment figures (Glikman 1992).[29] According to this view, while the recovery that began in March 1992 should eventually reduce cyclical unemployment in Poland, the shedding of what had been hidden unemployment (which then becomes structural unemployment) could continue for some time.[30]

On the other hand, there were numerous indications that unemployment was not the dire catastrophe implied by the official statistics. A survey of 2,500 employment offices by the Central Statistical Office in the spring of 1992 found that, according to the officials involved in monitoring unemployment cases and distributing benefits, only about one case of unemployment in six was genuine (Walicki and Adamczuk 1992). Labor shortages continued to exist in numerous areas, not only in highly technical fields such as computer programming, but also on low-skill labor markets in some of the large metropolitan areas with low unemployment rates. Only 24 percent of those classified as unemployed in March 1992 had lost their jobs as a result of group layoffs (*zwolnienia grupowe*) in which poor economic conditions at the place of employment were the unambiguous cause of unemployment (Dryll 1992). While the share of group layoffs (relative to total unemployment) rose continuously from 1990 to 1992, the figure of 24 percent suggested that the majority of people who lost their jobs during that time did so for individual (rather than macroeconomic) reasons. Finally, it is instructive that strikes over higher pay and better working conditions, rather than job security, continued to affect many industrial sectors; this was true of the strikes by automobile workers and coal and copper miners in mid-1992. In general, while rising unemployment rates might have been expected to reduce strike activity and improve labor discipline during 1990–1992, in fact the opposite occurred.

The rise in unemployment resulted in part from the decline of the state sector and the inability of the nascent private sector to absorb the workers laid off from state firms. Private-sector employment grew rapidly from 1990 to 1992, however; even according to official statistics, by 1991 more workers were employed in the private sector than in the public sector. In fact, job creation in the private sector in 1992 virtually compensated for declining employment in the state sector, which accounted for the slower growth in unemployment during 1992. On the other hand, the rights and privileges of workers in the state sector seemed much less available to employees of private firms. An unwritten rule seemed to be in effect throughout the private sector: workers who are too active in organizing unions, protesting poor working conditions, or pressing disability claims in privately owned workplaces were unlikely to keep their jobs. It is instructive to note that although approximately half the workforce was employed in the private sector in 1991, only 2 percent of *reported* workplace injuries took place in private firms (Gutkowska 1992). Still, the higher wages in the private sector and the competition for good jobs there implied that many workers were willing to accept this bargain.

One of the main factors behind the structural element of Poland's unemployment problem was the housing shortage. Here, relatively little changed between 1990 and 1992. Although the construction sector underwent a significant degree of privatization during this period—by 1993 about 78 percent of construction activities were accounted for by private firms (see Table 3.3)—part of this growth resulted from the reclassification of cooperative construction activities as private activities, even though these cooperatives were often rather large, bureaucratic institutions. In any case, while the privatization of construction activities may bode well for the future of the construction industry, it was unable in 1990–1992 to reverse the sizable drop in housing construction that occurred after 1987.[31] Without dramatic increases in the supply of housing, the chronic housing shortage will remain one of Poland's most painful social problems, especially for young people in urban areas.[32] In addition to construction problems, regulation of the sale and transfer of residential dwellings and uncertainties about land ownership and the rights of pre-1945 property owners (and their heirs), linked to the reprivatization controversy, constrained the marketization of the housing sector.

After largely neglecting housing in 1990, the Mazowiecki government (and later the Bielecki government) attempted to reduce housing subsidies and rationalize demand by dramatically raising rents in state-owned buildings, a move that evoked a firestorm of protest. While an improvement in the balance between supply and demand had to be an important part of any solution to Poland's housing problems, higher rents by themselves were unlikely to resolve anything beyond the central and local governments' budgetary woes. A comprehensive policy approach to the housing question was desperately needed—one that would integrate equilibrium (or near-equilibrium) prices with the genuine privatization of the erstwhile construction cooperatives, liberalization of property-transfer and land-ownership laws, banking reform,[33] and more innovative approaches to land use and environmental and local planning issues.

Summary judgments of Poland's labor market transformation from 1990 to 1992 are difficult to make. While the removal of most non-*popiwek* wage regulations can be seen as the most favorable development, two serious problem areas remained: the chaos and fragmentation of labor-management relations so noticeable during the strike waves of 1992 and 1993; and the failure to develop an active labor market policy and effectively refashion the social safety net. Judgments about the declines in real incomes, the rise in unemployment, the rapid increases in private-sector employment, and the development of workplace democracy are highly normative, since they imply trading off qualities that are hard to compare (e.g., more efficiency for less job security) or comparing gains for some groups with the cost of losses for others. Still, relative to the progress made in developing well-functioning capital markets and financial institutions, Poland's labor market transformation during this period looked rather impressive.

External Economic Relations

Foreign trade performance was one of the brighter spots of Poland's economic transition during 1990–1992. Trade flows were reoriented away from the former socialist countries toward the OECD and developing countries; the zloty became the most convertible currency in the region; foreign trade underwent a significant degree of liberalization and privatization; progress was made in restoring Poland's external creditworthiness. These accomplishments were all the more remarkable in light of the generally unfavorable macroeconomic conditions accompanying them, including high rates of inflation and the collapse of CMEA trade in 1991. On the other hand, some of the progress on restoring external creditworthiness and equilibrium in 1990 was subsequently squandered during 1991 and perhaps 1992. Declines in CMEA trade, especially with the former Soviet Union, were a major shock for hundreds of Polish firms that were largely, if not completely, reliant on the Soviet market. Major confusion in Poland's foreign trade statistics for 1992 introduced unprecedented difficulties into analyses of developments in that year.[34] Moreover, the external liberalization introduced in 1989–1990 was partially reversed after mid-1991, especially in agricultural trade. (Meanwhile, Poland began to encounter increased protectionist resistance to its exports on many OECD markets, including the EC and the United States ["Review of East European Foreign Trade Developments" 1993, 13–15].) Poland lagged behind Hungary and the Czech Republic in attracting foreign investment, and fears of Western and especially German economic influence were a strong policy undercurrent.

Restoring external balance while simultaneously increasing Poland's integration into the international economy were key external goals of the stabilization program introduced in 1990. The strong contractionary emphasis in fiscal and monetary policies and the large devaluation introduced in January 1990 (see Chapter 3) caused significant reductions in import volume in convertible-currency trade (see Table 4.7).[35] At the same time, declines in Soviet deliveries of energy products, as well as growing economic problems in the other CMEA countries, caused large reductions in Poland's CMEA imports in both financial and volume terms. This occurred despite the far-reaching import liberalization and significant increases in the zloty's current-account convertibility.[36] Most import quotas, licensing requirements, and other nontariff trade barriers in manufacturing had been effectively abolished by the end of 1990, and average nominal tariff rates were reduced from 13.3 to 8 percent (Dziewulski 1992). Although average nominal tariff rates in Poland still remained somewhat above EC levels (where average tariff levels on imports from other GATT signatories were 6.1 percent), the absence of overt protectionist schemes in manufacturing meant that Poland by late 1990 had become one of the most open economies in the region. Firms and farms were thus increasingly subjected to the bracing winds of international competition, while reductions in internal demand, central subsidies, and tutelage encouraged firms to export and find joint venture partners.

The end result was that Poland posted unprecedented current-account surpluses in both hard currencies and rubles in 1990 (see Table 4.7). In addition to arranging a $1 billion fund to stabilize the zloty-dollar exchange rate, the IMF approved a $1.5 billion adjustment loan to help underwrite the stabilization program,[37] and the IMF's imprimatur helped Poland gain access to as much as $8 billion in various forms of aid, credits, and loans from other Western and international public and private sources (Bieńkowski 1992a). The large hard-currency current-account surplus, the successes in reducing inflation and the budget deficit, and the IMF's seal of approval subsequently allowed Poland to conclude a landmark debt-reduction agreement with creditor governments (the Paris Club) in April 1991. Under this agreement, the governments holding the lion's share of Poland's foreign debt would forgive half the value of this debt,[38] provided Poland continued down the path begun in 1991 and was able to secure a similar debt reduction agreement with the London Club of private (commercial bank) creditors. This meant adhering to the targets agreed on with the IMF, resuming the servicing of the remaining Paris Club debts, and concluding a similar debt-relief agreement with the London Club.

TABLE 4.7
Foreign Trade Performance, 1990–1991

	1990	*1991*
CMEA Exports	13.5 billion TR[a] 28.3 trillion zl[b]	26.5 trillion zl.[c]
Percentage change from previous year	19.2[a]	−6.4[d]
Percentage in volume change from previous year	−13.3[a]	−42.9[e] −41.8[f]
CMEA Imports	6.9 billion TR[a] 14.5 trillion zl.[b]	31.2 trillion zl.[c]
Percentage change from previous year	−33.4[a]	115.9[d]
Percentage change in volume from previous year	−34.1[a]	−33.6[f]
CMEA terms of trade	104.4[a]	67.5[g]
CMEA current account balance	7.1 billion TR[a] plus $425 million (clearing)[a]	558 million TR[c] plus $130 million (clearing)[c] plus −$581 million[h]
Nonsocialist exports (includes clearing)	$10.9 billion[e]	$12.2 billion[e]
Percentage change from previous year	48.3[a]	11.3[i]
Percentage change in volume from previous year	40.5[a]	20.9[g] (26.4% to EC)[e] (−7.5% to non-EC)[g]
Nonsocialist imports (includes clearing)	$7.2 billion[e]	$12.4 billion[e]
Percentage change from previous year	17.7[a]	71.7[i]
Percentage change in volume from previous year	−2.9[a]	76.1%[e] 59.4% (from EC)[g] 60.0% (non-EC)[g]
Nonsocialist terms of trade	93.7[a]	89.9 (with EC)[g] 107.4 (non-EC)[g]
Dollar current account balance	$668 million[a]	−$1.359 billion[e]

Note: Figures for CMEA trade refer to the former members of the Council for Mutual Economic Assistance. TR stands for transferable ruble.

These successes on the current account were accompanied by an impressive reorientation of Polish trade away from the CMEA countries towards the OECD countries, and especally the European Community (EC). As Table 4.8 shows, the share of Polish exports to the former CMEA countries declined by about 54 percent between 1989 and 1992. While this decline reflects actual reductions in Poland's trade with the former CMEA countries in 1990 and 1991 (see Table 4.7), it illustrates first and foremost the rapid increase in trade with Western countries, expecially Germany. The agreement on Poland's associate EC membership, the first provisions of which became effective on March 1, 1992, symbolized this shift away from the former CMEA countries toward increased EC integration.[39]

This directional shift in trade was accompanied by the privatization of a significant share of Poland's trading activities. According to the official statistics, in 1991 private actors accounted for 49.9 percent of Polish imports, as well as 21.9 percent of exports. (These numbers were up from 14.4 and 4.9 percent, respectively, in 1990 [Telma 1992, 2]). These figures reflected the growth of indigenous private firms, since by 1993 only a handful of the traditional foreign trade organizations had been genuinely privatized (Walewska 1993). These statistics fail to record many small-scale private trading (not to mention smuggling) activities, so the private share of Poland's foreign trade was certainly higher than officially reported.

Notes for Table Continued

[a]Taken or derived from *Rocznik Statystyczny: Handel Zagraniczny* 1991, 7, 91, 92. 1990 data are in payments terms and refer to the first and second payment areas.

[b]Derived from corresponding TR figure by dividing the latter by the average TR-zloty exchange rate during 1990 (1 TR – 2,100 zloty).

[c]*Source: Rocznik Statystyczny: Handel Zagraniczny* 1992, 3, 69, 92. 1991 data include only trade with the European CMEA countries. 1990 data measure transactions conducted in rubles.

[d]Derived by subtracting (c) from (b) and dividing by (b).

[e]*Source:* Telma 1992, 6, 9, 10, 13, 27–28.

[f]*Source: Polski Handel Zagraniczny w 1991 Roku* 1992, 16.

[g]Taken or derived from data in *Polski Handel Zagraniczny w 1991 Roku* 1992, 12.

[h]Merchandise trade balance only. Derived by summing monthly data in Telma 1992, 13. TR balance may reflect some transactions made in 1990.

[i]Derived from data in preceding row.

TABLE 4.8
East-West Trade Reorientation, 1989–1992

	Share of Polish Imports (percentages)			*Share of Polish Exports (percentages)*		
	1989	*1991*	*1992*	*1989*	*1991*	*1992*
(Former) USSR	18.1	14.1	11.9	20.8	11.0	9.5
Germany[a]	15.7	26.5	23.9	14.2	29.4	31.3
(Former) CMEA[b]	32.2	19.0	16.3	34.8	16.8	15.4
European Community	33.8	49.9	53.1	32.1	55.6	57.9
(Former) socialist countries[c]	31.5	20.7	18.2	33.9	18.5	16.9
Nonsocialist countries[d]	68.5	79.3	81.8	66.1	81.5	87.1

Sources: Rocznik Statystyczny: Handel Zagraniczny 1991, 2–3, 8; Telma 1992, 6–7, "Review of East European Foreign Trade Developments in 1992" 1993, 62–63.

Note: Based on current prices.

[a] 1989 shares are for West Germany only.

[b] Includes European members only.

[c] 1989 shares are based on data for transactions conducted in the second currency area. 1991 and 1992 shares are based on data for former European CMEA countries, plus former Yugoslavia, China, Vietnam, North Korea, Cuba, and Mongolia.

[d] 1989 shares are based on data for transactions conducted in the second currency area. 1991 and 1992 shares are for all countries not included in (c).

On the other hand, Table 4.7 also shows that progress during 1990 in restoring external balance was followed by some backsliding in 1991. Despite continued rapid growth in exports to OECD and developing capitalist countries,[40] rapid increases in imports linked to the zloty's appreciation[41] and lower exports to the former CMEA countries in 1991 reduced the merchandise trade surplus from $2.2 billion to $51 million (*Rocznik Statystyczny: Handel Zagraniczny* 1992, 67). This smaller merchandise trade surplus was overwhelmed by the $2.8 billion in interest (debt-servicing) payments Poland made in 1991, and the hard-currency current account, which registered a $716 million surplus in 1990, fell into a deficit of $1.36 billion in 1991 (ibid.).

Although declines in CMEA exports certainly contributed to this slippage, the rapid increases in Western imports of consumer goods, which rose in real terms by an astounding 120 percent in 1991 (Telma 1992), almost certainly had more to do with it. On the one hand, these increases helped to reduce inflationary pressures and moderate the decline in consumption expenditures that occurred in 1990. On the other hand, the increases in domestic absorption underlying the higher imports were a deviation from

Poland's agreement with the IMF and contributed both to the suspension of payments from the IMF adjustment facility in mid-1991 and to a lack of progress in negotiations with the London Club. Whether developments during 1992 constituted a continuation or a reversal of these trends could not be ascertained, given the wide discrepancies between the customs and payments data mentioned above.

Poland's performance during 1990–1992 in attracting foreign capital was also rather disappointing. On the one hand, the number of partly and wholly owned foreign firms in Poland increased substantially after 1988. Between January 15, 1989, and March 31, 1990, 1,400 joint ventures applied for registration with the authorities and 1,146 applications were approved; 2,480 new joint ventures were registered in 1990 (P. Dabrowski 1991, 36) and the total number of joint ventures had risen to 11,473 by the end of March 1993 (*Statystyka Polski* 1993a, II). The amount of direct foreign investment approximately doubled in 1991, and important deals were concluded in the steel, paper, automobile, food processing, and telecommunications industries in 1991–1992. Estimates of the amount of capital committed to Poland from 1990 to 1992 were generally in the $4–4.5 billion range ("Polish Monthly Economic Monitor" 1993, 2). In aggregate terms, these numbers compare favorably with the other countries in the region.

On the other hand, the net value of the capital created through direct foreign investment was much less at the end of 1992, in the range of $0.8–1.5 billion (Mozolski 1992a). By way of comparison, Hungary, although a fraction of Poland's size, attracted $1.7 billion in direct foreign investment in 1991 alone (Denton 1992); Volkswagen's purchase of the Skoda automobile works in the Czech Republic will ultimately account for an estimated $6.5 billion in direct and financial foreign investment. According to Western press reports, Poland's direct foreign investment rate of $21 per capita in 1991 was 50 percent of the Czechoslovak level and only 10 percent of the Hungarian level (Fletcher 1992). The relatively small amount of direct foreign investment in Poland was also reflected in the small-scale nature of many projects; only 0.5 percent of which exceeded $3 million in value in 1991 (P. Dabrowski 1991).

This ambiguous record with joint ventures reflects in part the political instability that has buffeted postcommunist Poland. Between 1990 and 1992 Poland had four prime ministers, four finance ministers, three central bank presidents, four ministers for external economic relations, and five ministers of industry and trade. Despite progress in restoring Poland's external creditworthiness in 1990–1991, the disorder into which Poland's macroeconomic house fell after mid-1991 (during which time the budget deficit spiraled out of control and aid from the IMF was suspended) hardly raised Poland's stature in the eyes of the international financial community. The Suchocka government's successes during 1992 and 1993 in reducing this disorder and restoring Poland's agreement with the IMF seemed to repair some of the damage done in 1991–1992, and many observers were predicting significant increases in foreign investment in the years after 1993. Whether this optimism would survive the leftist government that emerged after the September 1993 elections remained to be seen.

Fears of foreign (and especially German) capital imposed additional constraints on policies toward foreign investment. Although Poland's need for capital, technology, and know-how is undeniable (and close proximity to Germany affords Poland certain advantages in this regard), opening the door to direct foreign investment raised political questions about possible reductions in Polish sovereignty. Simply put, preventing Poland from becoming an economic appendage of Germany has served as a justification for restrictions on foreign capital inflows.[42] These included the requirement (subsequently abolished) in the privatization legislation of July 1990 that foreign purchases of more than 10 percent of privatized state enterprises had to be approved by the central authorities. In May 1992 the Sejm passed legislation that forced foreigners to divest themselves of holdings in the most strategic of Poland's industries—gambling casinos. And foreign firms and individuals had to obtain permission from the Ministry of Internal Affairs in order to purchase land and real estate in Poland.[43] Not surprisingly, restrictions on property ownership were often cited as major obstacles to attracting foreign investment. The strong antiforeign capital element visible in the Polish labor movement was also a barrier. It is instructive that Fiat's $2 billion investment in the Polish automobile industry was nearly cancelled after wildcat strikes broke out in the FSM automobile plant in Tychy in July and August 1992.

Despite the problems, a great deal was accomplished in external economic relations between 1990 and 1992. Moreover, groundwork was laid for further expansion, if not rapid progress, in 1993 and beyond. It is noteworthy that in 1991 Polish per capita foreign trade turnover stood at $398. While this represented a substantial increase over the figure of $313 recorded in 1989, it was still ridiculously low by international standards and implied that Poland had only begun to tap the potential gains from international economic integration.[44]

In the longer term, success in continuing Poland's foreign trade transformation depends on two sets of issues. The first concerns Poland's prospects for continued integration into the European Community. This question is both economic and political, and concerns Poland, the governments of individual West European countries, and the EC in Brussels. In economic terms, the EC agreement, whose initial provisions went into effect March 1, 1992, offered Poland important opportunities for economic development and modernization.[45] The fact that many of the agreement's provisions were asymmetrical—EC duties on Polish products were to be lowered more rapidly than Polish duties on EC products—affords Poland a certain breathing space in adapting its economy to the rigors of EC competition. Poland's long border with Germany, its comparatively low labor costs, and the relatively high degree of zloty convertibility could make Poland an attractive site for foreign firms looking for low-cost ways of servicing EC markets.

On the other hand, the EC did not agree to significant liberalization of agricultural, steel, and textile imports, thus denying Poland access to markets in which it could have considerable export potential. More generally, the disarray into which the post-Maastricht EC had fallen in mid-1992, as well as rising protectionist trends within the EC vis-à-vis the Central European countries, implied that Poland, Hungary, the Czech Republic, and Slovakia were likely to remain in the EC's "waiting room" indefinitely, with many promises of increased market access going unfulfilled.[46] Nevertheless, the specter of direct competition with EC agricultural and industrial products by the end of the century did inspire terror in the hearts of many Polish farmers and managers. These fears, combined with concerns about reductions in economic sovereignty posed by the association agreement, formed the political basis for a more nationalist, protectionist external economic regime. Both left- and right-wing political groupings within Poland attempted to capitalize on this constituency during 1991 and 1992 to oppose ratification of the treaty on associate EC membership—a treaty which, in any case, was unlikely to come up for parliamentary ratification prior to 1994.

The second set of looming trade issues for Poland concerns trade relations with the former CMEA countries. The declines in trade volumes recorded during 1991 (and, to a lesser extent, 1990) were a hardship for hundreds of Polish firms specializing in the CMEA (especially the former Soviet) market. Most of these firms had neither the desire nor the ability to reorient their production to other markets and continued to export to the former USSR during 1991, even when payment from the bankrupt former Soviet authorities was not forthcoming. This left Poland with hundreds of millions of dollars in unpaid claims on the former USSR, adding yet another element to Poland's tangled web of debts and credits with the former socialist countries. As of early 1992 Poland was in debt to the former USSR to the tune of

4.8 billion transferable rubles, but had claims against it totaling some 2.5 billion transferable rubles, mostly the result of unpaid trade balances accumulated during 1990 and 1991 (Telma 1992, 28–30). Negotiations over the settlement of these issues were entangled with questions about the inheritance of the former USSR's external assets and liabilities and Polish demands for reparations or compensation for Soviet use of Polish labor during and after the Second World War (most recently in the construction of Siberian gas pipelines), as well as Soviet/CIS/Russian demands for compensation for the value of the Soviet military facilities in Poland returned to the Polish authorities in 1992.[47] Resolution of these issues seemed likely to drag on for years.

Despite these issues and the decline in the relative importance of trade with Poland's eastern and southern neighbors (shown in Table 4.7), the rationalization and reconstruction of these ties were of crucial importance. Although they were a painful shock for hundreds of Polish firms, the declines in the volume of CMEA trade from 1990 to 1992 were a part of this rationalization and reconstruction process. Indeed, the disappearance of CMEA markets in many cases resulted in the cessation of "value-subtracting" activities in Poland that could not be justified on efficiency grounds but instead arose from decisions made within the CMEA's singular political-economy framework.

The transitions from transferable-ruble to hard-currency trade accounting, and from intra-CMEA to world-market prices, were a painful way of ensuring that those trade flows that survived (or reappeared after) the shock had a solid economic rationale. Everything else equal, this restructuring should provide the basis for a healthier, and more sustainable reconstruction of Poland's "eastern" trade links. Rebuilding these links (on healthier footing) was especially important for such troubled sectors as agriculture and chemicals, whose exports to the former USSR in early 1992 comprised about 45 percent of Poland's total exports.

More immediate prospects for dynamizing Poland's trade with the former CMEA countries were found within the framework of the Central European Free Trade Agreement (CEFTA), which took effect March 1, 1993 (Okolicsanyi 1993).[48] Intra-CEFTA trade flows (between Poland, Hungary, the Czech Republic, and Slovakia) were to undergo symmetrical tariff reductions over a five-year period beginning in 1993. Tariff reductions were to occur at a different pace for each of three product groups, depending on their political "sensitivity." Trade would be carried out in national currencies. CEFTA thus represented a trade liberalization scheme that would be implemented parallel to the introduction of the Central European countries' EC association agreements as well as their EFTA free trade agreements. However, while the desire to prevent further declines in regional trade was a major force behind the conclusion of this agreement, political factors—especially the EC's desires to create new multilateral integration mechanisms in the former Eastern bloc—were probably more significant.

While the advent of CEFTA was certainly a hopeful development, numerous factors seemed likely to reduce its immediate impact on regional trade. First, because intra-CEFTA trade had fallen to ridiculously low levels by 1993, even voluminous intraregional trade creation would have only a limited impact.[49] Second, trade in some important products (e.g., automobiles) would be subject to the most gradual schedule of tariff reduction, others (e.g., pharmaceuticals and some light industrial products) would continue to enjoy nontariff trade, and the tariffs on others (e.g. agricultural and food products) not be liberalized at all. Third, important aspects of regional economic integration—closer macroeconomic policy coordination, the development of a common external tariff regime, and internal standards on health, safety, and financial issues—were not addressed by CEFTA. The failure to do so was unlikely to encourage outside investors to view the region as a single unified market instead of three (or four) submarkets. Finally, differing rates of inflation and different degrees of currency convertibility implied that exchange rate risk and profit repatriation concerns would also be important barriers to expanded intra-CEFTA trade.

Because of these initial problems, tangible gains from CEFTA were more likely to come in the long term. In the long run, however, the importance of CEFTA as a mechanism for promoting regional trade seemed likely to diminish, through integration with the EC and possible increased trade with the former Soviet republics. If and when the governments of the Russian Federation and Ukraine succeed in stabilizing their macroeconomies and introducing widely convertible currencies, Poland will become a gateway to markets of some 200 million consumers and rich mineral resources. In addition to Poland's proximity to these countries, the knowledge of these markets acquired by Polish firms (both state and privatized) over the past decades could be an extremely valuable commodity—if it can be retained.

CHAPTER V

The Lessons of the Polish Transition

QUESTIONS about the desirability and adequacy of the changes described in chapters 3 and 4 are heavily normative. As such, they both defy easy answers and motivate the search for other contexts in which to consider them. Comparisons with other postcommunist economies constitute one such context. In addition, Poland's pioneering role in this transition implies that the Polish experience may have lessons for other postcommunist economies, especially Russia and the other states of the former Soviet Union.[1] This chapter is devoted to these issues.

How Does Poland Compare?

Five criteria seem most appropriate in making international comparisons of the extent of systemic transformation: (1) macroeconomic stabilization; (2) the liberalization of the price system and commercial activity; (3) external liberalization, reorientation, and reintegration; (4) the development of new financial, regulatory, and legal mechanisms; and (5) privatization, in the sense of encouraging the growth of the private sector. Compared with other countries in the region, Poland scored well on all counts between 1990 and 1992. Although its inflation rates in late 1989 and early 1990 were the highest in the region after Yugoslavia, successes in bringing inflation under control and averting hyperinflation had, by 1993, made Poland one of the region's low inflation countries (a relative concept, to be sure). This success was also accompanied by extensive commercial and external liberalization, as symbolized by the relatively rapid price liberalization of 1990, and by the high degree of zloty convertibility established by mid-1991. While many of the postcommunist economies experienced similar (or worse) bouts of inflation and comparable declines in GDP during the initial years of their transition, it was instructive that Poland was the first economy to experience a sustained recovery from this decline.

To be sure, the dramatic growth in the budget deficit and the pathologies of the postcommunist banking and financial systems were major obstacles to

Poland's transition. However, it had become apparent by 1992 that Poland's banking and financial difficulties were not isolated events. Developments in Hungary, Russia, and elsewhere showed that problems of banking reform and interenterprise debt were present throughout the region (Whitlock 1992; Okolicsanyi 1992b), and the budgetary tensions Poland experienced beginning in mid-1991 subsequently became a feature common to the postcommunist economies (Bush 1992; Okolicsanyi 1992a). Indeed, as of early 1993 only the Czech Republic seemed to have escaped this "fiscal trap" (Kornai 1992).

Poland also fared comparatively well in terms of external economic reorientation. As Table 4.8 showed, the share of Poland's exports going to the former CMEA countries had fallen to 15.4 percent in 1992, while 57.9 percent went to the EC. The corresponding shares for Hungary were 19.4 and 49.8 percent, respectively, while for the Czech Republic[2] they were 43.5 and 36.4 percent, respectively ("Review of East European Foreign Trade Developments" 1993, 40, 50).[3] On the other hand, Hungary and the Czech Republic were more attractive than Poland as sites for foreign investment during this time. Poland's direct foreign investment of $21 per capita in 1991 was 50 percent of the Czechoslovak level and only 10 percent of the Hungarian level (Fletcher 1992), although these differences seem to have narrowed in 1992–1993. Finally, while the progress Poland made between 1990 and 1992 in restoring external balance and regaining external creditworthiness made an impressive contrast with the almost hopeless situation of the former Soviet republics, the Yugoslav successor states, and Bulgaria, Poland's external creditworthiness in early 1993 compared unfavorably with the status of the Czech Republic, Hungary, Slovakia, and perhaps even Romania.

In terms of privatization, at the end of 1992 Poland had the region's largest private sector (measured as the private share of GDP or employment), and the successes of Poland's liquidation and small privatization programs were widely acknowledged. Poland had clearly retained its "pioneer" status in these areas into 1993. However, the Hungarian and Czechoslovak approaches to the reprivatization question contrasted sharply with the lack of progress in Poland, and the confusion surrounding Poland's mass privatization program compared poorly with the more rapid progress made with mass privatization in the Czech Republic, Russia, Romania, and elsewhere.[4] As mentioned above, Poland proved to be a relatively unattractive site for foreign investment, compared both to Hungary and to other developing countries.

LESSONS OF THE POLISH EXPERIENCE

Compared to the other postcommunist economies, Poland was a pioneer in macroeconomic stabilization and adjustment, the expansion of the private sector, and domestic and external liberalization in the 1990–1992 period. What, then, were the more general lessons of the Polish transition? This is a difficult question to answer, since many factors significantly differentiated Poland from other countries in the former Soviet bloc. The most important of these were the following:

Ethnic homogeneity. In economic terms, the absence of secessionist movements or efforts to redefine the ethnic or geographic nature of the Polish state meant that Poland was not faced with questions concerning its national identity per se. The contrast with the problems of economic transformation in the post-Soviet ruble zone (Slay 1991b), economic relations among the Yugoslav successor states, or the economic difficulties of the "velvet divorce" in Czechoslovakia (Pehe 1993) could not be starker.

The relatively large size and vitality of Poland's private sector at the start of the transition.

The legacies of the economic and political reforms introduced during the communist period. In addition to discrediting Soviet-style socialism among the vast majority of the population, these reforms gave policymakers important insights into the problems of the transition and helped prepare Polish society for the downside of capitalism.

Poland's geographical proximity to the West and its historically Western orientation.

The relatively strong commitment of the postcommunist Polish political elite to political and economic transformation. While Poland's post-1989 politics have not been without their disappointments, elite conflicts have generally reflected personal ambition and disagreements over the correct strategy for effecting these transformations.

These differences go a long way toward explaining why the economic transition program in Russia during 1992 met with so many more difficulties than the Balcerowicz Plan in Poland in 1990–1991.[5] As Balcerowicz had done in January 1990, Yegor Gaidar, the Russian deputy prime minister in January 1992 liberalized most prices, deregulated the private sector, moved quickly to increase the extent of ruble convertibility, and attempted to introduce a macroeconomic stabilization program with the technical (and subsequently financial) assistance of the IMF. However, in contrast to

Poland, only a handful of state enterprises in Russia had any experience in dealing with Western firms and markets directly, and most of Russia's exports were narrowly concentrated in the natural-resources and energy sector. The absence of far-reaching economic reforms before 1990 meant that state enterprises were more accustomed to responding to administrative directives than to prices and financial indicators. It also meant that the private sector (lodged in the cooperative movement) was too small to exert a tangible macroeconomic impact on the economy. As a result, Russian enterprises responded less flexibly to the liberalized price and financial environment. Finally, in two respects the absence of a hard-currency fund to stabilize the ruble-dollar exchange rate magnified the difficulties faced by the Russian stabilization program. First, because the exchange rate could not be fixed it could not serve as a nominal anchor; this both added to inflation, since domestic price increases automatically produced new pressures for inflationary ruble devaluations, and placed additional burdens on other components of the stabilization program.[6] Second, the failure to stabilize the ruble-dollar exchange rate per force limited the extent to which ruble convertibility could be increased.

The small size of the private sector, the failure to significantly broaden ruble convertibility, and the inability to rapidly liberalize external economic relations prevented the introduction of import competition. Price liberalization therefore aggravated the monopoly problems inherited from the Soviet era without unleashing strong new competitive forces (Capelik 1992). The crumbling of the ruble zone added new elements of monetary and external instability (Hanson 1992). Politically, the Gaidar program in 1992 came under attack from many elements of the Russian political elite, resulting later in the year in changes in the government's policies and personnel at the behest of the military-industrial complex. These problems fed on one another, reducing the effectiveness of the stabilization program and preventing the realization of the critical mass attained by the Balcerowicz Plan in 1990. While much was accomplished in Russia in terms of liberalization and deregulation, progress in bringing inflation under control and restoring external balance was quite weak.

The Russian experience of 1992 was more or less typical of economic developments throughout the former Soviet bloc (outside of central Europe), in that the successes recorded in reducing inflation, liberalizing domestic prices and economic activity, and restoring external balance were generally modest. To be sure, there were important exceptions to this. For example, the introduction of national currencies in Estonia and Latvia during 1992–1993 produced significant reductions in inflation, improvements in external balance, and increases in convertibility (Girnius 1993). Also, the pace and extent of the privatization of small and medium-sized state enterprises in Russia during 1992 were in some respects more impressive than in Central Europe, not to mention the rest of the former USSR. Still, the many disadvantages (relative to Poland) with which these countries began their transitions—minuscule private sectors, state enterprises' lack of experience with market reforms or the international economy, collectivized agriculture, the monetary and financial tensions of belonging to the ruble and dinar zones—indicated that the relevance of the Polish experience to these countries was less than overwhelming.

Still, some general conclusions concerning the postcommunist transition may be drawn from the Polish experience, especially in the following areas: (1) macroeconomic stabilization and external adjustment, (2) privatization, (3) demonopolization, (4) industrial policy, and (5) labor relations.

Macroeconomic Stabilization and External Adjustment. The Polish experience during 1990–1991 illustrates the difficulties inherent in designing and implementing postcommunist macroeconomic stabilization programs. Differences between predicted and actual levels of inflation, production, and the budget deficit were substantial, while some of the protection built into the stabilization program, such as the $1 billion stabilization fund for the zloty, turned out to be of questionable utility. These differences provided political ammunition for opponents of the Balcerowicz Plan, especially during the election campaigns of 1990 and 1991.

With the passage of time, however, scholarly analysis has supplemented political rhetoric, so that by 1993 dispassionate scholarship on postcommunist stabilization programs pointed toward agreement on some important issues.

First, despite the populist criticisms of the Polish stabilization program's alleged "harshness," declines in Polish GDP between 1989 and 1992 were among the lowest in the region. As Table 5.1 shows, the smallest drops in GDP in Eastern Europe were recorded in Poland and Hungary; larger drops in output and incomes were measured elsewhere. And since consumption actually increased in Poland during 1991, these data imply that Polish living standards declined to a smaller extent than in other countries in the region. These data also indicate that, whatever mistakes may have been made in the stabilization program during the 1990–1992 period, they may have been less significant than the fact that a critical mass was attained in the areas of liberalization, privatization, external reorientation, and falling inflation rates.

TABLE 5.1
Decline in GDP in Eastern Europe, 1989–1992

	Approximate decline in GDP (percentages)
Poland	17
Hungary	17
Slovenia	20
Slovakia	23
Czech Republic	24
Bulgaria	28
Romania	32
Former Yugoslav Republics[a]	40–70

Source: "Slovenian Monthly Economic Indicator" 1993, 1.
[a] Slovenia not included.

Second, as Stanisław Gomulka pointed out, the "quality of macroeconomic control" can itself be understood as a choice variable in the stabilization process, to be traded off against the pace of structural adjustment (Gomulka 1992, 367–369). Thus, while the Polish stabilization program was essentially on target in 1990 (i.e., the "quality of macroeconomic control" was high), the large declines in real wages and the financial windfall that followed price liberalization meant that pressures on enterprises to restructure and adapt to the new environment were weak. By contrast, while the stabilization program encountered marked difficulties in 1991, as real wages rose and the zloty appreciated dramatically in real effective terms, the squeeze on state enterprises forced more rapid structural adjustment. This accelerated adjustment can be seen both in case studies on state enterprise behavior in 1991–1992 (Hume and Pinto 1993) and in the quickening of the pace of liquidation privatization after 1990.[7] Thus, if slippage in stabilization programs is accompanied by more rapid structural change, the benefits of the slippage may exceed the costs—especially if the resulting structural adjustment facilitates economic recovery, as occurred in Poland after February 1992.

Third, by 1993 a consensus was developing concerning the factors responsible for mistakes made in the design of stabilization programs (Gomulka 1992; Winiecki 1993). The initial windfall for state enterprises resulting from price liberalization (and, in the Polish case, from the depression in real wages and the sale of enterprise assets via liquidation privatization) produced large but temporary increases in enterprise profits, as occurred in Poland during the first half of 1990. In addition to reducing pressures for structural adjustment, higher profits produced marked but short-lived improvement in the state budget and in enterprise debt-servicing capabilities. Since the temporary nature of these stabilization triumphs were not foreseen at the time, excessively optimistic targets for the following year(s) were set. The ensuing failure to meet these targets (as occurred in Poland in 1991) was then portrayed as compromising the entire stabilization approach, whereas the real problem may have been the technical misestimation of this "windfall enterprise liquidity."

Fourth, while the successes of the Polish stabilization program in 1990 meant that the $1 billion stabilization fund did not have to be tapped to support the zloty, the argument that this fund went "unused" (and, by extension, was unnecessary) is somewhat misleading (Winiecki 1993, 114–115). To be sure, the stabilization fund was established to support the zloty at an exchange rate that instead undervalued the zloty during the first half of 1990, at least in terms of the merchandise trade balance. However, the creation of the stabilization fund had an unquantifiable but nonetheless visible psychological impact on Poland's nascent foreign-exchange market. This impact was probably instrumental in encouraging the transfer of the population's money holdings from dollars to zloty—a move that was crucial to the stabilization program's success.[8] Also, once obtained, the stabilization fund could subsequently be used to finance other aspects of the transition, such as the debt restructuring program. By contrast, the absence of a ruble stabilization fund in 1992 certainly contributed to the Gaidar government's inability to fix the ruble-dollar exchange rate at the start of the Russian transformation program, thus exacerbating inflationary pressures. Rather than being viewed as evidence of overshooting, then, the fact that the Polish stabilization fund did not have to be tapped to support the zloty can also be seen as confirmation of the validity of the stabilization program's basic design.

Finally, a central group of facts—that accurate predictions about the effects of fiscal policy changes on macroeconomic activity in developed capitalist countries are rare, that retreats from hyperinflation almost never occur without producing declines in output, and that virtually all other postcommunist economies experienced recessions similar to (or worse than) the Polish decline of 1990–1991—cannot be overemphasized. These factors argue for judging the Polish stabilization program of 1990–1992 less harshly than was common in Poland during 1991 and 1992.

Privatization. The Polish experience with privatization and with the development of the indigenous private sector since 1989 demonstrates the pitfalls of the former and the importance of the latter. It also shows the advantages of insider privatization via worker and/or manager buyouts over outsider privatization via public offer or mass privatization (Slay 1993b).

Although 2,478 state enterprises had "undergone" (begun) privatization by the end of 1992, only 668 had actually completed the privatization process and been removed from the register of state enterprises (*Prywatyzacja przedsiębiorstw państwowych* 1993, 21). This was a testimony to the lengthy delays and disappointments afflicting the privatization process. According to a former privatization minister, as many as 60 different central and local organs could block or impede the privatization process, as could powerful trade union and workers' council officials within firms. Instead, it was the rapid development of new private firms since 1989 (numbering 1.6 million in early 1993) that accounted for the bulk of the private sector. Thus, while many large state-owned industrial firms (the "dinosaurs") were rusting into oblivion, new private startups were popping up like mushrooms after a rain.

While this result may have been inevitable, it was not uniformly beneficial. Since the growth of new private firms exceeded the fiscal authorities' ability to tax them, this sort of privatization contributed to the postcommunist "fiscal trap." Because Poland's asset markets functioned quite imperfectly, the opportunity cost of the capital lost in rusting state enterprises may have been significant. Moreover, the effectiveness of this form of privatization hinged crucially on the relatively large size of the private sector in Poland at the start of the transition. In countries with smaller and less dynamic private sectors the costs of this approach to privatization would be much higher. In any case, since viable methods of transferring genuine ownership and control of large state enterprises to private actors on a broad front did not emerge anywhere in the postcommunist world between 1990 and 1992, there may have been little alternative to privatization via the expansion of the indigenous private sector.

Within the Polish state sector, insider privatization was more effective by far than outsider privatization. Of the 668 state enterprises that had completed privatization by the end of 1992, 617 of these (more than 92 percent) went via liquidation privatization (ibid.). In practice, this meant that these enterprises' physical assets were transferred to private firms in which a controlling packet of shares was usually held by the managers and/or the workers. (Most frequently, the transfer did not occur through sale, but instead took the form of a long-term lease with an option to buy.) Although an enterprise privatized in this manner formally remained in state hands—a major disadvantage, to be sure—the fact that its assets were transferred to a private firm with a small group of well-defined owners contrasted favorably with the confusion of ownership issues surrounding the mass privatization program and the fragmentation of ownership resulting from privatization via public offer.

In retrospect, it seems that although the advocates of spontaneous privatization (which empropertied state enterprise managers) and worker ownership may have lost the political battles in 1989 and 1990, the inevitability of these approaches was confirmed in 1991 and 1992 by the successes of the liquidation privatization program in practice. More generally, the Polish experience indicated that the expansion of private economic activity is best facilitated by the initial development of the indigenous private sector followed by insider privatization, rather by outsider privatization via public offers and mass privatization. On the other hand, if a majority of the "big nine" commercial banks had been sold via public offer (perhaps with controlling share packets going to institutional investors and/or foreign banks) in 1990, before the collapse of their balance sheets, the problems facing the debt restructuring program after 1992 might have been reduced considerably.

Demonopolization. According to some observers, the large, monopolistic firms typical of Soviet-style socialism posed two serious problems for the transition. First, because the behavior of privatized monopolies was unlikely to be less rapacious than the behavior of state monopolies, structural deconcentration activities should precede the privatization of large enterprises. Although they would slow the pace of privatization and structural adjustment, they would be a necessary first step (Grosfeld 1990; Schaffer 1990; van Brabant 1991). Second, once the transition began, monopolistic firms were alleged to reduce supply and increase prices in response to reductions in demand, thereby generating cost-push inflationary pressures (Capelik 1992; Modzelewski 1992).

The Polish experience of 1990–1992 shows that fears of the monopoly threat were exaggerated. Despite the highly concentrated industrial structures in place at the start of the transition, the rapid growth of new private firms, the advent of import competition, and the introduction of hard budget constraints for state enterprises produced widespread "spontaneous demonopolization" within Polish industry. As Table 4.3 showed, within the state sector alone the number of industrial firms increased by 42 percent between 1987 and 1991 (despite the completed privatization of some 550 firms during that time). This trend was also seen in falling concentration ratios for most industrial branches. Combined with entry by private firms (the numbers of which increased by 60 percent in industry between 1988 and 1991), these demonopolizing trends effectively deconcentrated Poland's industrial structures. This occurred largely in the absence of large-scale administrative deconcentration activities, since from 1990 to 1992 the Antimonopoly Office concentrated on merger control, anti-collusion policies, and (to a limited extent) supervision of the privatization of large state enterprises.

All of this indicated that the market power of large state enterprises proved to be much weaker than feared and that privatization was a prerequisite to demonopolization, not the other way around.[9] Likewise, fears of large enterprises generating cost-push inflationary pressures raised questions about the extent of accommodating macroeconomic policies—questions that could not be easily dismissed, in light of the post-1990 expansion of Poland's budget deficit.[10] The lesson of the Polish experience was that if privatization, liberalization, and convertibility can be effectively introduced, then significant demonopolization will result endogenously; it does not have to be a policy priority. On the other hand, important weaknesses in Polish competition policy were apparent during the 1990–1992 period, especially in such areas as the regulation of natural monopoly and preventing reductions in market competition in key sectors in order to attract direct foreign investment to those sectors (e.g., automobiles).

Industrial Policy. The debate on the nature and role of industrial policy in Poland's postcommunist transition has been highly charged, not only because of the ideological volatility of the subject but because the successes of the initially liberal and then more *dirigiste* approaches employed during 1990–1992 were mixed, at best (Slay 1993c). Poland's experience in this area teaches that both the liberals and the interventionists are simultaneously correct and incorrect, and that pragmatism is to be valued above all else. The liberal approach is unquestionably correct in postulating that a clean break must be made with the paternalism of the old system and that demands for central intervention are frequently window dressing for special-interest pleading. Nevertheless, opponents of the liberal "the market is our industrial policy" view are likewise correct in pointing out that market failures often require intervention even in developed market economies and that modern capitalism is based on the sophisticated and subtle cooperation between the private and public sectors.

The painful truth is that surmounting the numerous challenges facing the governments conducting the postcommunist transformation will certainly require such cooperation, but for a variety of financial, technical, and political reasons it is unlikely to be forthcoming. Postcommunist governments have neither the financial nor the human resources to salvage many of the enterprises inherited from the old system; furthermore, given the economic distortions contained therein, it is not clear why they should want to try. However, this does not change the fact that effecting a successful transition requires pragmatic government action in numerous areas. These include developing modern export promoting mechanisms, purging the financial and social-welfare systems of the legacies of the old regime, and supervising the rationalization of those branches of state industry and agriculture that *can* survive, once a clearer picture of their future emerges.[11] Fortunately, both financial and technical assistance is often available from Western and international organizations to facilitate these changes—although the adequacy of that assistance may be questioned.

This dilemma was illustrated by the Polish debt restructuring program. By 1992, policymakers had come to realize that there was no alternative to recapitalizing the state-owned commercial banks, since failure to do so could result in the collapse of the financial system. Such an operation would inevitably tax the country's financial, human, and organizational resources, since Poland possessed neither the funds, the know-how, nor the vulture capital markets required to make it work. And because the debt restructuring program was initially perceived by many in the state sector as "debt forgiveness" and as a weakening of the tight enterprise budget constraint, it exacerbated controversies about relations between the center and the enterprise during the transition. Nonetheless, policymakers during 1991 and 1992 were able to assemble a pragmatic program that addressed the threat to Poland's financial system while simultaneously respecting the country's financial constraints and avoiding a relapse into central paternalism. Although almost $1 billion in debt recapitalization was involved, the incentives for individual debtors and creditors were generally structured so as to minimize the problems of paternalism, credibility, and moral hazard implicit in such an operation. As such, the program was able to attract technical and financial support from Western and international agencies. This type of pragmatic, nonideological approach to solving the industrial-policy problems of the transition often represents the best, if not the only, method of dealing with these issues.

Labor Relations. The Suchocka government of 1992–1993, which in most economic policy areas attempted to return to the "orthodoxy" of 1990–1991, embarked on an unprecedented experiment in labor relations. Indeed, the emphasis on the "social pact" with state enterprise employees was the central microeconomic theme of the Suchocka government, to which many other policy initiatives (in privatization, industrial policy, debt restructuring, etc.) were formally subordinated. As such, it represented an attempt at combining pragmatic liberalism with what might be called participatory syndicalism.

Precisely because the social pact approach subordinated so many aspects of the transition to labor relations, it was difficult to be optimistic about its economic effects. Indeed, the pact was justified by the Suchocka government primarily on political grounds, as the cost of encouraging "responsible" trade union behavior. From a political standpoint, however, the corporatist element of the social pact also had major implications for Polish political development, not all of which were robustly consistent with the transition to democracy. Ironically, representatives of the very trade unions that stood to benefit from the social pact, had it been implemented, introduced the parliamentary motion of no confidence that led to the Suchocka government's downfall in May 1993. The government's fall, in turn, placed the future of the pact in doubt. The lesson of this experience was that in addition to being a doubtful economic proposition, the social pact as a political instrument for managing labor relations had eaten its own tail.

As of late 1993, it was impossible to ascertain whether the social pact represented a temporary tilt toward syndicalism or a reassertion of the fundamental role of working-class institutions in Polish political economy. History, and the results of the September 1993 parliamentary elections, would seem to argue for the latter, since parties to the left of center formed the resulting government. Continuing the social pact approach could have a fundamental impact on the microeconomics of the Polish transition. And because of Poland's pioneer status, this example could be significant for other countries in the region with relatively strong working-class movements, such as Russia. If the social pact were to prove an effective mechanism for defusing factory tensions and modernizing Poland's conflict-ridden labor relations system, its benefits could dwarf its costs.

In sum, the Polish experience should be taken as a hopeful one for reformers in other postcommunist economies. It shows that despite the (inevitable) mistakes made during transition, a heavily-indebted postcommunist economy can retreat from the brink of hyperinflation, be reoriented away from trade with its former political and economic allies, effect dramatic increases in the private share of economic activity, and experience the beginnings of recovery within two or three years. In this context, Poland's transition from socialism to capitalism looked quite successful in mid-1993. Whether the "Polish crisis" had finally ended remained to be seen.

Notes

Introduction

1. Until 1990, national income produced (*dochód narodowy wytworzony*) was the most common measure of aggregate economic activity used in Poland. It measures the value added (expressed in price terms) produced in the "material sphere" economy during a calendar year. National income produced differs from gross domestic product chiefly in that national income produced 1) is measured net of depreciation, and 2) excludes much of the service sector. Unless otherwise stated, all statistics are taken (or derived) from the official Polish statistical yearbooks.

2. Here, gross investment is calculated from national income used (*dochód narodowy podzielony*)—national income produced less net exports.

3. The decollectivization of agriculture in 1957 can be regarded as a successful reform and thus as an exception to this pattern.

Chapter 1

1. For a structural-institutional explanation of the collapse of Soviet-style socialism in Poland, see Kamiński 1991a.

2. While nationalities as understood today did not exist in medieval Europe, important national groupings in the Commonwealth included Germans, Ukrainians, Belarussians and Ruthenians, in addition to Poles and Lithuanians. Important religious denominations included the Ukrainian Uniate and Orthodox churches, the Russian Orthodox Church, various Protestant sects, and Judaism, as well as the dominant Roman Catholic Church.

3. The literature on nationalism in Eastern Europe and its attendant controversies is too extensive to allow a thorough discussion here. Suffice it to say that the author's conception of nationalism in the Polish context is consistent with that of Motyl (1992).

4. In 1915, for example, Imperial Russia "relocated" from Poland to Russia 150 factories, 70,000 industrial workers, and financial assets valued at more than 3.25 billion French francs (in gold). Restitution of these assets was prevented by the Bolshevik Revolution of 1917 (Małecka 1989, 47, 55).

5. Data from the 1921 census are neither complete nor noncontroversial. Population data from Upper Silesia and the *Wileńszczyzna* (the area around what is now Vilnius, the capital of Lithuania, which, until 1939, was predominantly Polish) were not included. Of course, issues concerning the definition of ethnicity and nationality are inevitably controversial, and were certainly so in the 1921 census (Tomaszewski 1985, 25–37). Data from 1921 on economic development are hardly beyond reproach either.

6. The "Tariff War," which followed the expiration of the most-favored-nation status for Polish exports to Germany (forced on the Weimar Republic by the Treaty of Versailles), represented German use of economic warfare to extract political and geographic concessions from Poland. In the Soviet case, the USSR's domestic market, toward which many firms in eastern Poland had been oriented before 1914, was now closed, and the USSR was unwilling to discuss claims for restitution of, or compensation for, Polish assets seized during the First World War.

7. Gross industrial production increased by 19.4 percent from 1922 to 1929; production of coal, iron ore, and steel during this time grew by 28.7, 46.2, and 22.4 percent, respectively (Davies 1984, 2:417).

8. The Polish state in 1939 owned 100 percent of the armaments and commercial aviation industries, 80–95 percent of the chemical, railroad, and merchant marine sectors, 50 percent of nonferrous metallurgy, and 40 percent of ferrous metallurgy (Taylor 1952, 91–92).

9. Gross industrial production increased by 41 percent from 1935 to 1938, with major increases in the production of steel and iron ore. Gross agricultural production increased by 19 percent from 1932 to 1938, with most of this growth coming after 1936 (Roszkowski 1989, 115; Drożdowski 1963, 11–13).

10. According to one estimate, the share of the labor force devoted to agriculture was reduced only slightly, from 65 to 61 percent, from 1921 to 1938 (Roszkowski 1989, 113).

11. According to Western recalculations, Soviet real GNP (measured in 1937 prices) grew at an average annual rate of 5.5 percent from 1928 to 1937, with industrial production growing at a much more rapid pace (Gregory and Stuart 1986, 329). Real GNP in Nazi Germany (in 1928 prices) grew by an average annual rate of nearly 12 percent from 1933 to 1938, and industrial production grew by an average annual rate of more than 14 percent (Overy 1982, 29).

12. By 1945–1946 agricultural production had declined by two thirds from its 1934–1938 levels; the caloric intake of the average Polish family in 1943 was 42 percent of the average American family's and 48 percent of the average British family's (Taylor 1952, 163, 173–174). On the other hand, the war's impact on Polish industry is more ambiguous, since a share of German industry was relocated into Polish territory to escape Allied air bombardment. According to one estimate, Polish industrial production under Nazi direction from 1941 to 1943 may have actually exceeded the 1938 level (Davies 1984, 2:454).

13. The forced resettlement of Poland's Ukrainian and Ruthenian populations from their homelands in southeastern Poland to the northern and western lands taken from Germany constituted a notable exception. Still, these forced migrations were not directly linked to collectivization and the imposition of Stalinism, and may have had more to do with the darker side of Polish nationalism.

14. Official statistics from People's Poland, especially during the 1950s, need to be viewed with a healthy skepticism. In addition to questions of outright falsification, the use of nonequilibrium prices and incentives for enterprises to exaggerate

reported production, use inputs wastefully, and reduce product quality in order to fulfill output plans make data produced under the old regime difficult to interpret. Official statistics in this period are probably best understood as depicting general trends in economic development rather than as accurate descriptions of economic activity.

15. These are official data taken from *Rocznik Statystyczny 1989*, XXXII. National income figures are in 1977 prices.

16. The exception here would be agriculture, which more than doubled its gross output from 1947 to 1950 despite massive labor outmigration and capital underinvestment. The fact that much of this labor was underemployed in agriculture, as well as the acquisition of the relatively good soils and developed agrarian culture in the formerly German lands, presumably account for a large share of this increase.

17. While there seemed to be a market-socialist consensus on many issues among most members of the Council, it should be noted that Stefan Kurowski represented on the Council what has been called a "christian liberal" viewpoint and did call for replacing the plan with the market. For more on the Economic Council's proposals, see Montias 1962, chapters 9–10.

18. For more on reform cycles in Poland and Hungary, see Bunce 1980, Iwanowska 1982, Jermakowicz 1988, Jermakowicz and Krawczyk 1985, Mieczkowski 1978, Mizsei 1987, Rychard 1980, Slay 1989 (Chapter 6), and Zielinski 1978.

19. Perceptions of reform in Poland by other members of the Soviet bloc were quite complicated and could not be interpreted merely as approbation of the PZPR's use of reform to stabilize political crises. Dislike of deviations from socialist unity and fears about the spread of "dangerous" reform ideas throughout the Soviet bloc were obviously strong; however, an analysis of reform cycles in Poland suggests that the antireform influence of "fraternal" socialist governments was most effectively exercised *after* the promise of reform had helped stabilize political crises, not before.

20. For more on reforms during the 1960s, see Feiwel 1971, vol. 2, and Zielinski 1973.

21. For more on the WOG reform, see Iwanowska 1982, Rychard 1990, Wanless 1980, and Woodall 1982.

Chapter II

1. The existence, extent, and implications of Poland's "inflationary overhang" (*nawis inflacyjny*) of forced savings became the subject of spirited debate during the 1980s. Identified originally in a 1981 article (Herer and Sadowski 1981) as a major disequilibrating force within the Polish economy, the overhang was estimated at 500 billion zloty in 1984 (G. W. Kołodko 1984). If accurate, this sum would have comprised almost 60 percent of the zloty in circulation (*obieg pieniężny*) in that year (*Rocznik Statystyczny* 1985, XXXVI), implying that the majority of zloty held by

Polish households and enterprises represented claims on goods and services that were unavailable. Topiński (1986), on the other hand, argued that the overhang was problematic in conceptual, measurement and policy terms. Topiński argued that many of the "hot" zloty were in fact servicing Poland's large second economy, where equilibrium prices absorbed much of the population's excess purchasing power. In any case, the overhang was certainly perceived as threatening by economists and policymakers during the 1980s.

2. The lack of institutional guarantees differentiated the official reform blueprint from the other, more radical, proposals developed at that time. The reform plan developed by Balcerowicz's group, for example, proposed that compromises such as the "temporary" retention of central supply rationing be subjected to yearly approval by the Sejm, and not just in general terms but on an item-by-item basis. The proposal drafted by economists at Warsaw University's Economics Department proposed fixed terms of service for high party and state officials (Krawczyk 1981).

3. Fear of unemployment led the Polish authorities in 1981 to introduce a number of measures that reduced the work force; however, this exacerbated the labor shortage that occurred after the resumption of economic growth in the second half of 1982.

4. This was the Council of Ministers' decree number 243, which delayed the reform's "full" implementation until 1983.

5. According to one source, real wages fell 26 percent during the first half of 1982 alone (Aaslund 1985, 114). According to official Polish statistics, consumer prices increased from 1982 to 1987 at yearly rates of 104.5, 21.4, 14.8, 15.0, 17.5, and 25.3 percent; money wages during those years rose by 46.2, 23.5, 29.4, 19.9, 22.6, and 21.9 percent (*Rocznik Statystyczny* 1987, 167, 413; *Rocznik Statystyczny* 1988, 156, 397). From a political standpoint, these increases in nominal wages represent an attempt by the PZPR to "buy off" working-class dissent, especially in the aftermath of martial law and the government's subsequent decision to recreate the "official" trade unions, the OPZZ.

6. This was Council of Ministers' decree number 278.

7. A smaller consortium, absorbing about one-third of the firms in the steel industry, was created instead.

8. In early 1986, for example, exporters were experiencing delays of up to 12 months in obtaining permission to use their "own" export receipts.

9. The ministries of Mining and Energy, Metallurgy and Machine Tools, and Chemicals and Light Industry were combined into a single Ministry of Industry, and the Supply Office and Ministry of Domestic Trade were combined into a single Ministry of the Domestic Market. The Ministry of Foreign Trade was combined with the Council of Ministers' Committee on International Economic Cooperation to form the Ministry of International Economic Cooperation. The Ministry of Construction and Spatial Affairs, as well as the Ministry of Agriculture, Foodstuffs, and Forestry, remained essentially unchanged, while the supervision of a significant number of state enterprises was transferred from the central to the local authorities.

10. In this regard, Milanovic's conclusion that "the exchange rate issue was left practically untackled, the trade regime was unchanged. . ." during the second stage is somewhat misleading (Milanovic 1992, 515).

11. Although legislation in 1981 and 1982 created the legal foundations for an interenterprise bond market, enterprise bond financing failed to develop during the 1980s. Reasons for this include pervasive inflationary conditions, reducing incentives to locate idle funds in fixed interest-bearing certificates; the presence of numerous regulations issued by the Ministry of Finance (and other central organs) restricting the types of bond emissions as well as the types of firms able to purchase them; and paper shortages that increased the difficulties of printing and issuing bonds.

12. According to Staniszkis, these traps included the "creation of an artificial reality, based upon a totalitarian utopia that included a myth of the unity of the interests of society and the state and the ideas of supercentralization in order to mobilize all resources," and the tendency toward "the attrition of the system's reserves" (Staniszkis 1984, 31).

13. The influence of workers' councils during the 1980s should not be exaggerated. Estimates of the number of councils functioning in a pro forma manner ran as high as 80 to 90 percent of the total in 1987 (Dryll 1987; Holland 1987, 136). Until late 1987, fully developed self-management organs were excluded from more than 20 percent of state enterprises on legal grounds; the number of firms on the list of "enterprises of essential importance for the national economy," in which the director was appointed by the central authorities without the councils' approval, expanded from 200 in 1981 to 1,372 out of 6,372 in 1984 (Holland 1987, 136; Kasten 1986, 67–101; Pełnomocnik rządu ds. 1985, 6–7). Before 1988 attempts at forming grass-roots confederations of workers' councils were frowned on and in some cases forcibly broken up by the authorities.

14. As one observer put it, Solidarity in the underground had become "a 'thousand-headed monster'—fracturing naturally into a multitude of either conspiratorial groupings or loose associations of devoted individuals. . . . Although fractured and uncoordinated, Solidarity was indestructible: the very looseness of its structures prevented the PZPR from developing an effective offensive against it" (Zubek 1991b, 357).

15. For more on Solidarity during the 1980s, see Holzer and Leski 1990. For more on the politics of the Roundtable Agreements, see Zubek 1991b, and Kamiński 1991b.

16. One of the more interesting questions raised by the Roundtable talks is the viability of a "neocorporatist" Polish political system in which PZPR hegemony would be supplemented by Solidarity as a "loyal opposition." The answer to this question hinges in part on the degree to which Solidarity in 1989 and 1990 was directed by intellectuals descended from KOR instead of being a strictly grass-roots working-class organization. For more on this, see Ost 1990 and Laba 1991.

17. The refusal by some of Solidarity's more radical elements to accept Wałęsa's

compromise strategy was mirrored on the other side by a near revolt of the PZPR rank and file, who accused Jaruzelski and Rakowski of "selling out socialism."

18. The stated desire of Solidarity's leadership that Solidarity's role in parliament be restricted to that of a limited opposition was apparently quite genuine and was maintained until the late summer of 1989.

19. This account of the behind-the-scenes political maneuvering prior to Mazowiecki's selection comes primarily from Echikson 1989 and Weschler 1989.

20. The issue of whether the cooperative sector should be included with the state sector is not addressed here. Prior to the 1990 data year, official Polish statistics included both cooperative and state enterprises in the "socialized sector" (*sektor uspołeczniony*). Also, in contrast to Hungary and the USSR during the *perestroika* period, most of the cooperatives in Poland functioned more like state enterprises than private firms. In any case, this is an important issue: in 1985 approximately 40 percent of the Polish population belonged to at least one cooperative and cooperatives comprised at least 75 percent of the productive capacity in such sectors as retail trade, restaurants, and housing construction (Chajęcki 1985, 3–4).

21. Suspicion is raised, for example, by the fact that official data on the shares of the state, cooperative, and private sectors' contribution to national income, industrial production, and other indicators of aggregate economic activity in Poland rarely sum to 100 percent, and the deviations from 100 percent (up to 0.8 percent) are presumably too great to be attributed to rounding off.

22. Economic working groups were groups of state enterprise workers who contracted with management to perform certain tasks that would not be profitable during the regular workday. Through this arrangement workers received additional income (not subjected to normal wage taxation), while management gained increased flexibility and output.

23. The 1934 Commercial Code, which was never formally annulled by the PZPR, also served as the legal basis for creating *spółki*.

24. By way of comparison, in 1981 meat, gasoline, cigarettes, vodka, sugar, cheese, rice, butter, and many other consumer goods were also rationed.

25. Under the old system, non-equilibrium prices, shortages, and central pressures on enterprises to exaggerate increases in output and underreport price increases contributed to "hidden inflation" by giving firms incentives to repackage old products to sell as "new" products at higher prices. Statistically, such repackaging was measured as increased production rather than as inflation.

26. The degree to which Polish labor productivity is affected by the business cycle is seen in the fact that in 1981 and 1982, labor productivity fell by 11.8 and 2.4 percent (*Rocznik Statystyczny* 1985, 77).

27. Western economic sanctions against Poland were not without a silver lining, as they allowed Poland to suspend debt-servicing payments to Western governments during martial law and its aftermath.

28. The water-quality statistics for 1987 are the most favorable of the various

possible water-quality indicators. They reflect measurements of emissions collected during periods other than those of maximum production and pollution (*okresy pozakampanijne*). Measurements of pollution gathered during these peak periods (*okresy kampanijne*) show that in 1964–1967 the share of "highest quality" rivers was 31.6 percent and that of "excessively polluted" rivers 28.2 percent. By 1987 the "highest quality" share had fallen to 4.7 percent, while the "excessively polluted" share had risen to 41.7 percent. Moreover, the above data reflect *chemical* measurements of water quality. If *biological* measurements are taken, the share of "highest quality" rivers in 1987 falls to 0.0 percent (both during and after periods of peak pollution), while the share of "excessively polluted" rivers in 1987 rises to 64.7 and 65.2 percent for nonpeak and peak pollution periods, respectively (*Ochrona Środowiska* 1989, 56).

29. Eberstadt reports that the share of Polish "public consumption funds allocated to free public health and physical education" declined from 26.9 to 21.7 percent between 1975 and 1985 (Eberstadt 1989, 118).

30. According to Eberstadt, Polish life expectancy at birth declined by 0.6 years during this time. For Polish men, life expectancy declined by 1.3 years during the same period (Eberstadt 1989, 110). The official statistics tell a similar, if less stark, story.

31. As shown in the chart below, Polish per-capita consumption of both alcohol and cigarettes in the 1980s was among the highest in Europe. It is noteworthy that of the countries in which distilled spirits account for at least one-third of total alcohol consumption, Poland in 1980 had the highest level of per-capita alcohol consumption (Eberstadt 1989, 117).

	Estimated per capita cigarette consumption[a]	*Estimated per capita alcohol consumption*[b]
Poland	3,438	5.9
Soviet Union	—	6.8
Hungary	3,160	4.3
Yugoslavia	3,155	—
East Germany	2,350	4.3
Czechoslovakia	2,295	3.5
Bulgaria	2,225	2.0
Western Europe[c]	2,239	2.2

[a]Preliminary data for 1987.

[b]Measured in liters of pure alcohol consumed in 1980.

[c]Unweighted averages. Cigarette data are for France, West Germany, Greece, Italy, Norway, and the United Kingdom. Alcohol data are for the nine NATO countries.

32. National income produced registered a 0.2 percent decline in 1989; GDP increased by 0.2 percent (*Rocznik Statystyczny* 1991, 117, 127).

Chapter III

1. The significance of these issues is hardly limited to Poland, of course; their relevance and implications have been discussed in terms of all the postcommunist economies. While a voluminous literature has appeared on these questions since 1989, for an overview see Blommestein and Marrese 1991, Campbell 1991, Killick and Stevens 1991, Kornai 1990, van Brabant 1990, Wade 1992, Williamson 1991, and Winiecki 1993.

2. The plan was first made public, in the form of a general outline of goals and strategies, and discussed in the Polish press, in October 1989 (see *Rzeczpospolita*, October 12, 1989).

3. An alternate liberal program was prepared in late 1989 and early 1990 by a different group of Solidarity economists, including Janusz Beksiak, Jan Winiecki, and Tomasz Gruszecki. Among other things, this program contrasted with Balcerowicz's in its greater emphasis on rapid privatization, the absence of wage controls, and the retention of limited controls on food prices (Beksiak et al. 1989).

4. A 0.2 coefficient meant that firms could raise wages by only 20 zloty for every 100-zloty increase in the general price level. Larger wage increases were subject to prohibitive taxation.

5. The official exchange rate was set at 9,500 zloty per dollar on January 1, 1990, following a series of devaluations from 1,775 zloty per dollar in October to 5,200 zloty per dollar in December 1989 (Milanovic 1992, 521).

6. These and subsequent references are to nominal, rather than effective, tariff rates.

7. I am passing over here the numerous populist and demagogic political attacks made on Balcerowicz and, by extension, the Mazowiecki and Bielecki governments in general, since Balcerowicz served as a lightening rod for criticism of these governments' economic policies.

8. The National Bank of Poland reduced its base monthly lending rate for commercial banks from 4.0 to 2.5 percent and shifted from monthly to annual interest compounding in the summer of 1990. Wage taxation became more lenient during the second half of 1990: in addition to raising the *popiwek* coefficients, the number of firms obtaining exceptions to (or exclusions from) these taxes began a steady increase (Winiecki 1992, 192).

9. After falling to under 2 percent in August 1990, consumer prices increased 38 percent from September 1990 to January 1991. The NBP responded by increasing the base (annual) interest rate to 43 percent (from 34 percent) in October 1990, to 55 percent in November, and to 72 percent in January 1991 (Winiecki 1992, 193, 196).

10. On the other hand, other observers have claimed that the specific methodology adopted by the Central Statistical Office understated the decline in GDP in 1990–1991 (Misiak 1992; Felbur 1992). According to this view, the GDP deflators chosen during these years were excessively low, while data on changes in the struc-

ture of production and transportation services imply larger declines in production than those depicted in the official statistics.

11. Poland actually concluded two agreements with the IMF in 1990 and 1991. The first, a standby agreement, was in effect from February 1990 through March 1991.

12. Funds in enterprise bank accounts doubled in real terms between December 1989 and November 1990 (Winiecki 1992, 198).

13. The poor quality of many state enterprise managers, as well as conflicts between managers, workers' councils, and trade union officials, also weakened the stabilization program's microeconomic impact.

14. A slight upturn in industrial production was, in fact, recorded from September to November 1991 (*Eastern Europe* 1992, 14).

15. At the end of 1990, the degree of decapitalization of Polish industrial "machines, technical equipment, and tools" was listed as 72.5 percent (*Rocznik Statystyczny* 1991, 258).

16. Poland ended 1991 with a current-account surplus of $130 million in clearing, and a transferable ruble deficit of 25 million rubles (Telma 1992, 27–28).

17. According to various arguments, the absence of a "real" owner in the state sector made the *popiwek* necessary to forestall "excessive" wage demands, while the *dywidenda* ensured that returns to capital in the state sector would accrue to the state budget instead of being wasted. On the other hand, these tax schemes contained microeconomic distortions of their own: the *popiwek* discriminated against firms with above-average rates of labor productivity (*ceteris paribus*), while the *dywidenda* deterred investment by penalizing firms with the newest, most highly valued capital stock.

18. According to PlanEcon, the zloty appreciated against the dollar by "a staggering 136 percent in real effective terms" between January 1990 and April 1991. The zloty's real effective appreciation between January 1990 and April 1992 was 128 percent, despite the two devaluations and the adoption of the crawling peg regime in October 1991 ("East European Currency Exchange Rates" 1992, 1–2).

19. Import prices on the whole increased by 30.2 percent in 1991, and Poland's terms of trade for that year registered an 8.8 percent decline (*Rocznik Statystyczny: Handel Zagraniczny* 1992, 5).

20. Beginning in 1990, the Polish statistical authorities at least attempted to include private activities in the official data for 1990–1991. (Most other postcommunist economies did not do this.) According to official statistics, the private share of Polish import and export activity at the end of 1991 had grown to 46.1 and 19.8 percent, respectively (up from 14.4 and 4.9 percent, respectively, at the end of 1990).

21. In current prices, the shares of Polish imports to, and exports from, the former USSR were 14.1 and 11.0 percent, respectively in 1991 (*Rocznik Statystyczny: Handel Zagraniczny* 1992, 2).

22. For more on privatization in Poland, see Poznański 1992; Sachs and Lipton 1990a; and Slay 1992b.

23. While the official statistics are notorious for underreporting private activities, in at least two respects they also exaggerate the extent of the private sector. First, a new statistical methodology was adopted in 1990, according to which the activities of cooperatives, foundations, and other socioeconomic organizations (such as labor unions) are listed in the private sector. Second, activities linked to state enterprises and properties leased to private actors are also included in the private sector. In addition to producing a discontinuity in the post-1989 official data on the size of the private (and state) sectors, these conventions also raise questions about what is, and what is not, private enterprise in Poland.

24. The new ministry was preceded by the Office of the Plenipotentiary for Ownership Transformation, which was established in Balcerowicz's Finance Ministry in October 1989.

25. "Managerial contracts" operated according to this logic, with the exception that managers submitted bids to restructure firms not immediately slated for privatization (subordinated usually to the Ministry of Industry and Trade). Managers in this case faced a less restrictive regulatory environment and, since there was no prospect of a capital gain at the end of the restructuring process, they did not have to put up as much collateral.

26. Of the 668 state enterprises completely privatized during this period, 617 were privatized via liquidation. Of the 2,478 firms "undergoing privatization" (*objęte procesem prywatyzacji*) during this time, 1,459 (about 60 percent) were undergoing liquidation privatization (*Prywatyzacja przedsiębiorstw państwowych* 1993, 21).

27. In the spirit of the traditional *liberum defaecatio*—the right to vilify one's rivals—some parliamentary opponents of the Balcerowicz Plan claimed that this decimation had been intentional, as part of a plan by the IMF and Western governments to destroy the Polish economy.

28. Regulations issued on December 7, 1991 restricting private firms' rights to produce, import, and sell alcoholic beverages, nonferrous metals, and intellectual property constituted a partial exception (Niezgódka-Medvoda 1992). A system of concessions for the private import of spirits, tobacco, and fuels came into effect on March 31, 1992 ("Obowiązują koncesje" 1992). This system subsequently proved to be quite unwieldy and controversial, and almost led to the removal of the Olszewski government's minister for external economic relations, Adam Glapinski.

29. In an interview with *Gazeta Wyborcza* on July 10, 1992, Suchocka praised Balcerowicz, saying that "eventually everyone will give him credit for enacting a revolution."

30. While industrial production originating in the public sector declined by 4.8 percent in 1992, private sector industrial production increased by 32.2 percent (*Statystyka Polski* 1993b, v).

31. Nominal household income declined some 3 percent during the first quarter of 1993 (*Statystyka Polski* 1993a, II).

32. On the other hand, it can be argued that the intellectuals' unwillingness to secure some sort of compromise with Wałęsa demonstrated their own political ambition and shortsightedness.

33. By abandoning the PZPR and voting to install Mazowiecki's government in August 1989, the PSL had played a crucial role in the collapse of the old political system.

34. Numbers of MPs in the different parties later changed slightly, due to inter-party defections and electoral challenges.

35. This is roughly triple the levels in developed Western countries ("Żyjemy coraz krócej" 1991). Infant mortality in rural regions actually increased in 1990 from 15.8 deaths per thousand live births to 16.2 (*Ochrona Środowiska* 1991, 14).

36. Despite the large declines in real incomes in 1990, the quantity of cigarettes sold in 1990 increased by 9.4 percent (*Rocznik Statystyczny* 1991, 395).

37. For example, the quantity of particulate (*pyłowy*) and gaseous (*gazowy*) wastes emitted in 1990 declined by some 354,000 and 945,000 tons, respectively (*Ochrona Środowiska* 1991, 17).

38. One survey conducted by Warsaw's Center for Public Opinion Research in mid-July 1992 asked the question, "Do any organizations, associations, or unions currently existing in Poland represent your interests?" Of those who responded, 53 percent answered no and only 26 percent answered yes ("CBOS" 1992).

39. Fines and electronic identification cards had to be introduced to increase attendance at parliamentary sessions, in order to guarantee the quorum necessary to conduct state business.

40. At the time of the dissolution of that parliament in May 1993, some 5 percent of the deputies were under investigation for various crimes. One senator was immediately arrested and charged with embezzling $3 million (Vinton 1993a, 10–11).

41. Instead of indicating a complete reversal of public attitudes, these changes may have represented the rise of one set of deeply held negative attitudes toward capitalism alongside another set of deeply held positive attitudes. Sociological research indicates that throughout the 1980s Poles held quite inconsistent attitudes toward capitalism. For example, poll respondents had no difficulty in simultaneously agreeing with the statements that "inefficient workers should be fired" and that the state should be concerned with "ensuring work for all those wanting to work" (Morawski 1992, 287).

Chapter IV

1. While private firms in 1990 accounted for 98.5 percent of the production units (*przedsiębiorstwa i zakłady przemysłowe*) in the engineering sector, 99.5 percent of those in light industry, and 97.3 percent of those in food processing, they accounted for less than 0.01 percent of the production units in the energy and fuels sector (*Rocznik Statystyczny: Przemysł* 1991, 2).

2. These were *nieuspołecznione zakłady przemysłowe* ("unsocialized industrial production units") (*Rocznik Statystyczny: Przemysł* 1988, 38–39).

3. These were *prywatne jednostki prowadzące działalność gospodarczą w przemyśle* ("private units conducting economic activity in industry") (*Rocznik Statystyczny: Przemysł* 1992, 1). These included first and foremost proprietorships and partnerships (comprising some 98 percent of the total number of firms), cooperatives, plants owned by labor unions and social and political organizations, corporations with limited and unlimited liability, foundations and, joint ventures.

4. The liquidation privatization program also made important contributions to the growth of the private sector in industry.

5. Production of energy and fuels declined (in real terms) by 26 percent in 1990 (*Rocznik Statystyczny: Przemysł* 1991, 26–27). The price index for production in the energy and fuels complex in 1990 was 1033.0, relative to 1989's base of 100.0 (ibid., 31). Net profit rates (*wskaźniki rentowności*, defined as gross pre-tax profits divided by total cost) for the coal, fuels, energy, and ferrous and nonferrous metallurgical branches in 1990 averaged 39.7 percent, while the average rate of profit for all industrial branches was 30.9 percent (ibid., 86).

6. The *popiwek* was absorbing some 25 percent of the profits earned by the *Polska Miedź* copper monopoly at the time of the strikes in mid-1992 (Lipiński 1992a).

7. More than 11 million tons of coal were stockpiled at the mines and various other locations in June 1992, in contrast to a total coal output in 1991 of 507,000 tons ("Górnictwo" 1992).

8. Similar developments were occurring, for example, in the steel industry, where 20 of 26 firms lost money in 1992 (Andrejewski and Gołata 1992). Accelerated competition from EC steel producers was expected to force a reduction in yearly steel output from 19 to 11 million tons per year by the end of the decade. According to a government restructuring program, as many as seven foundries were to be closed, and 80,000 steel workers were expected to lose their jobs (Kwiatkowski 1993; "Wspólnota losu węgla i stali" 1992).

9. For this reason, the task of transforming postcommunist agriculture in Poland differs in important ways from the situation in other countries. For more on this transition, see Brooks et al. 1991.

10. Monthly interest rates for farmers in early 1990 were in the neighborhood of 40 percent (Turska 1992).

11. Despite the popular impression that large increases in imported foodstuffs helped to depress post-1989 farm incomes, the official statistics do not bear this out. Imports of food and agricultural products in 1990 were respectively only 63.5 and 29.9 percent of 1989 levels, in real terms (*Rocznik Statystyczny: Handel Zagraniczny* 1991, 9). While imports in these two groups increased, in nominal terms, by 124.3 and 170.5 percent, respectively, in 1991 (*East European Agriculture*, March 1992, 19), these figures should be deflated by the 30 percent growth recorded in the agricultural price index in 1991, giving approximated real import growth of 73 and 108 percent for that year. This indicates that in real terms food imports remained

essentially constant from 1989 to 1991 and imports of agricultural products fell by about one-third.

12. This additional 100,000 would produce about a 0.5 percent increase in the overall unemployment rate. It would be unlikely to exhaust hidden unemployment in the countryside, however.

13. Part of the problem may be the sheer number of small farmers who would be doomed to extinction by the adoption of a farmerization strategy. According to one observer, some 83 percent of Poland's 2.1 million peasant farmers operate on a scale too small (less than 10 hectares) to survive in the long term under a farmerization policy (Mozolski 1992c).

14. For more on banking issues in the postcommunist transition, see Brainard 1991, Kemme and Rudka 1992, and McKinnon 1991. For more on Poland's pre-reform banking system, see Podolski 1972.

15. The role of the private sector in Poland's banking system was somewhat ambiguous, since ownership in many banks is shared among various public, private, and cooperative fiduciary institutions. According to the Ministry of Ownership Transformation, a majority of stock was privately held in more than one-third of the 90 banks operating in Poland during the second half of 1991 ("Prywatyzacja banków" 1991, 3). The number of banks stood at 99 at the end of 1992 (Żuławnik 1993).

16. In 1991, according to the Ministry for Ownership Transformation, these nine banks controlled 45 percent of the total amount of credit and all "state banks still service[d] more than 95 percent of the credit flowing into the economy" ("Prywatyzacja banków" 1991, 3). While the role of these banks (and of state banks in general) in commercial lending declined in 1992–1993, the decline was gradual.

17. According to press reports, the share of bank credits devoted to loans for investment purposes between 1990 and 1992 did not rise above 30 percent (Bińczak 1993).

18. While the privatization of the Export Development Bank did begin in July 1992, this was a specialized bank, not one of the "big nine" commercial banks.

19. This would apply only to debt issued prior to the implementation of the law.

20. This condemnation of Poland's postcommunist financial system does not extend to its financial policymakers who, in general, did an exemplary job in making the best of a bad institutional situation during this period.

21. For an overview of issues associated with the transformation of postcommunist labor markets, see Coricelli and Revenga 1992, Brown 1992, and Vodopivec 1991.

22. Private firms and some state-owned joint-stock companies were exempted after mid-1990, and since then the *popiwek* has been applied to state firms in an increasingly discretionary manner (Brown 1992; Winiecki 1992). By the end of 1991, enterprises owed the Finance Ministry some 13 trillion zloty in unpaid *popiwek* charges ("Wzrosło zadłużenie przedsiębiorstw" 1992). This sum was equal to approximately one-third of the budget deficit for 1991.

23. By contrast, the portion of funds allocated to unemployment compensation, as opposed to active labor market programs, ranged from 57 percent in Germany to 40 percent in Greece to 30 percent in Sweden (Kraus 1992).

24. According to preliminary data, these trends were reversed in 1992, as peasant households' real incomes increased by about 3 percent and pensioners experienced a 7 percent decline in their real incomes (Polish Television, April 15, 1993).

25. The absurdity of this situation was nicely captured by Balcerowicz, who remarked in May 1993 that Poland had "made the transition from a situation of hidden unemployment to a situation of hidden employment" (*Polska Agencja Prasowa*, May 18, 1993).

26. These subsidies more than doubled as a share of ZUS revenues between 1989 and 1992, from 12.5 percent to an estimated 28 percent (Vinton 1993b, 4–5).

27. For example, the official retirement ages for both men and women in Great Britain and Germany in 1993 were 56 and 57, respectively. European workers must generally work 40 years in order to be eligible for state pensions (Kowalska 1993).

28. Women comprised some 45.7 percent of the labor force at the end of 1990 (*Rocznik Statystyczny* 1991, 92).

29. On the other hand, the combination of falling real wages and substantial increases in the cost of capital significantly reduced the relative cost of labor during 1990–1991 (M. Rutkowski 1991). Since this would tend to increase the quantity of labor demanded by Polish enterprises, the slow decline in employment (relative to production) may not necessarily have constituted increases in hidden unemployment.

30. The upward trend in the unemployment rate from March 1992 (12.6 percent) to March 1993 (14.2 percent) would tend to confirm this hypothesis (*Statystyka Polski* 1993a, II; *Statystyka Polski* 1993b, IV).

31. The number of apartments completed (*mieszkania oddane do użytku*) declined by 29.9 percent between 1988 and 1990 (*Rocznik Statystyczny* 1991, XXXVII).

32. By 1991, the waiting time for housing supplied by state and bureaucratized cooperative firms in cities like Warsaw and Cracow exceeded 30 years. The boom in private housing construction did little to make housing more affordable for the majority of Polish citizens.

33. Although an expanded mortgage loan program to make home purchases more affordable was introduced during the first half of 1992, this program seemed most likely to increase the demand for housing without producing commensurate increases in its supply.

34. While Polish foreign trade statistics have never been beyond reproach, data problems worsened dramatically with the introduction in 1992 of SAD (standard administrative document), customs-based procedures intended to make Polish trade statistics more consistent with EC norms. This led to major discrepancies between the foreign trade data released by the Central Statistical Office (which were based on customs declarations) and data released by the NBP (which were based on payment flows). According to the former, Poland ran a $2.7 billion merchandise trade deficit

in 1992; according to the latter, the merchandise trade balance registered a $400 million surplus ("Review of Eastern European Trade Developments" 1993, 57–58). Since these different figures have vastly different implications for Polish external developments in 1992, analysis of these developments is omitted from the discussion.

35. For a variety of reasons, the 1991 data in Table 4.7 should be interpreted with care. First, because of lapses in the quality and completeness of the official foreign trade statistics for 1991, preliminary data from a variety of sources, not all of which were compatible, had to be used. Second, the transition in 1991 from transferable-ruble to dollar accounting in CMEA trade complicated comparisons of 1990 and 1991 CMEA trade data, owing to the essentially arbitrary nature of the official dollar-zloty-ruble cross exchange rates implicit in these comparisons. (According to PlanEcon, ruble-denominated trade flows accounted for 17 percent of total exports and 15 percent of total imports in 1990, while the relevant figures for 1991 were 2 and 1 percent, respectively [Telma 1992, 7].) The zloty's undervaluation vis-à-vis the transferable ruble in 1991 implied that this conversion exaggerated the decline in CMEA imports and exports in that year. Third, there are indications that many private trading transactions, as well as barter deals concluded among state enterprises, were not captured by the official statistics. This too would tend to exaggerate post-1990 declines in CMEA trade. Data for 1991 are therefore best viewed with an eye to the trends they depict rather than as accurate representations of levels of trade flows.

36. The Rakowski government initiated increases in zloty convertibility in early 1989 by decriminalizing black-market currency transactions for nonresidents. The systems of enterprise foreign-exchange retention accounts and hard-currency auctions created during the 1980s were also expanded during 1989. These changes had the effect of legalizing the multiple exchange-rate regime that had existed during the 1980s, in that the "official" exchange rate (at which commercial transactions were conducted within the first economy) was quite a bit above (i.e., the zloty was significantly overvalued relative to) the bank auction and "market" rates. The "introduction of internal convertibility" commonly dated at January 1, 1990 thus consisted of the unification of these three rates. This was achieved by introducing resident current-account convertibility, abolishing administrative barriers separating private citizens' and enterprises' use of foreign exchange, devaluing the official rate so that it converged with the market and bank rates, and prohibiting the use of foreign exchange within Poland. By mid-1991 repatriation of zloty profits in foreign exchange for foreign firms had been effectively guaranteed, thus providing virtual complete current-account convertibility for the zloty.

37. Poland concluded two agreements with the IMF in 1990 and 1991. The first, a standby agreement, was in effect from February 1990 through March 1991; the second, the three-year adjustment agreement, was to be in effect from January 1991 through March 1994. While these agreements could have provided credits totalling some 2.4 billion SDR, Poland qualified for only 0.6 billion of these before being

declared out of compliance with the adjustment agreement during the summer of 1991. Another standby agreement, concluded in March 1993, runs through the first quarter of 1994 and could release up to 476 billion SDR (Możejko 1993).

38. At the end of 1991 Poland's gross convertible-currency debt stood at $48.4 billion. $31.5 billion was owed to the Paris Club of government creditors; $11.7 billion was owed to the London Club of commercial banks; and $2.5 billion was owed to the former USSR and two CMEA banks. By mid-1992, debt write-off agreements worth more than $3 billion had been concluded with the governments of 14 of Poland's 16 creditors (Telma 1992, 28; "Do podpisania" 1992).

39. Poland also concluded a free-trade agreement with the European Free Trade Association (EFTA) that went into effect on April 1, 1993.

40. In dollar terms, Poland's exports to the EC in 1991 were almost double the 1989 level (Telma 1992, 1, 9).

41. According to PlanEcon, the zloty's real effective appreciation between January 1990 and April 1992 was 128 percent, despite devaluations in May 1991 (when the zloty was tied to a market basket of currencies) and February 1992, and the adoption of a crawling-peg regime in September 1991 ("East European Currency Exchange Rates" 1992, 1–2).

42. These fears were exacerbated by the rapid increases in Germany's share of Polish foreign trade from 1989 to 1992 (see Table 4.8), but fears of German penetration through investment were not borne out. Instead, Italian, American, and Swedish firms all invested more in Poland between 1990 and 1992 than did German firms ("Polish Monthly Economic Indicator" 1993).

43. Perhaps for this reason, only 1,100 hectares of Polish land passed into foreign ownership in 1990–1991. While Germans constituted the largest group of owners, they received only 18.5 percent of the purchase permits issued. ("Low Demand for Land among Foreigners in 1991," *East European Markets*, March 1992, 17).

44. By contrast, Poland's per capita foreign trade turnover in 1980 was $508 (*Polish Economy in the External Environment* 1988, 45–46).

45. Identical agreements were simultaneously initialed with Hungary and Czechoslovakia (Brada 1991).

46. Turkey has been an associate member of the European Community since 1964 and has little prospect of attaining full membership in the near future.

47. In addition to these issues, Poland was also in debt to Hungary, Czechoslovakia, and Germany for 1.2 billion transferable rubles and had assets worth 778 million transferable rubles in Albania, Bulgaria, Mongolia, Romania, Cuba, North Korea, Laos, and Cambodia (Telma 1992, 28–30). The murky prospects for settling these claims and counterclaims suggested that the bulk of them would ultimately be written off.

48. For more on CEFTA, see *Russian and East European Finance and Trade*, January-February 1994.

49. According to one source, Polish exports to the Czech Republic, Hungary, and Slovakia in 1992 accounted for only 2.8, 1.3, and 0.9 percent of total Polish

exports, respectively. The corresponding import figures were 2.3, 0.9, and 0.8 percent, respectively ("Review of East European Foreign Trade Developments" 1993, 62.)

Chapter V

1. References to the postcommunist economies in this chapter do not generally pertain to eastern Germany, both because the GDR ceased to exist as an independent country and because the nature of the East German transition differs crucially from other postcommunist economies in many important respects.

2. Transactions with Slovakia are included in the former CMEA share for the Czech Republic.

3. Because the aggregation of trade data within the former CMEA countries prior to 1991 occurred at exchange rates that generally overvalued the transferable ruble and undervalued the dollar, the 1991 transition to dollar-denominated trade within the CMEA produced a revaluation of regional trade flows. By depressing the dollar value of intraregional trade that had previously been measured in rubles (and therefore increasing the share of extraregional dollar-denominated trade in total trade) this revaluation statistically inflated the share of trade with the West in the former CMEA countries' total trade, while simultaneously reducing the share of regional trade. Thus, some of the post-1990 increase in shares of Western trade was a statistical, not an economic, phenomenon. While the exact relationship between this statistical rejigging and its effects on changes in individual CMEA countries' trade shares is unclear, the decline in the share of regional trade for any given country would have been positively related to the share of that country's total trade accounted for by regional trade, ceteris paribus. The relatively low share of CMEA imports and exports in Polish trade for 1990 (less than 25 percent [*Rocznik Statystyczny: Handel Zagraniczny* 1991, 2–3]) implied that the post-1990 increases in the share of Western trade for Poland were more genuine, and less a statistical artifact, than for other countries in the region. By contrast, the share of Hungary's CMEA imports and exports in total imports and exports for 1990 were 34 and 32 percent, respectively (*Külkeresdelmi Statisztikai Évkönyv 1990* 1991, 28–29).

4. For a comparison of programs for mass privatization and privatizing large firms, see Djelic 1992 and Fischer 1992.

5. For an interesting evaluation of Gaidar's economic transformation program and a comparison with the Balcerowicz Plan, see Ellman 1992. For more on economic transformation in Russia during 1992, see Noren 1992, Heymann 1992, and Ash 1992.

6. Indeed, whereas the Polish stabilization program originally included three nominal anchors—the nominal exchange rate, nominal interest rates, and the *popiwek* tax on nominal wage growth (Gomulka 1992)—these anchors were essentially absent in the Russian program. Wage taxation was avoided throughout 1992 (and most of 1993) in favor of labor market liberalization, and while interest rates

trended upward in nominal terms, they remained negative in real terms. Finally, although the Russian Central Bank not infrequently intervened to support the ruble on foreign exchange markets during 1992 and 1993, the resulting dirty float could hardly be described as a nominal anchor. While three nominal anchors may, theoretically, have been excessive in terms of designing a consistent stabilization program in Poland, from a practical point of view, the absence of any effective anchors in the Russian program almost certainly was a mistake.

7. The extent to which the characteristics of this structural adjustment were uniformly desirable is another matter, one discussed in Chapter 4.

8. According to Gomulka, the share of dollar-denominated deposits in the total money supply (presumably M1) fell from 59 percent in December 1989 to 25 percent at the end of 1991 (Gomulka 1992, 363).

9. To be sure, large state firms seriously endangered the transition during 1990–1992 with threats such as the interenterprise debt problem. The linkage between enterprises' unwillingness to pay their bills and their monopoly status was unclear, however, since at least two other factors—the absence of effective bankruptcy procedures and, more generally, the inefficiencies of state ownership—played an important role in the rise of enterprise indebtedness. A more serious monopoly problem was presented by the monopsony power over local labor markets held by large employers in small towns.

10. For an overview of issues pertaining to monopoly and cost-push inflation, see Scherer 1980, Chapter 13.

11. Other functions may legitimately be assigned to the postcommunist state, depending upon the normative role envisioned for it once the transition has been completed.

Bibliography

In the listings below, multiple works by one author are arranged in reverse chronological order (the most recent first). Multiple works by one author published in the same year in the same publication are also listed in reverse chronological order; others published in the same year are arranged alphabetically.

The titles of two frequently cited journals are abbreviated in the listings, as follows:

Radio Free Europe/Radio Liberty Research Report	RFE/RLRR
Radio Free Europe Report on Eastern Europe	RFEREE

"10 bilionów z prywatyzacji" (10 trillion from privatization). 1992. *Gazeta Wyborcza*, February 3.

Aaslund, A. 1985. *Private Enterprise in Eastern Europe*. New York: St. Martin's Press.

Aleksandrowicz, P. 1992a. "Inwestycje zamiast konsumpcji" (Investment instead of consumption). *Rzeczpospolita*, March 20.

———. 1992b. "Trzeba podejmować męskie decyzje" (Firm decisions must be made). *Rzeczpospolita*, August 6.

Ancerowicz, W., and A. Cylwik. 1984. *Działalności zrzeszeń a interesy przedsiębiorstw* (Association activities and enterprise interests). Warsaw: Institute of Organization, Management and Personnel Training.

Andrzejczak, J., P. Ćwikliński, and J. Ziarno. 1991. *Art-B Bluff*. Warsaw: Polska Oficyna Wydawnicza BGW.

Andrzejewski, P., and K. Gołata. 1992. "Punkt zerowy" (Ground zero). *Wprost*, November 8.

Ash, T. N. 1992. "Problems of Ruble Convertibility." RFE/RLRR 29:26–32.

Baczyński, J. 1986. "FAZowanie na gorąco" (FAZing it on hot). *Polityka*, October 25.

Baka, W. 1982. *Polska reforma gospodarcza* (The Polish economic reform). Warsaw: Państwowe Wydawnictwo Ekonomiczne.

Balcerowicz, L. 1992. *800 dni szok kontrolowany* (800 days: Controlled shock). Warsaw: Polska Oficyjna Wydawnicza "BGW."

Balcerowicz, L., *et al.* 1981. "Reforma gospodarcza: Główne kierunki i sposoby realizacji" (Economic reform: Central principles and methods of implementation). In *Reforma gospodarcza: Propozycje, tendencje, kierunki dyskusji* (Economic reform: Proposals, tendencies, directions of discussion). Ed. Rafał Krawczyk. Warsaw: Państwowe Wydawnictwo Ekonomiczne.

Balicka, M. 1993. "Gilotyna" (Guillotine). *Wprost*, March 14.

———. 1992. "Trzech na jednego" (Three on one). *Wprost*, October 4.

———. 1991. "Dziecko z kąpielą" (Throwing out the baby with the bath water). *Wprost*, October 6.

"Banki w prywatne ręce" (Banks in private hands). 1991. *Gazeta Wyborcza*, July 12.

Beksiak, J., T. Gruszecki, A. Jędraszczyk, and J. Winiecki. 1989. "Zarys programu stabilizacyjnego i zmian systemowych" (Outline of a program for stabilization and systemic change). Unpublished paper for Solidarity Parliamentary Club, Warsaw.

"Bezrobocie po polsku" (Unemployment in the Polish way). 1992. *Sztandar Młodych*, May 29–31.

Białkowska, A. 1992. "Kosztowne oddłużanie" (Costly debt relief). *Gazeta Wyborcza*, July 23.

Bielasiak, J. 1983. "The Party: Permanent Crisis." In *Poland: Genesis of a Revolution*, ed. Abe Brumberg. New York: Vintage Books.

"Bielecki: System bankowy największą słabością gospodarki" (Bielecki: The banking system is the economy's greatest weakness). 1991. Polska Agencja Prasowa, October 15.

Bieńkowski, W. 1992. "Poland's Bermuda Triangle." RFE/RLRR, no. 17:22–24.

"Bilans prywatyzacji" (A privatization balance sheet). 1991. Polska Agencja Prasowa, December 16.

Bińczak, H. 1993. "Nie lubiane inwestycje" (Unloved investments). *Gazeta Bankowa*, June 4.

———. 1992. "Szok po roku" (The shock after a year). *Gazeta Bankowa*, March 8–14.

Biuletyn Statystyczny (*Statistical Bulletin*) no. 2. 1993. Warsaw: Główny Urząd Statystyczny.

Biuro Pełnomocnika Rządu d/Przekształceń Własnościowych, Warsaw. 1990. "Propozycje działań na rzecz rozwoju drobnego sektora prywatnego /handel, usługi, produkcja/" (Proposed activities to develop the small-scale private sector [trade, services, production]). Unpublished government working paper.

Blazyca, G., and R. Rapacki, eds. 1991. *Poland in the 1990s: Economy and Society in Transition*. New York: Saint Martin's Press.

Blommestein, H. J., and M. Marrese. 1991. *Transformation of Planned Economies: Property Rights Reform and Macroeconomic Stability*, ed. Hans J. Blommestein and Michael Marrese. Paris: Organisation for Economic Co-operation and Development.

Bobinski, C. 1992. "Poland's Tough Draft Budget Cuts Subsidies." *Financial Times*, March 24.

Boffito, C. 1988. "Reforms and Export Promotion." In *Creditworthiness and Reform in Poland: Western and Polish Perspectives*, ed. Paul Marer and Włodzimierz Siwiński. Bloomington: Indiana University Press.

Bogus, M., and W. Kasperkiewicz. 1983. "Zaopatrzenie quid pro quo" (Supply quid pro quo). *Przegląd Techniczny*, February 13.

Bożyk, P. 1988. *Raporty dla Edwarda Gierka* (Reports for Edward Gierek). Warsaw: Państwowe Wydawnictwo Ekonomiczne.

Brabant, J. M. van. 1991. "Property Rights Reform, Macroeconomic Performance, and Welfare." In *Transformation of Planned Economies: Property Rights Reform and Macroeconomic Stability*, edited by Hans J. Blommestein and Michael Marrese. Paris: Organisation for Economic Co-operation and Development.

———. 1990. *Remaking Eastern Europe: On the Political Economy of Transition*. Dordrecht: Kluwer Academic Publishers.

Brada, J. C. 1991. "The European Community and Czechoslovakia, Hungary and Poland." RFEREE, no. 49:27–32.

Brada, J. C., and A. E. King. 1992. "Is There a J-Curve for the Economic Transition from Socialism?" *Economics of Planning*, no. 1:37–53.

Brainard, L. 1991. "Strategies for Economic Transformation in Central and Eastern Europe: Role of Financial Market Reform." In *Transformation of Planned Economies: Property Rights Reform and Macroeconomic Stability*, ed. Hans J. Blommestein and Michael Marrese. Paris: Organisation for Economic Co-operation and Development.

Brooks, K., J. L. Guasch, A. Braverman, and C. Csaki. 1991. "Agriculture and the Transition to the Market." *Journal of Economic Perspectives*, no. 5:149–161.

Brown, B. 1992. "Post-Communist Labor Markets in Transition: The Polish Case." RFE/RLRR, no. 32:50–56.

Brumberg, A., ed. 1983. *Poland: Genesis of a Revolution*. New York: Vintage Books.

Brus, W. 1983. "Politics and Economics: The Fatal Link." In *Poland: Genesis of a Revolution*, ed. Abe Brumberg. New York: Vintage Books.

Brzeg-Wieluński, S., and M. Urbaniak. 1992. "Stan świadomości kierownika (resortu)" (The state of consciousness of the driver [of the ministry]). *Gazeta Bankowa*, January 26–February 1.

Bunce, V. 1980. "The Political Consumption Cycle: A Comparative Analysis." *Soviet Studies*, no. 2:280–290.

Bush, K. 1992. "The Russian Budget Deficit." RFE/RLRR, no. 40:30–32.

Campbell, R. W. 1991. *The Socialist Economies in Transition: A Primer on Semi-Reformed Systems*. Bloomington: Indiana University Press.

Capelik, V. 1992. "The Development of Anti-Monopoly Policy in Russia." RFE/RLRR, no. 34:66–70.

"CBOS: Opinie respondentów o representacji ich interesów" (CBOS: Respondent opinions about the representation of their interests). 1992. Polska Agencja Prasowa, July 30.

"Centralny Urząd Planowania: O prywatyzacji i zmianach strukturalnych w gospodarce" (The Central Planning Office on privatization and structural changes in the economy). 1991. *Wspólnota*, October 5.

Chajęcki, A. 1985. *Zmiany w strukturach organizacyjnych spółdzielczości: Ewolucja form koncentracji* (Changes in organizational structures in the cooperative sector: The evolution of forms of concentration). Warsaw: Institute of Organization, Management and Personnel Training.

Chmiel, J., and Z. Żółkiewski. 1990. "Przeciw Recesji" (Against the recession). *Życie Gospodarcze*, July 22.

Cook, E. 1984. "Agricultural Reform in Poland: Background and Prospects." *Soviet Studies*, no. 3:406–426.

Coricelli, F., and A. Revenga. 1992. *Wage Policy during the Transition to a Market Economy: Poland 1990–1991*. World Bank Discussion Paper 158. Washington: World Bank.

Crane, K. 1991. "Polish Foreign Trade in 1990 and the First Half of 1991." *PlanEcon Report*, August 30.

"Cud się nie nadarzył" (The miracle did not occur). 1993. *Trybuna*, March 25.

"CUP o 1991 r.: Recesja" (The Central Planning Office on 1991: The recession). 1992. Polska Agencja Prasowa, January 13.

"CUP o handlu zagranicznym w ubr." (The Central Planning Office on foreign trade last year). 1992. Polska Agencja Prasowa, May 13.

"CUP prognozuje zahamowanie recesji w przemyśle" (The Central Planning Office forecasts a bottoming out in industry). 1992. Polska Agencja Prasowa, July 29.

Curry, J. L. 1992. "The Puzzle of Poland." *Current History*, November, 385–389.

———. 1984. *The Black Book of Polish Censorship*. New York: Vintage Books.

Cylwik, A. 1984. *Ogólna charakterystyka zrzeszeń przedsiębiorstw* (A general characterization of enterprise associations). Warsaw: Institute of Organization, Management, and Personnel Training.

Czechowski, D., and B. Raczko. 1993. "Fundusz dla klientów 'Westy'" (A fund for the clients of 'Westa'). *Spotkania*, April 8–14.

Dabrowski, P. 1991. "The Foreign Investment Boom." RFEREE, no. 30:36–42.

Dąbrowski, M. 1992a. "Interventionist Pressures on a Policy Maker during the Transition to Economic Freedom (Personal Experience)." *Communist Economies and Economic Transformation*, no. 1:59–73.

———. 1992b. "Polska stabilizacja (1)" (Polish Stabilization [1]). *Gazeta Bankowa*, February 2–8.

———. 1991. "The Polish Stabilisation Programme: Accomplishments and Prospects." 1991. *Communist Economies and Economic Transformation*, no. 1:121–133.

———. 1990. "Co dalej?" (What next?). *Życie Gospodarcze*, November 25.

"Dalszy wzrost liczby bezrobotnych" (Further growth in the number of unemployed). 1992. *Polska Agencja Prasowa*, July 14.

Davies, N. 1984. *God's Playground: A History of Poland*. 2 vols. New York: Columbia University Press.

Denton, N. 1992. "A Kiss of Life from across the Border." *Financial Times*, April 21.

"Developments in the Direction of Trade in Eastern Europe and the Former Soviet Union in 1991." 1992. *PlanEcon Report*, July 21.

Djelic, B. 1992. "Mass Privatization in Russia: The Role of Vouchers". *Radio Free Europe/Radio Liberty Research Institute*, no. 41:40–44.

"Do podpisania—jeszcze dwie umowy o redukcji długów" (Two debt-reduction agreements still unsigned). 1992. Polska Agencja Prasowa, July 20.

Domańczyk, Z. 1990. *100 dni Mazowieckiego* (Mazowiecki's 100 days). Warsaw: Wydawnictwo Andrzej Bonarski.

Doliniak, K. 1992. "Strefa cienia" (The shadow sphere). *Kurier Polski*, March 26.

———. 1991. "Ekspert droższy od . . . rolls royse'a" (An expert is more expensive than a Rolls Royce). *Kurier Polski*, December 5.

Dowda, H. 1992. "W pułapce: Raport o zadłużeniu rolników" (In a trap: Report on farmers' indebtedness). *Trybuna*, January 22.

Drożdowski, M. 1963. *Polityka gospodarcza rzadu polskiego 1936–1939* (Economic policy of the polish government, 1936–1939). Warsaw: Państwowe Wydawnictwo Naukowe.

Dryll, I. 1993. "Bezrobocie—bez programu" (Unemployment—no program). *Życie Gospodarcze*, April 25.

———. 1992. "Spadek statystyczny, czy faktyczny?" (Statistical or factual decline?). *Życie Gospodarcze*, June 7.

———. 1991. "Bezrobocie: Fikcja, czy dramat?" (Unemployment: Fiction or drama?), *Życie Gospodarcze*, February 3.

———. 1990, "Oswoić . . . bezrobocie" (Getting used to unemployment). *Życie Gospodarcze*, July 22.

Dzierżawski, K. 1991. "Dwa oblicze gospodarki" (The two faces of the economy). *Rzeczpospolita*, September 5.

Dziewulski, K. 1992. "Kogo protegować?" (Whom to protect?). *Życie Gospodarcze*, February 2.

"East European Currency Exchange Rates: Recent Developments and Near Term Outlook." 1992. *PlanEcon Report*, April 28.

Eastern Europe: Struggling to Stay on the Reform Track. 1992. Central Intelligence Agency paper, prepared for the Subcommittee on Technology and National Security of the Joint Economic Committee of the U.S. Congress.

Eberstadt, N. 1989. "Health and Mortality in Eastern Europe: 1965 to 1985." In *Pressures for Reform in the East European Economies: Study Papers Submitted to the Joint Economic Committee of the U.S. Congress*, vol. 1. Washington, D.C.: Government Printing Office.

Echikson, W. 1989. "How Solidarity Did the Impossible." *Christian Science Monitor*, August 22.

Ellman, M. 1992. "Shock Therapy in Russia: Failure or Partial Success?" RFE/RLRR, no. 34:48–61.

Eysymontt, J. 1990a. "Rozwój rynków towarowych w Polsce w 1990 r." (The development of goods markets in Poland in 1990). In *Realizacja polskiego programu gospodarczego 1990 r.* (The implementation of the polish economic program in 1990). Warsaw: Stefan Batory Foundation.

———. 1990b. *Ocena stanu i dynamiki niektórych rynków na tle ogólnej sytuacji gospodarki polskiej w 1989 roku* (An evaluation of the state and dynamics of certain markets in the context of the general situation of the Polish economy in 1989). Warsaw: Stefan Batory Foundation.

Falkiewicz, K. 1989. "Kapitalny pomysł . . . ?" (A Capital Idea?). *Zmiany*, June 4.

Fallenbuchl, Z. M. 1991. "The New Government and Privatization." RFEREE, no. 12:11–16.

———. 1989. "Poland: The Anatomy of Stagnation." In *Pressures for Reform in the East European Economies: Study Papers Submitted to the Joint Economic Committee of the U.S. Congress*, vol. 1. Washington, D.C.: Government Printing Office.

———. 1986. "The Economic Crisis in Poland and Prospects for Recovery." In *East European Economies: Slow Growth in the 1980s*, vol. 3. Joint Economic Committee, U.S. Congress. Washington, D.C.: Government Printing Office.

———. 1984. "The Polish Economy under Martial Law." *Soviet Studies*, no. 4:513–527.

———. 1982. "Poland's Economic Crisis." *Problems of Communism*, March-April, 1–21.

Federowicz, M. 1992. *Trwanie i transformacja: Ład gospodarczy w Polsce* (Continuity and transformation: The economic order in Poland). Warsaw: Ifis Publishers.

———. 1990. *Social Barriers to Ownership Transformations: Case Study*. Warsaw: Stefan Batory Foundation.

Feiwel, G. R. 1971. *Poland's Industrialization Policy: A Current Analysis*. 2 vols. New York: Praeger.

Felbur, S. 1992. "Wątpliwości do obliczeń GUS" (Doubts about the Central Statistical Office's calculations). *Życie Gospodarcze*, June 7.

Fischer, B. J. 1992. "Large Privatization in Poland, Hungary, and Czechoslovakia." RFE/RLRR, no. 44:34–39.

Fletcher, P. 1992. "Investment Eludes East European Reform Pioneer." Reuters, April 22.

Gadomski, W. 1992. "Prywatyzacja przez oddłużenie" (Privatization through debt restructuring). *Gazeta Bankowa*, June 21–27.

Gąsiorowska, K. 1986. "Zespoły gospodarcze: Korzystny rachunek" (Economic working groups: A positive account). *Życie Warszawy*, March 24.

"Geografia bezrobocia w czerwcu br." (The geography of unemployment in June 1992). 1992. Polska Agencja Prasowa, July 15.

Girnius, S. 1993. "Establishing Currencies in the Baltic States." RFE/RLRR, no. 22:35–39.

Glikman, P. 1992. "Ukryte bezrobocie" (Hidden unemployment). *Życie Gospodarcze*, March 29.

Gmyż, C. 1992. "Nie da się zmienić praw ekonomii" (The laws of economics cannot be changed). *Życie Warszawy*, July 25–26.

Golinowska, S. 1992. "Polityka 'społecznych cięć'" (The policy of 'social cuts'). *Życie Gospodarcze*, June 7.

Gomulka, S. 1992. "Polish Economic Reform, 1990–91: Principles, Policies and Outcomes." *Cambridge Journal of Economics*, no. 16:355–372.

———. 1986. *Growth, Innovation and Reform in Eastern Europe*. Madison: University of Wisconsin Press.

Gomulka, S., and J. Rostowski. 1984. "The Reformed Polish Economic System, 1982–83." *Soviet Studies*, no. 3:386–405.

"Gospodarka 1991 w ocenie GUS: Mniej wytwarzamy, więcej konsumujemy" (The economy in 1991 according to the Central Statistical Office: Producing less, consuming more). 1992. *Rzeczpospolita*, February 1–2.

"Górnictwo" (Mining). 1992. *Trybuna Śląska*, July 17.

Grabowski, M. H., and P. Kulawczyk. 1991. "Ciężka stopa" (High interest rates). *Polityka*, October 19.

Gregory, P. R., and R. C. Stuart. 1986. *Soviet Economic Structure and Performance*, 3d edition. New York: Harper and Row.

Grosfeld, I. 1990. "Prospects for Privatization in Poland." *European Economy*, March, 139–150.

Grzegorzewski, Z. 1991. "Przez likwidację" (Via liquidation). *Życie Gospodarcze*, December 8.

Gruszecki, T. "Privatization in Poland in 1990." *Communist Economies and Economic Transformation*, no. 2:141–154.

Gutkowska, A. 1992. "Z winy ludzi?" (Operator error?). *Życie Gospodarcze*, May 17.

Guzicki, L., and S. Żurawicki. 1984. *Polscy ekonomiści XIX i XX wieku* (Polish Economists of the Nineteenth and Twentieth Centuries). Warsaw: Państwowe Wydawnictwo Ekonomiczne.

Hanson, P. 1992. "The End of the Ruble Zone?" RFE/RLRR, no. 30:46–48.

Henzler, M. 1991. "Nostalgia?" *Polityka*, September 14.

Herer, W., Z. Landau, A. Muller, M. Nasiłowski, W. Rydygier, W. Sadowski, and A. Woś. 1985. *U źrodeł polskiego kryzysu* (At the source of the Polish crisis). Warsaw: Państwowe Wydawnictwo Naukowe.

Herer, W., and W. Sadowski. 1981. "Nawis inflacyjny" (The inflationary overhang). *Życie Gospodarcze*, August 9.

Heymann, H. 1992. "Russia's Economic Reform: A Comment." *Soviet Economy*, no. 1:42–45.

Holland, D. C. 1988. "Workers' Self-Management before and after 1981." In *Creditworthiness and Reform in Poland: Western and Polish Perspectives*, ed. Paul Marer and Włodzimierz Siwiński. Bloomington: Indiana University Press.

Holzer, J., and K. Leski. 1990. *Solidarność w podziemiu* (Solidarity underground). Łódź: Wydawnictwo Łódzkie.

Hough, J. F. 1982. *The Polish Crisis: American Policy Options*. Washington, D.C.: Brookings Institution.

Hume, I. M., and B. Pinto. 1993. "Prejudice and Fact in Poland's Industrial Transformation". *Finance and Development*, no. 2:18–20.

Iwanowska, A. 1982. *Dynamika systemu zarządzania gospodarką* (The dynamics of the system of economic management). Warsaw: Książka i Wiedza.

Jacukowicz, Z. 1986. *Płace w zakładzie pracy* (Wages in the workplace). Warsaw: Państwowe Wydawnictwo Ekonomiczne.

Janacek, K. 1992. "Czechoslovak Economy in Transition: A Survey of Major Trends in 1991." RFE/RLRR, no. 12:31–33.

Jermakowicz, W. 1988. "Reform Cycles in Poland, the USSR, the GDR, and Czechoslovakia." In *Creditworthiness and Reform in Poland: Western and Polish Perspectives*, ed. Paul Marer and Włodzimierz Siwiński. Bloomington: Indiana University Press.

———. 1983. "Gra o instrumenty" (A Game of Instruments). *Przegląd Techniczny*, November 2.

Jermakowicz, W., and R. Krawczyk. 1985. *Reforma gospodarcza jako innowacja społeczna* (*Economic Reform as a Social Innovation*). Warsaw: Młodzieżowa Agencja Wydawnicza.

Jezierski, A., and B. Petz. 1988. *Historia gospodarcza Polski Ludowej 1944–1985* (An economic history of People's Poland, 1944–1985). Warsaw: Państwowe Wydawnictwo Naukowe.

Kamiński, B. 1991a. *The Collapse of State Socialism: The Case of Poland*. Princeton: Princeton University Press.

———. 1991b. "Systemic Underpinnings of the Transition in Poland: The Shadow of the Round-table Agreement." *Studies in Comparative Communism*, no. 2:173–190.

Kasten, M. 1986. *Vadecum konkursów na stanowiska kierownicze* (Competitions for managerial positions). Warsaw: Institute of Labor and Social Affairs.

Kemme, D., ed. 1991. *Economic Reform in Poland: The Aftermath of Martial Law, 1981–1988*. Greenwich: JAI Press.

Kemme, D., and A. Rudka. 1992. *Monetary and Banking Reform in Post Communist Economies*. New York: Institute for East-West Studies.

Kharas, H. J. 1991. *Restructuring Socialist Industry: Poland's Experience in 1990*. World Bank Discussion Paper 142. Washington: World Bank.

Killick, T., and C. Stevens. 1991. "Eastern Europe: Lessons on Economic Adjustment from the Third World." *International Affairs*, no. 4:679–696.

Kołodko, A. 1992a. "Ciężkie, ogromne i . . . zacofane" (Heavy, Gigantic, and Obsolete). 1992. *Kurier Polski*, February 18.

———. 1992b. "Kołos na glinianych nogach" (Colossus on legs of clay). *Kurier Polski*, February 18.

———. 1992c. "Ziemia do wzięcia" (Land for the taking). *Gazeta Bankowa*, June 14–20.

———. 1991. "Sekrety nadprodukcji" (The secrets of overproduction). *Gazeta Bankowa*, September 15–21.

Kołodko, G. W. 1993. "Transition from Socialism and Stabilization Policies: The Polish Experience." In *Trials of Transition: Economic Reform in the Former Communist Bloc*, ed. Michael Keren and Gur Ofer. Boulder: Westview Press.

———. 1992. *Transformacja polskiej gospodarki Sukses czy porażka*) (The transformation of the Polish economy: Success or failure?). Warsaw: Polska Oficyjna Wydawnicza "BGW."

———. 1991. "Po roku i po szoku" (After the year and the shock). *Życie Gospodarcze*, January 13.

———. 1984. "Inflacyjna alternatywa" (The inflationary alternative). *Życie Gospodarcze*, February 26.

Komisja Reformy Gospodarczej. 1981. *Kierunki reformy gospodarczej* (Principles of economic reform). Warsaw: Książka i Wiedza.

"Koniec pogody dla reformy?" (The end of clear sailing for reform?). 1992. *Gazeta Wyborcza*, February 4.

Korbonski, A. 1981. "Victim or Villain: Polish Agriculture since 1970." In *Background to Crisis: Policy and Politics in Gierek's Poland*, ed. Maurice Simon and Roger Kanet. Boulder: Westview Press.

———. 1965. *Politics of Socialist Agriculture in Poland, 1945–1960*. New York: Columbia University Press.

Kornai, J. 1992. "The Postsocialist Transition and the State: Reflections in the Light of Hungarian Fiscal Problems." *American Economic Review*, May, 1–21.

———. 1990. *The Road to a Free Economy*. New York: Norton.

Kostrowicka, I., and P. Przeciszewski. 1989. "Bilans otwarcie" (A preliminary balance). In *Problemy gospodarcze Drugiej Rzeczypospolitej* (Economic problems of the Second Republic), ed. Zbigniew Landau and Jerzy Tomaszewski. Warsaw: Państwowe Wydawnictwo Ekonomiczne.

Kostrz-Kostecka, A. 1992. "GUS o handlu zagranicznym w 1991 roku: Wzrost importu, spadek eksportu" (The Central Statistical Office on foreign trade in 1991: Imports grew, exports fell). *Rzeczpospolita*, February 10.

Kowalik, T. 1991. "The Costs of 'Shock Therapy'." *Dissent*, Fall, 497–504.

Kowalska, M. 1993. "Koniec życia ponad stan" (No more living beyond one's means). *Życie Gospodarcze*, May 30.

———. 1992. "Gra na czerwonych liczbach" (A game in red numbers). *Życie Gospodarcze*, February 2.

———. 1991. "Próba generalna" (Dress rehearsal). *Życie Gospodarcze*, January 13.

———. 1990. "Prywatyzacyjny rachunek sumienia" (Privatization and the conscience). *Życie Gospodarcze*, November 18.

———. 1987. "Zmiany w ustawach" (Changes in the laws). *Życie Gospodarcze*, November 1.

Kozak, M. 1991. "Social Support for Privatization in Poland." *Communist Economies and Economic Transformation*, no. 2:155–167.

Kraus, K. 1992. "Bezrobocie—co dalej?" (Unemployment—what next?). *Trybuna*, June 25.

Krawczyk, R., ed. 1981. *Reforma gospodarcza: Propozycje, tendencje, kierunki dyskusji* (Economic reform: Proposals, tendencies, directions of discussion). Warsaw: Państwowe Wydawnictwo Ekonomiczne.

Kruszewski, R. 1992. "Czy warto było obalać komunę?" (Was it worth overthrowing communism?). *Prawo i Życie*, June 6.

Kuczyński, W. 1981. *Po Wielkim Skoku* (After the great leap). Warsaw: Państwowe Wydawnictwo Ekonomiczne.

Külkereskedelmi Statisztikai Évkönyv 1990 (Foreign trade yearbook 1990). 1991. Budapest: Központi Statisztikai Hivatal.

Kwiatkowski, P. 1993. "Hartownie stali" (The steel crucible). *Wprost*, January 17.

Laba, R. 1991. *The Roots of Solidarity: A Political Sociology of Working Class Democratization*. Princeton: Princeton University Press.

Lamentowicz, W. 1992a. "Czy nastąpi wybuch. . . . " (Will there be an Explosion?). *Kurier Polski*, February 26.

———. 1992b. "Schyłek naszych elit" (The decline of our elites). *Tygodnik Solidarność*, February 7.

Landau, Z., and J. Tomaszewski, eds. 1989. *Problemy gospodarcze Drugiej Rzeczypospolitej* (Economic problems of the second republic). Warsaw: Państwowe Wydawnictwo Ekonomiczne.

Leśnicka, H. 1992. "Żyć bez zasiłku" (To live without unemployment benefits). *Życie Warszawy*, July 16.

Levitas, A., and P. Strzałkowski. 1990. "What Does 'uwłaszczenie nomenklatury' ('Propertisation of the Nomenklatura') Really Mean?" *Communist Economies*, no. 3:413–416.

Lewandowski, J. 1991. *Neoliberałowie wobec współczesności* (Neoliberals and the contemporary world). Gdynia: Wydawnictwo BGZT.

Lewandowski, J., and J. Szomburg. 1989. "Uwłaszczenie jako fundament reformy społeczno-gospodarczej" (Propertization as a foundation of socioeconomic reform). In *Propozycje przekształceń polskiej gospodarki* (Proposals to Transform the Polish Economy). Polish Economics Association: Warsaw.

Lindemann, M. 1992. "New Government Signals Intention to Slow Down Privatization Process." Associated Press, January 6.

Lipiński, S. 1992a. "Wszystko możliwe" (Anything is possible). *Gazeta Bankowa*, July 25.

———. 1992b. "Jak pozbyć się balastu" (How to dump the ballast). *Gazeta Bankowa*, February 2.

Lipko, A. 1992. "Co tam Panie w Polityce?" (What's new in politics, Mister?). *Polityka*, April 25.

Lipowski, A. 1988. *Mechanism rynkowy w gospodarce polskiej* (The market mechanism in the Polish economy). Warsaw: Państwowe Wydawnictwo Naukowe.

Lipski, J. J. 1985. *KOR: A History of the Workers' Defense Committee in Poland, 1976–1981*. Berkeley: University of California Press.

Loch, J. 1986. "Tęsknota za konsekwencją" (A yearning for consistency). *Polityka*, June 14.

Lubowski, A. 1981. "Diplomacja i gospodarka." *Życie Gospodarcze*, no. 6:13.

Lukomska, A. 1992. "Cud mniemany" (The promised miracle). *Wprost*, May 24.

Magyar Statisztikai Évkönyv 1991 (Hungarian statistical yearbook 1991). 1991. Budapest: Központi Statisztikai Hivatal.

Małachowski, A. W. 1992. "Wędka bez haczyka" (A line without a hook). *Prawo i Życie*, May 2.

Małecka, T. 1989. "Przemysł. Warunki rozwoju" (Industry: conditions of development). In *Problemy gospodarcze Drugiej Rzeczypospolitej* (Economic problems of the second republic). ed. Zbigniew Landau and Jerzy Tomaszewski. Warsaw: Państwowe Wydawnictwo Ekonomiczne.

Mały Rocznik Statystyczny 1992 (Small statistical yearbook 1992). 1992. Warsaw: Główny Urząd Statystyczny.

Mapes, T., and A. Mitraszewska. 1992. "Warsaw's Slowing Pace of Economic Reform Frustrates Poles and Foreign Financiers." *Wall Street Journal* (European edition), May 11.

Marer, P., and W. Siwiński, eds. 1988. *Creditworthiness and Reform in Poland: Western and Polish Perspectives*. Bloomington: Indiana University Press.

Mazurkiewicz, Z. 1982. *Polska reforma gospodarcza: Rolnictwo i gospodarka żywnościowa* (The Polish economic reform: Agriculture and the food economy). Warsaw: Państwowe Wydawnictwo Ekonomiczne.

McKinnon, R. J. 1991. "Financial Control in the Transition from Classical Socialism to a Market Economy." *Journal of Economics Perspectives*, no. 4:107–122.

McQuaid, D. 1991a. "The Political Landscape before the Elections." RFEREE, no. 42:11–17.

———. 1991b. "Art-B and the Pathology of Transition." RFEREE, no. 38:15–21.

———. 1991c. "The 'War' over the Election Law." RFEREE, no. 31:11–28.

Michnik, A. 1985. *Letters From Prison and Other Essays*. Translated by Maya Latynski. Berkeley: University of California Press.

Michta, A. A. 1990. *Red Eagle: The Army in Polish Politics, 1944–1988*. Stanford: Hoover Institution.

Mieczkowski, B. 1978. "The Relationship between Changes in Consumption and Politics in Poland." *Soviet Studies*, no. 2:262–269.

Mieszczańkowski, M. 1987. "Krótka historia reformy" (A short history of the reform). *Życie Gospodarcze*, May 17.

Milanovic, B. 1992. "Poland's Quest for Economic Stabilisation, 1988–91: Interaction of Political Economy and Economics." *Soviet Studies*, no. 3:511–532.

Misiak, M. 1992. "Jaki PKB w 1991 r." (What kind of GDP in 1991). *Życie Gospodarcze*, May 24.

Misiak, M., and B. Żukowska. 1992. "Walizka do negocjacji" (Materials for negotiation). *Życie Gospodarcze*, March 22.

Mizsei, K. 1993. *Bankruptcy and the Post-Communist Economies of East Central Europe*. New York: Institute for EastWest Studies.

———. 1990. *Lengyelország: Válságok, reformpotlékok, és reformkok* (Poland: Crises, reform-substitutes, and reforms). Budapest: Közgazdasági és Jogi Könyvkiadó.

———. 1986a. *A valutavisszatérítés lengyel rendszer* (The Polish currency-retention system). Budapest: Institute for World Economy.

———. 1986b. *The Dynamics of Change in East European Economic Systems*. Budapest: Institute for World Economy.

Montias, J. M. 1962. *Central Planning in Poland*. New Haven: Yale University Press.

Morawski, Witold. 1991. "Reform Models and Systemic Change in Poland." *Studies in Comparative Communism*, no. 3:281–294.

Morawski, Wojciech. 1989. "Polityka pieniężna" (Monetary policy). In *Problemy gospodarcze Drugiej Rzeczypospolitej* (Economic problems of the Second Republic), ed. Zbigniew Landau and Jerzy Tomaszewski. Warsaw: Państwowe Wydawnictwo Ekonomiczne.

Moskwa, A., M. Socha, and J. Wilkin. 1981. "Kierunki reform polityczno-gospodarczych w Polsce" (Foundations of political and economic reforms in Poland). In *Reforma gospodarcza: Propozycje, tendencje, kierunki dyskusji* (Economic reform: Proposals, tendencies, directions of discussion), ed. Rafał Krawczyk. Warsaw: Państwowe Wydawnictwo Ekonomiczne.

Motyl, A. J. 1992. "The Modernity of Nationalism: Nations, States, and Nation-States in the Contemporary World." *Journal of International Affairs*, no. 2:307–323.

Mozolski, A. 1992a. "Zniechęcenie" (Disincentive). *Polityka*, August 1.

———. 1992b. "Upadek Kołosa" (The Fall of the Colossus). *Polityka*, June 27.

———. 1992c. "Zabawa w długi" (A Game of Debt). *Polityka*, May 16.

Możejko, E. 1993. "Pomoc uwarunkowana" (Conditional assistance). *Życie Gospodarcze*, March 28.

Myant, M. 1992. "Economic Reform and Political Evolution in Eastern Europe." *Journal of Communist Studies*, no. 1:107–127.

Nasierowska, G. 1991. "Sprawa jakich wiele" (So many matters). *Firma*, no. 12:35.

Niezgódka-Medvoda, M. 1991. "Zmiany ustawy o działalności gospodarczej." *Firma*, no. 12:20–21.

Noren, J. H. 1992. "Russia's Economic Reform: Progress and Prospects." *Soviet Economy*, no. 1:3–42.

Nowak, S. 1988. "Polish Society in the Second Half of the 1980s: An Attempt to Diagnose the State of Public Consciousness." Princeton: International Research and Exchanges Board.

"Obowiązują koncesje na import alkoholu, tytoniu i paliw" (Concessions are in force for the import of alcohol, tobacco, and fuels). 1992. Polska Agencja Prasowa, April 1.

Ochrona Środowiska 1991 (Environmental Protection, 1991). 1991. Warsaw: Główny Urząd Statystyczny.

Ochrona Środowiska 1989 (Environmental Protection, 1989). 1989. Warsaw: Główny Urząd Statystyczny.

"Oczyszczenie finansów i polityka strukturalna" (Financial cleansing and structural policy). 1992. *Rzeczpospolita*, February 25.

"Oddzielić reprywatyzację od budżetu" (Separating reprivatization from the budget). 1992. Polska Agencja Prasowa, March 1.

OECD Economic Surveys: Poland 1992. 1992. Paris: Organisation for Economic Co-operation and Development.

Okolicsanyi, K. 1993. "The Visegrad Free Trade Zone." RFE/RLRR, no. 3:19–22.

———. 1992a. "The Hungarian Budget Deficit." RFE/RLRR, no. 29:53–55.

———. 1992b. "New Hungarian Bank Laws Maintain Political Influence." RFE/RLRR, no. 8:41–45.

Ost, D. 1991. *Solidarity and the Politics of Anti-Politics: Opposition and Reform in Poland since 1968*. Philadelphia: Temple University Press.

Overy, R. J. 1982. *The Nazi Economic Recovery, 1932–1938*. London: Macmillan.

Pajestka, J. 1984. *Polski kryzys 1980–1981: Jak do niego doszło i co rokuje* (The Polish crisis of 1980–1981: How it happened and what it portends). Warsaw: Książka i Wiedza.

Pataki, J. 1993. "Hungary: Domestic Political Stalemate." RFE/RLRR, no. 1:92–95.

Patterson, P. L., ed. 1993. *The Re-emergence of the Private Sector in Eastern Europe and the Former Soviet Union*. Boulder: Westview Press.

Pawłowski, W. 1991. "Wątły Gąszcz" (A frail bush). *Polityka*, November 23.

Pehe, J. 1993. "The Czech-Slovak Currency Split." RFE/RLRR, no. 10:27–32.

Pełnomocnik rządu ds. reformy gospodarczej. 1985. *Raport o realizacji reformy gospodarczej w 1984 roky* (Report on the implementation of the economic reform in 1984). Warsaw: Rzeczpospolita

Piesiewicz, Z. 1987. "Biurokracja nam rośnie" (Our bureaucracy is growing). *Polityka*, January 10.

Plesiński, K. 1987. "I chciałabym i boję się" (I want to, but I'm afraid). *Życie Gospodarcze*, November 1.

"Podatki bez mitów" (Taxes without myths). Polska Agencja Prasowa, October 24.

Podolski, T. M. 1972. *Socialist Banking and Monetary Control: The Experience of Poland*. Cambridge: Cambridge University Press.

Podrąża, H. "Koniec monopolu w handlu" (The end of the state monopoly in trade). *Życie Gospodarcze*, July 22.

"Poland: Country Report." 1992. *The Economist Intelligence Unit*, May 30.

"Poland's Economic Performance in 1989 and the First Half of 1990." 1990. *PlanEcon Report*, September 28.

"Polish Monthly Economic Monitor." 1993. *PlanEcon Report*, April 5.

Polish Economy in the External Environment in 1980s. 1988. Warsaw: World Economy Research Institute, Central School of Planning and Statistics.

Polska 1918–1988 (*Poland, 1918–1988*). 1989. Warsaw: Główny Urząd Statystyczny.

Polski Handel Zagraniczny w 1991 Roku (Polish foreign trade in 1991) 1992. Warsaw: Instytut Koniunktur i Cen Handlu Zagranicznego.

Pomfret, J. 1993. "Poland Rushes to Make a Market." *Washington Post*, June 17.

Poznański, K. 1992. "Privatisation of the Polish Economy: Problems of Transition." *Soviet Studies*, no. 4:641–664.

———. 1986. "Economic Adjustment and Political Forces: Poland since 1970." *International Organization*, no. 2:455–488.

Prochnicka, M. 1992. "Jak się zarejestrować i dostać zasiłek?" (How to register for and obtain unemployment benefits). *Sztandar Młodych*, May 29–31.

"Produkt krajowy brutto" (Gross domestic product). 1992. *Polska Agencja Prasowa*, May 12.

Program realizacyjny drugiego etapu reformy gospodarczej (Implementation program for the second stage of the economic reform). 1987. Warsaw: Rzeczpospolita.

"Prywatnych przybywa" (The private sector is growing). 1991. *Gazeta Wyborcza*, September 7–8.

"Prywatyzacja banków" (The privatization of the banks). 1991. *Prywatyzacja*, November, 3.

"Prywatyzacja połączona z restrukturyzacją" (Privatization combined with restructuring). 1991. *Prywatyzacja*, November, 1, 16.

Prywatyzacja przedsiębiorstw państwowych według stanu na 31.12.92 r. (The privatization of state enterprise, as of December 31, 1992). 1993. Warsaw: Główny Urząd Statystyczny.

"Prywatyzacja restrukturyzacyjna" (Restructuring privatization). 1991. *Prywatyzacja*, October, 1, 8–10.

"Przy fundamentach" (Present at the creation). 1991. *Gazeta Bankowa*, December 22–28.

Radek, A., and J. Welter. 1992. "Dwa lata zamętu" (Two years of turmoil). *Polityka*, May 30.

"Review of East European Foreign Trade Developments in 1992." 1993. *PlanEcon Report*, June 29.

Rocznik Statystyczny 1991 (Statistical yearbook 1991). 1991. Warsaw: Główny Urząd Statystyczny.

Rocznik Statystyczny 1990 (Statistical yearbook 1990). 1990. Warsaw: Główny Urząd Statystyczny.

Rocznik Statystyczny 1989 (Statistical yearbook 1989). 1989. Warsaw: Główny Urząd Statystyczny.

Rocznik Statystyczny 1988 (Statistical yearbook 1988). 1988. Warsaw: Główny Urząd Statystyczny.

Rocznik Statystyczny 1987 (Statistical yearbook 1987). 1987. Warsaw: Główny Urząd Statystyczny.

Rocznik Statystyczny 1986 (Statistical yearbook 1986). 1986. Warsaw: Główny Urząd Statystyczny.

Rocznik Statystyczny 1985 (Statistical yearbook 1985). 1985. Warsaw: Główny Urząd Statystyczny.

Rocznik Statystyczny: Handel Zagraniczny 1992 (Statistical yearbook: Foreign trade, 1992). 1992. Warsaw: Główny Urząd Statystyczny.

Rocznik Statystyczny: Handel Zagraniczny 1991 (Statistical yearbook: Foreign trade, 1991). 1991. Warsaw: Główny Urząd Statystyczny.

Rocznik Statystyczny: Handel Zagraniczny 1990 (Statistical yearbook: Foreign trade, 1990). 1990. Warsaw: Główny Urząd Statystyczny.

Rocznik Statystyczny: Handel Zagraniczny 1989 (Statistical yearbook: Foreign trade, 1989). 1989. Warsaw: Główny Urząd Statystyczny.

Rocznik Statystyczny: Handel Zagraniczny 1988 (Statistical yearbook: Foreign trade, 1988). 1988. Warsaw: Główny Urząd Statystyczny.

Rocznik Statystyczny: Handel Zagraniczny 1987 (Statistical yearbook: Foreign trade, 1987). 1987. Warsaw: Główny Urząd Statystyczny.

Rocznik Statystyczny: Handel Zagraniczny 1986 (Statistical yearbook: Foreign trade, 1986). 1986. Warsaw: Główny Urząd Statystyczny.

Rocznik Statystyczny: Przemysł 1992 (Industrial statistical yearbook 1992). 1992. Warsaw: Główny Urząd Statystyczny.

Rocznik Statystyczny: Przemysł 1991 (Industrial statistical yearbook 1991). 1991. Warsaw: Główny Urząd Statystyczny.

Rocznik Statystyczny: Przemysł 1988 (Industrial statistical yearbook 1988). 1988. Warsaw: Główny Urząd Statystyczny.

Rosati, D. K. 1993. "Czy koniec recesji (1)" (Is the Recession Over [1]). *Życie Gospodarcze*, January 17.

Rostowski, J. 1992. "Dźwignia" (Crane). *Gazeta Bankowa*, June 28-July 4.

———. 1989. "The Decay of Socialism and the Growth of Private Enterprise in Poland." *Soviet Studies*, no. 2:194–214.

Roszkowski, W. 1989. "Rolnictwo i leśnictwo" (Agriculture and forestry). In *Problemy gospodarcze Drugiej Rzeczypospolitej* (Economic problems of the Second Republic), ed. Zbigniew Landau and Jerzy Tomaszewski. Warsaw: Państwowe Wydawnictwo Ekonomiczne.

Rutkowski, A. 1991. "Reanimacja" (Reanimation). *Przegląd Tygodniowy*, September 15.

Rutkowski, M. 1991. "Is the Labour Market Adjustment in Poland Surprising?" *Labour*, no. 3:79–103.

Rychard, A. 1980. *Reforma gospodarcza: Socjologiczna analiza związków polityki i gospodarki* (Economic reform: A sociological analysis of the links between politics and the economy). Warsaw: Wydawnictwo Polskiej Akademii Nauk.

Rymarczyk, J. 1985. "Próba diagnozy" (An attempt at diagnosis). *Życie Gospodarcze*, August 18.

Sabbat-Swidlicka, A. 1992. "Summer Strikes: First Test for New Polish Government." RFE/RLRR, no. 34:9–14.

———. 1991. "Mazowiecki's Year In Review." RFEREE, no. 1:25–31.

———. 1990a. "Polish Peasant Party Withdraws Support for Mazowiecki's Government." RFEREE, no. 41:22–25.

———. 1990b. "Walesa Moves to 'Tidy Up' Solidarity." RFEREE, no. 25:26–29.

———. 1990c. "After the Peasants' Unity Conference: A New Political Constellation?" RFEREE, no. 21:33–36.

———. 1990d. "The Walesa Factor." RFEREE, no. 17:14–17.

———. 1990e. "Poland's Provisional Constitution." RFEREE, no. 14:32–36.

———. 1990f. "Peasant Party Politics." RFEREE, no. 5:14–18.

Sachs, J., and D. Lipton. 1990a. "Privatization in Eastern Europe: The Case of Poland." *Brookings Papers on Economic Activity*, no. 2:293–333.

———. 1990b. "Creating A Market Economy in Eastern Europe: The Case of Poland." *Brookings Papers on Economic Activity*, no. 1:75–148.

Schaffer, M. E. 1992. "The Polish State-Owned Enterprise Sector and the Recession of 1990." *Comparative Economic Studies*, no. 1:58–85.

———. 1990. "State-Owned Enterprises in Poland: Taxation, Subsidization, and Competition Policies." *European Economy*, March, 183–201.

Scherer, F. M. 1980. *Industrial Market Structure and Economic Performance*. Boston: Houghton Mifflin.

Secomski, K. 1950. *Analiza wykonania planu trzyletniego* (An analysis of the three-year plan's fulfillment). Warsaw: Polskie Wydawnictwo Gospodarcze.

Semprich, Ż. 1993. "Robotnicy w ciąży nie dojadają" (Pregnant workers are under-nourished). *Rzeczpospolita*, March 16.

Siemaszko, A. 1993. "Dziki wschód" (The wild east). *Gazeta Wyborcza*, February 23.

Singer, D. 1981. *The Road to Gdansk*. New York: Monthly Review Press.

Slay, B. 1993a. "The Dilemmas of Economic Liberalism in Poland." *Europe-Asia Studies*, no. 2:237–257.

———. 1993b. "Poland: The Role of Managers in Privatization." RFE/RLRR, no. 12:52–56.

———. 1993c. "Evolution of Industrial Policy in Poland since 1989." RFE/RLRR, no. 2:21–28.

———. 1992a. "The Polish Economy: Between Recession and Recovery." RFE/RLRR, no. 36:49–57.

———. 1992b. "The Banking Crisis and Economic Reform in Poland." RFE/RLRR, no. 23:33–40.

———. 1992c. "Privatization in Poland: An Overview." RFE/RLRR, no. 17:15–21.

———. 1992d. "Poland: The Rise and Fall of the Balcerowicz Plan." RFE/RLRR, no. 5:40–47.

———. 1991a. Poland: The 'Mass Privatization' Program Unravels." RFE/RLRR, no. 44:13–18.

———. 1991b. "The USSR: On the Economics of Interrepublican Trade." *Radio Liberty Report on the USSR*, no. 48:1–7.

———. 1990. "Monopoly and Marketization in Polish Industry." *Jahrbuch der Wirtschaft Osteuropas*, no. 1:58–83.

———. 1989. *Economic Reform: A Comparison of the Polish and Hungarian Experiences*. Ph.D. dissertation, Indiana University.

———. 1988. "Foreign Trade Reforms since 1981." In *Creditworthiness and Reform in Poland: Western and Polish Perspectives*, ed. Paul Marer and Włodzimierz Siwiński. Bloomington: Indiana University Press.

"Slovenian Monthly Economic Indicator." 1993. *PlanEcon Report*, May 18.

Smolar, A. 1983. "The Rich and the Powerful." In *Poland: Genesis of a Revolution*, ed. Abe Brumberg. New York: Vintage Books.

Smuga, T. 1986. "Polityka płacowa przedsiębiorstw" (Enterprise wage policy). *Życie Gospodarcze*, May 4.

Smulska, G. 1989. "Signum temporis" (A sign of the times). *Życie Gospodarcze*, January 1.

Sonntag, K. 1992. "Życie codzienne w transformacji" (Daily life in transformation). *Życie Gospodarcze*, no. 35:2.

Staniszkis, J. 1992. "Oni sami się czają" (They are stalking themselves). *Tygodnik Solidarność*, February 7.

———. 1984. *Poland's Self-Limiting Revolution*. Princeton: Princeton University Press.

"Statystyka mówi" (Statistics speak). 1992. *Sztandar Młodych*, May 29–31.

Statystyka Polski. 1993a. Supplement to *Rzeczpospolita*. May 8.

Statystyka Polski 1993b. Supplement to *Rzeczpospolita*. February 7.

Svitek, I. 1992. "An Assessment: Czechoslovak Economic Reform in 1991." RFE/RLRR, no. 21:45–49.

Szot, E. 1992. "Rolnictwo: Serce gospodarki" (Agriculture: The heart of the economy). *Rzeczpospolita*, July 18–19.

Szwarc, K. 1987. "Reforma centrum" (Reform of the central administration). *Życie Gospodarcze*, October 25.

Szyszło, M., and P. Stefaniak. 1992. "Wystartowaliśmy dobrze" (We began well). *Nowy Swiat*, June 25.

Tarnowski, P. 1987. "Przetargi w 'Szwarcbanku'" (Auctions in the 'Szwarcbank'). *Polityka*, June 20.

Tarr, D. G. 1992. "Problems in the Transition from the CMEA: Implications for Eastern Europe." *Communist Economies and Economic Transformation*, no. 1:23–44.

Taylor, J. 1952. *The Economic Development of Poland, 1919–1950*. Ithaca: Cornell University Press.

Telma, T. 1992. "Polish Foreign Trade in 1991 and Early 1992." *PlanEcon Report*, June 19.

———. 1991. "The Polish Economy in 1991." *PlanEcon Report*, December 30.

"Tezy w sprawie drugiego etapu reformy gospodarczej" (Theses of the second stage of economic reform). 1987. *Rzeczpospolita*, April 17.

"To nie będzie spacerek" (It won't be a cakewalk). 1992. *Rzeczpospolita*, April 3.

Tomaszewski, J. 1985. *Rzeczpospolita wielu narodów* (The republic of many nations). Warsaw: Czytelnik.

Topiński, A. 1986. "Gdzie ten nawis?" (Where's that overhang?). *Życie Gospodarcze*, April 27.

Turska, A. 1992. "Wziąć głodem" (To take by hunger). *Życie Gospodarcze*, May 3.

"Uwiąd sektora państwowego, rozwój—prywatnego" (The state sector atrophies, the private sector develops). 1992. Polska Agencja Prasowa, January 31.

Vinton, L. 1993a. "Polish Government Faces New Strike Challenge." RFE/RLRR, no. 21:25–30.

———. 1993b. "Poland's Social Safety Net: An Overview." RFE/RLRR, no. 17:3–11.

———. 1992a. "Polish Government Proposes Pact on State Firms." RFE/RLRR, no. 42:10–18.

———. 1992b. "Poland's Government Crisis: An End in Sight?" RFE/RLRR, no. 30:15–25.

———. 1992c. "Olszewski's Ouster Leaves Poland Polarized." RFE/RLRR, no. 25:1–10.

———. 1992d. "Poland: The Anguish of Transition." RFE/RLRR, no. 1:91–95.

———. 1991a. "Poland: Disparate Responses to Democracy and the Market." RFEREE, no. 13:29–37.

———. 1991b. "Balancing Continuity and Change: Walesa Forms a Government." RFEREE, no. 3:17–20.

———. 1990a. "The Debate Over the 'Political Calendar'." RFEREE, no. 44:13–19.

———. 1990b. "Solidarity's Rival Offspring: Center Alliance and Democratic Action." RFEREE, no. 38:15–25.

———. 1990c. "Government Contends with Collapse of Governing Coalition." RFEREE, no. 30:29–35.

———. 1990d. "Political Parties and Coalitions in the Local Government Elections." RFEREE, no. 26:26–30.

Vodopivec, M. 1991. "The Labor Market and the Transition of Socialist Economies." *Comparative Economic Studies*, no. 2:123–158.

Wade, R. 1992. "East Asia's Economic Success: Conflicting Perspectives, Partial Insights, Shaky Evidence." *World Politics*, no. 2:270–320.

Walewska, D. 1993. "Prywatyzacja z oporami" (Privatization with resistance). *Rzeczpospolita*, April 8.

Walicki, R., and L. Adamczuk. 1992. "Bezrobocie: prawda i urzędowa fikcja" (Unemployment: The truth and administrative fiction). *Życie Warszawy*, July 9.

Wandycz, K. 1990. "Lech Walesa, meet Alexander Hamilton." *Forbes*, November 26.

Wandycz, P. S. 1974. *The Lands of Partitioned Poland, 1795–1918*. Seattle: University of Washington Press.

Wanless, P. T. 1980. "Economic Reform in Poland: 1973–79." *Soviet Studies*, no. 1:28–57.

Wedel, J. R. 1989. "Lech's Labors Lost?" *World Monitor*, no. 11:44–54.

"Welcome to Poland." 1991. *Rynki zagraniczne*, October 23.

Wellisz, C. 1991a. "Warsaw's Bears and Bulls." *Radio Free Europe Report on Eastern Europe*, no. 24:18–21.

———. 1991b. "The Perils of Restitution." *Radio Free Europe Report on Eastern Europe*, no. 22:1–5.

Wellisz, L. 1938. *Foreign Capital in Poland*. London: Allen and Unwin.

Weschler, L. 1990. "A Reporter At Large: Shock." *New Yorker*, December 10.

———. 1989. "A Reporter At Large: A Grand Experiment." *New Yorker*, November 13.

———. 1985. *Solidarity: Poland in the Season of Its Passion*. New York: Simon and Schuster.

———. 1982. *The Passion of Poland*. New York: Pantheon Books.

Weydenthal, J. B. de. 1990a. "Finding a Place in Europe." RFEREE, no. 52:21–24.

———. 1990b. "Communists Dissolve Party, Set Up New Social Democratic Group." RFEREE, no. 7:23–27.

———. 1986. *The Communists of Poland: An Historical Outline*. Stanford: Hoover Institution.

Whitlock, E. 1992. "A Borrower and a Lender Be: Interenterprise Debt in Russia". RFE/RLRR, no. 40:33–38.

Wieczorkowska, A. 1992. "Rozbudzenie nadziei" (Building false hopes). *Życie Gospodarcze*, July 26.

Wielopolska, A. 1993, "Restrukturyzacja będzie przyspieszona" (Restructuring will be accelerated). *Rzeczpospolita*, March 16.

———. 1992. "PGR łatwiej wydzierżawić niż sprzedać." *Rzeczpospolita*, August 6.

Williamson, J., ed. 1991. *Currency Convertibility in Eastern Europe*. Washington, D.C.: Institute for International Economics.

Winiecki, J. 1993. *Post-Soviet Type Economies in Transition*. Aldershot: Avebury.

———. 1992. "The Polish Transformation Programme: Stabilisation under Threat." *Communist Economies and Economic Transformation*, no. 2:191–213.

———. 1991. "The Inevitability of a Fall in Output in the Early Stages of Transition to the Market: Theoretical Underpinnings." *Soviet Studies*, no. 4:669–676.

Woodall, J. 1982. *The Socialist Corporation and Technocratic Power*. Cambridge: Cambridge University Press.

Wrąbec, P. 1992. "Tajna liga przedsiębiorstw" (The secret enterprise league). *Gazeta Wyborcza*, March 6.

"Wschodni filar pozostaje" (The eastern pillar remains). 1992. *Rzeczpospolita*, July 4–5.

"Wspólnota losu węgla i stali" (The common fate of coal and steel). 1992. *Rzeczpospolita*, August 28.

Wykrętowicz, K. 1992. "Dezercja kontrolowana" (A controlled desertion). *Tygodnik Solidarność*, February 28.

"Wystąpienie Premiera Olszewskiego" (Prime Minister Olszewski's speech). 1992. Polska Agencja Prasowa, February 26.

"Wzrosło zadłużenie przedsiębiorstw" (Enterprise debt has grown). 1992. Polska Agencja Prasowa, March 12.

"Zadłużenie opóźnia przekształcenie PGR-ów" (Indebtedness slows the transformation of the state farms). 1992. Polska Agencja Prasowa, August 12.

"Założenia polityki społeczno-gospodarczej" (Principles of Socioeconomic Policy). 1992. Polska Agencja Prasowa, February 15.

Zaryczny, Z. 1992. "Polska marnuje swój czas" (Poland is wasting her moment). *Prawo i Życie*, June 27.

Zarzycki, Z. 1985. "Tanio kupić" (Buy cheap). *Życie Gospodarcze*, December 1.

Zielinski, J. 1978. "On System Remodelling in Poland: A Pragmatic Approach." *Soviet Studies*, no. 1:3–37.

———. 1973. *Economic Reforms in Polish Industry*. London: Oxford University Press.

Zienkowski, L., editor. 1993. *Polish Economy in 1990–1992: Experience and Conclusions*. Warsaw: Research Centre for Economic and Statistical Studies.

Zubek, V. 1991a. "The Rise and Fall of Rule by Poland's Best and Brightest." *Soviet Studies*, no. 4:579–608.

———. 1991b. "The Threshold of Poland's Transition: 1989 Electoral Campaign as the Last Act of a United Solidarity." *Studies in Comparative Communism*, no. 4:355–376.

Żmuda, A. 1986. "Zakładowe zespoły gospodarcze: Złotówki z Wolframu" (Enterprise working groups: Zloty from Wolfram). *Życie Warszawy*, April 3.

Żukowska, B. 1992. "Trójkąt handlowy" (The trade triangle). *Życie Gospodarcze*, May 10.

———. 1991. "Niech ma rację optymista" (May the optimists be right). *Życie Gospodarcze*, February 3.

———. 1990. "Wyśpiański kontra Waszyngton" (Wyśpiański versus Washington). *Życie Gospodarcze*, August 12.

Żuławnik, B. 1993. "Liczbowe harce" (Numerical rankings). *Gazeta Bankowa*, March 12.

"Żyjemy coraz krócej" (Our lives are getting shorter and shorter). 1991. *Gazeta Wyborcza*, October 8.

Index